The Renaissance of the Scottish Economy?

The Renaissance of the Scottish Economy?

CHARLOTTE LYTHE
University of Dundee
and
MADHAVI MAJMUDAR
Paisley College of Technology

London
GEORGE ALLEN & UNWIN
Boston   Sydney

George Allen & Unwin (Publishers) Ltd,
40 Museum Street, London WC1A 1LU, UK

George Allen & Unwin (Publishers) Ltd,
Park Lane, Hemel Hempstead, Herts HP2 4TE, UK

Allen & Unwin Inc.,
9 Winchester Terrace, Winchester, Mass 01890, USA

George Allen & Unwin Australia Pty Ltd,
8 Napier Street, North Sydney, NSW 2060, Australia

First published in 1982

British Library Cataloguing in Publication Data

Lythe, Charlotte
   The renaissance of the Scottish economy?
1. Scotland – Economic conditions – 1918–
I. Title   II. Majmudar, Madhavi
330.9411′0855   HC257.S4
ISBN 0-04-339032-3

Library of Congress Cataloging in Publication Data

Lythe, Charlotte.
   The renaissance of the Scottish economy?
1. Scotland – Economic conditions – 1918–1973.
2. Scotland – Economic conditions – 1973–
I. Majmudar, Madhavi.   II. Title.
HC257.S4L88   1982   330.9411′085   82-8733
ISBN 0-04-339-032-3   AACR2

Set in 10 on 11pt Times by Typesetters (Birmingham) Ltd
and printed in Great Britain by Biddles Ltd, Guildford, Surrey

Contents

List of Tables

List of Figures

Preface

This book springs from a continuing programme of research on the Scottish economy. The Social Science Research Council sponsored this work, at the University of Dundee, from 1973 to 1980, and it has continued there with funding from the Manpower Services Commission. Out first and main debt is therefore to the SSRC and MSC for enabling this research to be undertaken, and specifically for bringing us together as co-workers on this programme. What we try to do in this book is to present in a form which we hope will be accessible to the general reader the main conclusions of the work, and to put its evidence into the context of what has been shown in other studies.

The text is presented as six chapters. Chapter 1 is intended to set the scene, by discussing the main features of the political and economic history of Scotland to identify in what sense Scotland has an economy that is a proper object of study and how its fortunes declined in UK terms up to the mid 1960s. Chapters 2 and 3 set out the evidence on which the case for arguing that the economy has experienced a renaissance can be based. Chapter 2 considers the levels of income and output and expenditure in the economy, and Chapter 3 looks at what is implied about the productivity with which inputs have been used. Chapter 4 goes into greater analytical depth, by offering a full discussion of how far the economic performance of Scotland differs from that of the UK, and what conclusions should be drawn. In Chapter 5 we discuss what we believe to be the most important factor in accounting for these differences – the role of government, which we define more broadly than is usual. Chapter 6 starts with an overview of some of the special considerations not analysed earlier and then moves on to a discussion of the outlook for the Scottish economy.

We have tried to make our arguments accessible to a variety of readers. Chapters 1 and 6 will, we hope, be readily comprehensible to readers with no formal understanding of economics. Chapters 2 to 5 undertake what is inevitably a rather more technical discussion, as we present evidence and offer analysis of it. Although we believe that the general reader will be able to follow the thrust of our arguments in these chapters, it may be that some of the details are somewhat abstruse to non-economists. Lastly, we have relegated to an Appendix the more technical issues of measurement which lie behind some of our evidence, in the belief that while our professional colleagues will wish to satisfy themselves about the sources of our data, other readers will not wish to have the text cluttered by formal treatment of sources and methods.

In writing an extended work on an empirical topic, there is always the problem that data becomes obsolete, as series (that is runs of officially published data) are revised and updated. With the intention of making our study as up-to-date as possible, we did not impose an arbitrary cut-off date for the whole book, ignoring all new data published after, say, December 1979. Instead, we have tried in each chapter to incorporate as much recent evidence as we dared, consistent with meeting our publication target date. That has led to a little inconsistency between and indeed within chapters, but we hope we have avoided acute problems of that nature by fixing fairly early in the writing process what output and employment data we were going to use in the analysis in Chapters 4 and 5, and leading up to that information in Chapters 2 and 3. As far as employment details are concerned, there are no awkward consequences. In the case of output data, however, there have been some important changes in the most recently published series, affecting manufacturing industries since 1970, and we have been unable fully to incorporate these in our discussion. The revisions to the data do not, we are confident, affect our general conclusions, but they do have some effect on the more detailed regression analysis evidence. To avoid the necessity of listing sources of data in detail for each table, we have adopted the convention of labelling data drawn from published sources specifically for this book with a note of origin: all tables not so labelled are based on information in the data bank constructed as part of the research programme, and available on request as computer print-out from the University of Dundee.

We have incurred many debts of gratitude in the long- and short-term preparation of this book, and are pleased to acknowledge the assistance we have received. All those who have worked at various stages on the project – Hugh Begg, Robert Sorley, David Macdonald, Morag Maclaren, John Dewhurst, Mark Cox, Sam Parrillo, Jennifer Devlen, Robert Gausden, Richard Miller, Evelyn Calley and David Forbes – have contributed so much towards the pooling of ideas and towards the construction of numerous data series used in this book that it is very difficult for us to identify any proprietorship in ideas or in data. Lucy Docherty of Paisley College of Technology has done the bulk of computing work for Chapters 4 and 5. We have been fortunate in enjoying the constructive support of our departmental colleagues, at Dundee and at Paisley, and especially of our Heads of Department, Professor Blake and Professor Sloane, in their encouragement. The Libraries at our two institutions could not have been more co-operative in obtaining material for us.

The list of people who have helped us with specific problems is very lengthy indeed, and we hope we have acknowledged their help in our more technical publications, but we would like here to mention the extensive assistance we have received from all branches of the government economic statistical service, and especially from Scottish Office.

We indicate at appropriate points in notes to the text when we have received, and we hope profited from, guidance specifically for this book.

Lastly, we would like to acknowledge the help we have been given for the production of this book. The typescript was prepared by Mrs Margaret Jamieson and Miss Laura Handy and their patience in coping with successive drafts and indecipherable handwriting was outstanding. The diagrams were drawn by Mrs Carolyn Bain; and Mr Nicholas Brealey of Allen & Unwin has guided us through various points, and encouraged us to complete the text on time. Without financial guarantees from the Carnegie Trust for the Universities of Scotland this book could not have been published.

Lastly, we add the customary disclaimer. We have drawn widely for advice and information, but the use we have made of that help is, of course, solely our responsibility, and the views expressed in this book should be attributable to us alone.

Dundee and Paisley   Charlotte Lythe
October 1981   Madhavi Majmudar

1

The Renaissance of the Scottish Economy?

Introduction

To ask whether the Scottish economy has experienced a renaissance is to beg two questions, whether there is anything that can be called the Scottish economy and whether it has in the past enjoyed a period of prosperity followed by one of decline. Both questions seem simple, but as we shall try to show in this chapter the answers are not straightforward.

The Scottish Economy

An English tourist visiting Scotland for the first time cannot fail to be aware that in some respects he is in alien territory, and that this alienness reflects official recognition of differences. If he buys ordinary postage stamps to put on his postcards, he will find that they bear a lion rampant as well as the Queen's head. If he visits ancient monuments, he will find that the notice warning him about the penalties for damaging them are in the name of the secretary of state for Scotland. He will find that the banknotes in circulation are not just those of the Bank of England – there are also notes issued by the three Scottish banks, and for ordinary transactions it is a matter of complete indifference to all parties which of the four different banks has issued a note. If he wishes to draw cash from a bank, he will normally be unable to find a branch of his own bank, and will have to use instead a branch of one of the Scottish banks.

Some of these differences reflect relatively trivial gestures towards regions in the UK – like the differentiated postage stamps – whilst others, like the relevance of the secretary of state, are the consequence of historical influences. Later in this section we will offer a thumb-nail sketch of the more important historical factors, and what they entail for the present administration of Scotland. But even differences which are firmly rooted in history and which affect the economic institutions of the area, like the existence of the Scottish banks, do not of themselves make that area an economic entity, and there are obvious senses in which Scotland is not an economic unit. Our English tourist did not pass through a customs barrier as he crossed the border into Scotland. He did not exchange his English currency for Scottish currency. He can remit income freely between England and Scotland, and can operate as an economic agent on much the same terms in the two countries. If there is such a thing as the economy of Scotland as an entity, Scotland's economy is fully integrated with that of England so that there are no barriers to the transmission of goods or of money across their mutual frontier – in more technical language, the two economies are in complete customs and monetary union, both being part of the larger economy of the United Kingdom (UK). Further, as we shall show later in this book, the scanty evidence that exists about Scotland's external trade suggests that the vast bulk of such trade is with the rest of the UK, and since the Scottish economy accounts for around a tenth of the economic activity of the UK it follows that Scotland's economic fortunes are inextricably linked with those of the UK and that, as a small part of the total, Scotland has very little control over her economic destiny. We will return to these issues when we consider the outlook for the Scottish economy. The implications we wish to draw here are twofold: first, that there is some connection between the political framework and the extent to which an economy can be described as independent – although, as we shall show, that connection is a little complex: and second, that in the present political framework the relationship of Scotland to the UK is that normally labelled in economics as that of a region to a nation, and so when we refer to Scotland in this book as a region we will simply be using the most appropriate economic terminology and we do not mean in any sense to decry the sense of national identity felt by the Scots.

At the same time, there are institutional elements which actually or potentially give coherence to the Scottish economy and separate it from that of the rest of the UK. There is in practice a substantial devolution of administration, covering among other things economic matters, to the secretary of state for Scotland and his officials. In many important respects, the extent and nature of this devolution is the result of the constitutional history of the UK. Because of a dynastic marriage that had taken place a century earlier, the throne of England and Wales was united with that of Scotland in 1603, but the Scottish Parliament remained quite separate from that of England and Wales till 1707. The Act of Union that brought about the united Parliament was, like most such treaties, accompanied by considerable horse-trading, but for whatever reason its clauses guaranteed the perpetual existence of certain Scottish institutions as separate from their counterparts in England and Wales and as separately administered. The institutions thus given a separate Scottish identity were the Scottish Presbyterian Church, the legal system, and the universities. From the independence of the legal system has flowed both the necessity for a lot of what is really UK legislation to be separately enacted for Scotland and the continued existence in Scotland of laws, courts, and lawyers all quite different from those in England and Wales. From the independence of the universities and churches has grown an independent educational system in Scotland, where paradoxically the Scottish universities are now very like their English counterparts (and financed in the same way), whereas the school system is quite separate.

From these peculiarly Scottish institutions there has developed a correspondingly peculiar Scottish administration. After the Union a secretary of state for Scotland was responsible generally for the conduct of government in Scotland, while the lord advocate was the chief government law officer. In 1746 the former office was abolished, and the lord advocate took over responsibility for the administration of government in Scotland, this new arrangement working satisfactorily for about a century. The mid-nineteenth century, however, saw a steady expansion of local government responsibilities in the administration of poor law relief, public health, environmental improvement, and education, and since some of these activities were financed from central government funds, various co-ordinating bodies, notably the Board of Supervision for Poor Relief and the Scotch Education Department, were created to supervise the expanding expenditure of the local authorities. These Boards were ultimately the responsibility of the UK home secretary, but the lord advocate was still generally regarded as being in charge of Scotland's affairs. In the late nineteenth century, Scotland's MPs became increasingly critical of the lack of a Scottish secretary with clear responsibility for Scotland, and the 1880s saw a flowering of nationalist sentiment in Scotland. In 1884 Gladstone responded to this combination of practical and political pressures, and a bill was enacted to set up a Scottish Office, headed by a Scottish secretary.

The new Scottish Office took over most of the Scottish functions of the Home Office, and also responsibility for education. The Scottish Boards continued to exist, but the Scottish secretary was now generally answerable to Parliament for their activities, and gradually the functions of the Boards were transferred to statutory departments under his control.

The status of the Scottish secretary was raised by his elevation to the level of secretary of state, with a seat in the Cabinet. A more physical symbol of the devolution of power was the opening in 1939 of St

Andrew's House in Edinburgh as the headquarters of the administration of government in Scotland. The size of the administration controlled by the Secretary of state has steadily increased, and now his office is organised into five departments – Agriculture, Education, Health, Home and, the most recent creation, the Scottish Economic Planning Department.

We will consider in Chapter 6 how far these institutional arrangements provide the potential for economic development in Scotland: our point here is simply that there is already substantial administrative devolution. The corresponding public accountability is, however, much more diffuse. A Member of Parliament for a Scottish seat must fulfil the same functions as his counterpart from any other part of the UK. But he is in practice a member not of one legislature but of two. Scottish MPs, in addition to their other work, discuss their own Bills, sit on their own committees and question their own ministers. The Scottish committee system gives Scottish MPs considerable opportunities to discuss Scottish legislation and affairs, but most of the work of the Scottish committees is uncontroversial and ultimately the committees cannot overturn the wishes of the government of the day. After reviewing the present system, the Royal Commission on the Constitution's Study of Parliament Group concluded that 'while the Select Committee on Scottish Affairs has been a useful addition to the Scottish Committees, the present arrangements still do not provide adequately for the proper performance by Parliament of its inquisitive, deliberative, redressive and controlling functions in relation to Scottish business viewed as a whole'. (Report of the (Kilbrandon) Royal Commission on the Constitution, Vol. 1, 1973, para 1062.)

Laying aside for the rest of our discussion these questions of democratic control, it is clear that even administratively Scotland is not an independent economic unit. There is no real control within or on behalf of Scotland of taxation and of the money supply, and so the major instruments of management of an economy cannot be exercised independently for Scotland. It is true that there are some decisions about taxation taken by local authorities when they determine the rate levy, but even before the recent confrontations between certain local authorities and central government about local expenditure plans it was obvious that the extent of local freedom was fairly heavily circumscribed by the dependence of local authorities on central government grants towards their expenditure, and by the extent to which the local authorities are required by statute to provide certain services at prescribed standards. So local rates cannot realistically be envisaged as providing any room for an independent fiscal policy for Scotland. The existence of a Scottish banking system might be taken to imply that there could be an independent monetary policy, but that is not so: no body exercises separately for Scotland the central banking role of the

Bank of England. The Scottish banks operate in more or less the same relationship to the Bank of England as do the English clearing banks, and are subject in the normal ways to interest rate and discount market policies. Their note-issue, which makes the Scottish banks look different, give them only a very slight technical freedom for manoeuvre as apart from a fiduciary issue, which is tiny in modern terms, they have to have a one-for-one Bank of England note banking for every note they issue, and so the only advantages note-issuing powers give the Scottish banks are the small technical bonus of being able to count their Bank of England note-holding for two purposes (against their note issue and against the required cash holdings) and what they regard as the more important benefit of advertisement.

The limitations we have described so far are at least superficially institutional. If, as some people in Scotland want, Scotland were to have her own government, independent of the UK government, then that government would exercise monetary and fiscal control like any other government, and so, the argument runs, it is an accident of history that Scotland is a region in the sense described so far. But there is more to being a region in the economic sense than not having a government charged with decisions about monetary and fiscal policy. In the economic sense, a region is characterised by membership of and interconnection with a larger entity. As we can see in Table 1.1, Scotland's population is now a little under a tenth of that of the UK. Even if Scotland's purchasing power per head were exactly at the UK average (and we will see in Chapter 2 that it is fractionally lower), that would mean that Scotland is in economic terms a small part of the UK. We will show in Chapter 6 that the evidence suggests that the vast bulk of Scotland's trade is with the rest of the UK. The picture is of a small country heavily dependent on trade with larger and more prosperous neighbours. An interesting analogy lies in the relationship of Eire to the UK. Since 1927, the Irish punt has been separate from the UK £ sterling and its par value could consequently fluctuate. In fact, it is only in the last few years that the Irish punt against sterling and the £ sterling have not been at parity. The reason for the long parity, and for the recent change, is simple: as long as the Irish economy was heavily dependent on and closely linked to the UK economy, whatever determined the economic fortunes of the UK determine also the economic fortunes of Eire, and so it was in the Irish interest to keep parity between the countries. In the words of a governor of the Central Bank of Ireland, 'Fundamentally, the maintenance of a monetary union in the form of a fixed link between the Irish pound and sterling reflects the openness of the Irish economy and the high degree of economic interdependence between Ireland and the UK. Openness . . . favoured the *principle* of a pegged exchange rate with the currency of larger area. Interdependence between the two independence, the economy has managed sufficiently to sever its link with the UK economy that, in a regime of generally floating exchange rates, the Irish currency can move freely against sterling.

The implication of this argument is that, even if Scotland were over-night to acquire complete nominal economic independence from the rest of the UK, it would be hard for her, without incurring very great adjustment costs, to operate her economy without very close regard to the plans of the UK government. As was concluded by Tait (1977) discussing the context of Scottish economic independence, 'it does appear that to have a viable Scottish monetary policy requires enormous changes in the way in which all business (financial and mercantile) is conducted . . . Basically, if the Scots are not prepared to face up to as yet unthought of change in their financial dealings, Scottish monetary policy cannot exist in practice.' (Tait, 1977, p. 127.) Much the same conclusions were reached by Corden (1972). Discussing the possibility of Scotland's depreciating her currency against the English pound to reduce employment, he argues,

> if Scotland had never been joined to England, one could well conceive of Scotsmen accepting wage settlements fixed in their own currency irrespective of prospective exchange-rate changes. But this is less likely if Scotland, after more than 200 years of union, were newly turned into a separate country . . . A very small open economy is not really a feasible area, since there would be no signifi-cance in its having its own exchange rate. Its own currency would have no liquidity value, and the population would choose to strike wage bargains in terms of foreign currency. (Corden, 1972, p. 13.)

Whilst not suggesting that the Scottish economy is so small that the last two sentences would apply to it without modification, we would suggest that in the foreseeable future the close historic links between Scotland and England would cause a noticeable population movement from Scotland to England if Scottish real wages were to be reduced in an attempt to reduce Scottish unemployment, whilst English real wages were unchanged. Political independence would not very easily or quickly bring about economic independence.

It is, we hope, clear from the foregoing discussion that whether there is a Scottish economy depends on what we take the phrase to mean. Sheer regional sentiment could justify the claim that there must be an identifiable economy for any area which can reasonably claim that it is a unit, and of course it must be true in that sense that Bognor Regis, or Govan, have economies of their own. Sentiment alone, however, whilst it might explain the decision of an individual to devote his research effort to the analysis of a local economy, can hardly be offered as a reason for inviting the controllers of public funds or the readers of a book to interest themselves in the output of such research projects. There is a Scottish economy in a more profound sense than there is an economy of Bognor Regis because of the institutional framework we have described. There is a separate Scottish dimension in the central administrative structure of the UK. There are central government civil servants whose sole job it is to analyse the effects on Scotland of proposals for the UK. Parliamentary machinery exists that could bring about economic effects on Scotland different from those on the rest of the UK. As we have suggested, there may be severe practical limits to the differential impact that can be achieved, but the facility to nudge the Scottish economy towards a preferred path makes it not just a matter of academic interest but also a matter of practical importance to undertake studies of the characteristics of the Scottish economy.

Prosperity and Decline

The move from a predominantly agricultural to a predominantly manufacturing economy that is labelled the Industrial Revolution took place at much the same time and at much the same pace in the lowland areas of Scotland as in the north of England and Midlands. As in England, agricultural advances and improvements in communications were followed by developments in textiles, coal, iron and steel. The most useful indicator of economic growth in the nineteenth century is perhaps population: as the historical data in Table 1.1 show, the home population of Scotland grew in the period 1801–1911 a little faster than that in the British Isles as a whole, particularly from 1841. In terms of output, perhaps the most reliable measure is pig iron, where Scottish production rose from 22,000 tons in 1806 to 196,000 tons in 1839, and reached a peak in 1904–8 at 1,358,000 tons (Lythe and Butt, 1975, p. 254). Scottish coal output shows a less dramatic but similar pattern, rising from 7.4 million tons in 1854 to an all-time peak of 41.3 million tons in 1910 (op. cit. p. 253).

The geographical impact of the industrialisation of Scotland was very uneven. Partly because of the physical limitations of terrain outside the lowland areas, and partly because of the geographical accidents of where deposits of coal and iron are located, the industrial development has concentrated in the strip of terrain from Glasgow to Edinburgh, especially around Glasgow, and outside that only Aberdeen and Dundee constituted significant areas of industrialisation and consequent foci of population. This pattern, which established itself in the nineteenth century, persists today, as the second half of Table 1.1 shows. Nearly half of the population of Scotland lives in the Strathclyde region (see Figure 1.1), dominated by Glasgow, and the

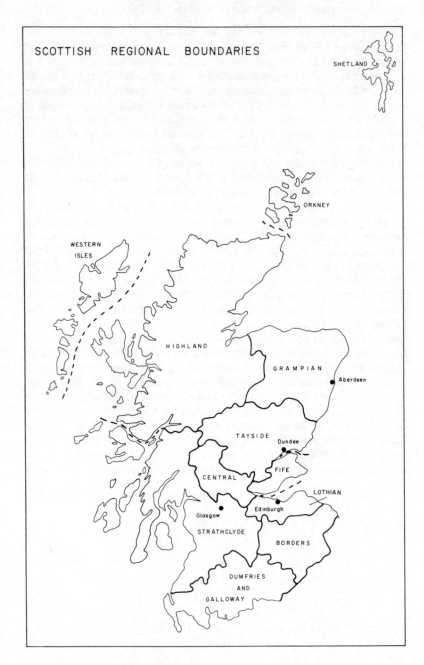

SCOTTISH REGIONAL BOUNDARIES

SHETLAND

ORKNEY

WESTERN
ISLES

HIGHLAND

GRAMPIAN

Aberdeen

TAYSIDE

Dundee

FIFE

CENTRAL

LOTHIAN

Edinburgh

Glasgow

STRATHCLYDE

BORDERS

DUMFRIES
AND
GALLOWAY

Figure 1.1   *The regions of Scotland*

Lothian region around Edinburgh accounts for another 15 per cent. Thanks to the presence in their areas of Aberdeen and Dundee respectively, Grampian and Tayside come next in order of importance in contributing to Scottish population. The physically large Highland and Borders regions together contain only just over a twentieth of the total population of Scotland. One drawback of the industrialisation of Scotland was, therefore, that it was restricted in area, and led to the coexistence of industrialised and rural areas and the pressures on the rural areas entailed by the proximity of populous, more thriving, urbanised neighbours. We shall examine these problems and the approach to solving them when in Chapter 6 we consider the role of the Highlands and Islands Development Board.

The second major drawback in the pattern of industrialisation in Scotland is that in the late nineteenth century there was too little flexibility. The persistence of an outdated industrial structure has been generally argued to be the fundamental cause of the industrial problems of the UK: what is true here of the UK is even more apparent for Scotland. The symptoms of industrial decline in Scotland are familiar, and illustrated in Tables 1.2 and 1.3. Table 1.2 brings out the extent to which Scotland has suffered from the emigration of her labour force. The outflow of labour has since the First World War gone far towards cancelling the natural increase in population (that is the number of live births minus the number of deaths): perhaps more important, emigration has probably been of the most ambitious and most skilled. Table 1.3 shows that for as long as reliable figures are available, from 1930, Scotland's unemployment rate (despite emigration) has been persistently higher than that of Great Britain. (It should be noted that the unemployment data presented in Table 1.3 contain many discontinuities. The evidence for the years up to 1960 is drawn from the Expenditure Committee (Trade and Industry Sub-Committee) *Minutes of Evidence* on Regional Development Incentives

Table 1.2   *Net loss of the Scottish population by migration, 1881–1979*

Period	Net loss by migration ('000)	Percentage of natural increase for period
1881–91	217	43
1891–1901	53	11
1901–11	254	47
1911–21	239	66
1921–31	392	111
1931–51	220	44
1951–61	282	83
1961–71	327	95
1971–9	37	82

(July 1973) Appendix 5, and the reader should consult the text there for details of the problems of measurement and comparison). The unemployment relative – the proportion of the Scottish to the British unemployment rates – has varied countercyclically, being particularly adverse in times of low unemployment rates – but except in 1930 the Scottish unemployment rates has never been less than 25 per cent greater than the British rate. An interesting analysis of this behaviour is presented in *Scottish Economic Bulletin*, no. 9 (Winter 1976). We will return in Chapter 2 to the identifications of symptoms of

Table 1.3 *Scottish unemployment rates: annual average, including school-leavers*

	Scotland %	GB %	Scotland/(GB) (GB = 100)
1930	18.5	16.0	116
1932	27.7	22.0	126
1934	23.1	16.6	139
1936	18.7	12.9	145
1938	16.3	12.6	129
1946	4.6	2.4	192
1948	3.0	1.6	188
1950	3.1	1.5	207
1952	3.3	2.0	165
1954	2.8	1.3	216
1956	2.4	1.2	200
1958	3.8	2.1	181
1960	3.6	1.6	225
1961	3.1	1.5	207
1962	3.8	2.0	169
1963	4.8	2.5	192
1964	3.6	1.6	225
1965	3.0	1.4	214
1966	2.9	1.5	193
1967	3.9	2.4	163
1968	3.8	2.4	158
1969	3.7	2.4	154
1970	4.2	2.6	162
1971	5.8	3.5	166
1972	6.4	3.8	168
1973	4.5	3.8	142
1974	4.0	2.6	154
1975	5.2	4.1	127
1976	7.0	5.7	123
1977	8.1	6.2	131
1978	8.2	6.1	134
1979	8.0	5.8	138
1980	10.0	7.3	137

industrial weakness of Scotland, but at present take the existence of economic problems for granted and turn to the evidence that their origins lie in the late nineteenth and very early twentieth centuries.

The only way in which we can attempt to identify the structure of economic activity in Scotland in the late nineteenth and early twentieth centuries is by the use of statistics of employment. Output would be a much more direct measure, but as we shall show in Chapter 2 statistics of output in Scotland are not available for years before the 1950s. Further, the employment series we must use is not ideal, because it ignores the self-employed, which, as we will argue in Chapter 3, is an important omission. Nevertheless, the evidence on employment structure presented in Table 1.4 can give us some broad indication of trends, although not too much should be read into its detail. In Table 1.4, we present the structure of employment in Scotland in 1881, 1921, 1931 and 1951, and we set out also the corresponding structure in Great Britain (GB) all in terms of the percentage of total employment. We can draw some conclusions about the whole period by comparing 1881 with 1951 by means of some intermediate year – say 1921, and by looking at the 1921 pattern in terms of how far the 1881 structure of employment had adapted towards that appropriate for 1951. On that criterion we can see that in some industries Scotland's record was significantly different from that of GB as a whole.

In mining and quarrying; metal manufacture; and shipbuilding and marine engineering, Scotland increased her specialisation between 1881 and 1921 (by GB standards) in industries which were to show marked short-term declines in the depression of 1931 and long-term decline by 1951.

In insurance, banking and finance, which later proved to be a growth industry, Scotland increased her employment relatively slowly between 1881 and 1921. Although she was as successful as GB in shedding employment in agriculture, forestry and fishing and in textiles, Scotland remained over-concentrated in these declining industries, just as one of the major growth industries, vehicles, was constantly under-represented in her employment structure. Only in clothing did she manage to do markedly better than the British average in keeping her employment consistently low in a declining industry. In short, she showed in 1921 a structure of employment which had changed less to meet the changing pattern of demand and competitive pressures than that of GB as a whole. Although, as we shall show in later chapters, there has been a very marked change in the structure of Scottish output and employment since 1951, these changes have partly been a delayed response to long-term declines rather than a reaction to the stimulus of growth industries.

The evidence that we have discussed in this section points, we think, fairly clearly to a decline in Scotland's economic fortunes from some time in the late nineteenth century. Whether before that decline began the Scottish economy was more or less prosperous than other parts of the UK economy is very hard to assess, simply because the kind of statistical evidence economists would use to answer the question is lacking. The backwards parts of the economy – the Highlands particularly – appear to have been in material terms very poor. But the late nineteenth century explosion in urban development, particularly in and around Glasgow, and the high quality of the public buildings of that period, suggest levels of prosperity and confidence at least the equal of those of the major English manufacturing towns. On the whole, the proposition that the industrial parts of Scotland were flourishing as well as the industrial parts of England towards the close of the nineteenth century is hard to resist. It follows that a recent revival in Scotland's economic fortunes, if such a revival were firmly based, could indeed be labelled as a renaissance.

The Alternative Hypothesis

The question which our title does *not* beg is that of whether this renaissance has occurred. The rest of this book will be devoted to answering this question, particularly in the light of the counter-claim that such recovery as has taken place is the consequence of government policy which has, by accident or by design, affected Scotland in a special way. Because of the importance of this counter-claim, we devote the concluding section of this chapter to a quick outline of its argument.

Some of the measures which have been designed to promote economic, especially industrial, development in Scotland are conventionally lumped together under the heading of 'regional policy', which is usually taken to mean specific measures taken by government to effect various kinds of price discrimination within the UK so as to make industrial activity, primarily in manufacturing industries, more profitable in the favoured regions than it otherwise would be. Thus, regional policy consists of arrangements like grants and tax allowances for investment (its commonest form), or subsidies towards labour costs, or the provision of advance factories and serviced sites to reduce the time involved to set up production. More widely defined, and we argue in Chapter 5 that greater width of definition should be used, regional policy would also include less clearly measurable items such as the provision of infrastructure in advance of development (roads, housing and so on), policy about the regional distribution of contracts to private industry, and policy about the dispersal of public-sector employment. In the rather narrower sense, the history of regional policy in the UK has been well documented, and in the

Table 1.4 *Percentage structure of employment in Scotland, 1881, 1921, 1931 and 1951*

	1881		1921		1931		1951	
	Scot.	GB	Scot.	GB	Scot.	GB	Scot.	GB
Agriculture, forestry and fishing	18.1	12.5	9.5	6.6	10.0	6.4	7.4	5.1
Mining and quarrying	4.8	4.5	8.1	6.6	5.9	5.6	4.5	3.8
Total: primary	22.9	17.0	17.6	13.2	15.9	12.0	11.9	8.9
Food, drink and tobacco	0.9	1.0	3.7	3.2	4.2	3.4	4.4	3.4
Chemicals and allied industries	0.4	0.4	0.8	1.1	1.0	1.2	1.7	2.0
Metal manufacturing	4.3	3.9	4.3	2.8	2.7	2.2	2.9	2.6
Engineering and electrical goods	2.2	1.9	5.2	4.5	3.0	3.6	6.1	7.4
Shipbuilding and marine engineering	1.1	0.6	5.7	2.0	1.8	0.8	3.5	1.3
Vehicles	0.2	0.5	0.8	1.9	0.9	1.8	3.0	4.5
Metal goods not elsewhere specified	0.3	1.0	0.6	1.8	1.4	2.0	1.3	2.1
Textiles	11.8	9.0	6.9	6.7	6.4	5.8	5.4	4.5
Leather, leather goods and fur	0.4	0.5	0.3	0.4	0.3	0.4	0.3	0.4
Clothing and footwear	6.8	8.5	3.1	4.4	2.2	4.4	2.0	3.2
Bricks, pottery, glass and cement	0.7	1.1	0.7	1.2	0.7	1.3	1.0	1.4
Timber, furniture	1.5	1.5	1.9	1.5	2.0	1.5	1.8	1.5
Paper, printing and publishing	1.6	1.3	2.0	1.9	2.5	2.5	2.4	2.3
Other manufacturing industries	0.3	0.4	0.8	0.9	1.1	1.1	0.9	1.2
Total: manufacturing	32.7	31.6	36.8	34.3	30.2	32.0	36.7	37.7

Construction	6.9	6.8	3.4	3.6	4.2	5.0	6.9	6.3
Gas, electricity and water	0.2	0.2	0.8	0.9	0.8	1.2	1.2	1.6
Transport and communication	5.4	5.8	7.1	6.0	7.2	6.9	8.2	7.7
Distributive trades	7.1	6.9	11.9	10.9	16.2	15.0	12.4	12.1
Insurance, banking and finance	0.6	0.6	1.3	1.6	1.5	1.7	1.5	2.0
Professional and scientific services	2.9	3.6	3.0	2.7	4.0	3.5	7.5	6.9
Miscellaneous services	12.1	17.2	9.7	11.0	11.5	14.1	7.7	9.1
Public administration and defence	1.3	1.8	6.5	6.3	7.6	8.2	6.0	7.7
Total: services (including construction)	36.3	42.0	43.7	43.0	53.0	55.6	51.4	53.4
Not classified	8.1	8.4	1.9	9.5	1.0	0.3	0.1	0.1

Appendix we offer a brief chronology of the more important measures affecting Scotland (see pp. 196–204). In the broader sense, very little academic study has been satisfactorily completed.

Regional policy, in all its senses, has in the UK undergone a complex pattern of change in nature and in intensity. Although some of the instruments of regional policy – particularly the mechanisms of using planning legislation to reduce congestion – were available before the 1939–45 war, regional policy in its current sense did not effectively start till after that war. It was a response to two complementary forces – the coexistence in some areas of congestion and in others of unemployment, and the nationally high levels of employment and dangers of inflation. The rationale was thus to reduce the pressure of demand in areas experiencing congestion by transferring the demand to areas where there was spare capacity, in the belief that in that way more output would be available in the economy without fuelling inflation.

This argument rests on the assumption that the moving of industry to what is not its most preferred location does not involve any significant long-run output loss, or that if there are such losses they are more than compensated by the savings in using spare social capital (housing, etc.) rather than building anew in already congested areas. Thus, regional policy is conceived not as an instrument of charity towards the less prosperous regions but as a method of achieving higher national output (taking into account social costs and benefits). It follows that if national unemployment levels, or spare capacity measured by some other indicator, get so high that no area experiences congestion, regional policy loses its immediate rationale (though it still might have a place in forestalling pressure when recovery occurs).

Throughout the post-war period, or at least once the immediate post-war boom in activity for heavy industry in replacing wartime losses had passed, Scotland has been an obvious candidate for the receipt of regional policy assistance – the unemployment rates in Table 1.3 make the point. The method of defining areas for assistance has varied – between identifying very small areas as 'unemployment blackspots' and earmarking quite large areas as development centres – but in effect nearly all of Scotland has been eligible for favourable treatment under the terms of regional policy for most of the period in which a recognisable regional policy has existed. As we shall try to show later in this book, especially in Chapters 4 and 5, whilst it is clear that in general terms regional policy has helped the Scottish economy it is difficult to demonstrate its successes in a quantitative way. This is partly because the very sharp and frequent changes in policy have made it difficult both for industrialists to respond to its incentives and for economists to identify its effects, but also partly because, as we have tried to illustrate in this chapter and will consider in more detail in the next three chapters, the successes of regional policy in Scotland have been against a background of important economic problems.

2

Scottish Income and Output since 1954

The Concepts

The most direct way to examine how an economy is performing is to look at the level and at the rate of growth of its income – the income of its inhabitants, the goods and services made available to them, the amount of their expenditure. We should, however, make it clear from the outset that this does not tell the full story: even if we had completely reliable income figures – and we shall show in this chapter that we do not – there are still important parts of the well-being of the inhabitants of an economy that national income cannot portray, such as the amount and quality of their leisure, their personal and political freedoms, the quality of their environment. Despite the acknowledged limitations of national income as a measure of welfare (documented for example in Nordhaus and Tobin, 1972), it remains the closest approximation we have to an indicator of the success of the inhabitants of an economy in maximising their welfare. It is therefore natural to start the detailed discussion of this book by considering the behaviour of national income in Scotland since 1954, that is, since the end of the distortions associated with the Second World War.

There are three ways in which social accountants try to measure national income – as the sum of incomes (that is, as the incomes generated or received in the economy – income from employment, from self-employment, from profit, etc), as the sum of outputs (that is, all the output made in or available to the economy, usually reckoned as the total value added at each stage of production), and as the sum of expenditures (that is, all the final expenditures in or on behalf of the economy by consumers, firms, government, etc.). Each of these three measures has associated with it two distinct concepts – territorial income and residents' income. The distinction between the two concepts, and the importance of being sure what is being measured, can be illustrated very strikingly from the work of Phyllis

Table 2.1 *National Income of Northern Rhodesia, 1938 (£'000)*

Sum of incomes		Sum of outputs		Sum of expenditures	
Residents' incomes		**Residents' outputs**		**Residents' expenditure**	
Incomes of individuals	7,371	Net output of mining	2,484	Personal cash expenditure at factor cost	4,162
Incomes of local companies	303	Net output of agriculture	2,000	Subsidence consumption	1,891
Income of government (including receipts from foreign tax payers)	820	Net output of manufacturing	321	Expenditure abroad by individuals	774
		Net output of distribution and transport	1,304	Total personal consumption	6,827
		Net output of other goods and services	974	Government current expenditure	1,343
		Net output of government	627	Savings etc.	322
		Net income from abroad	784		
Total residents' incomes	8,494	Total residents' output	8,494	Total residents' expenditure	8,494
Territorial income		**Territorial output**		**Territorial expenditure**	
Incomes of individuals	7,371	Net output of mining	7,353	Personal cash expenditure at factor cost	4,162
Incomes of companies	5,954	Net output of agriculture	2,000	Subsidence consumption	1,891
Incomes of government	175	Net output of manufacturing	321	Expenditure abroad by individuals	774
		Net output of distribution and transport	1,811	Total personal consumption	6,827
		Net output of other goods and services	977	Government current expenditure	1,245
		Net output of government	899	Savings etc.	5,428
		Net income from abroad	139		
Total territorial income	13,500	Total territorial output	13,500	Total territorial expenditure	13,500

Source: Deane (1953) pp. 63 and 64.

Deane (Deane, 1953) on the social accounts of what was then Northern Rhodesia (now Zambia) for 1938. We present a version of Deane's summary tables as Table 2.1.

It is obvious from Table 2.1 that Northern Rhodesia's territorial income was, in 1938, much greater than its residents' income. The main reason for this was that in the concept of territorial income it was proper to treat mining companies registered in the UK and operating in Northern Rhodesia as wholly (except for their London head office) within the Northern Rhodesian economy. So, in the sum of incomes calculations, undistributed profits, income earned by shareholders, and royalties of such companies were treated as part of the territorial income, but not of course of residents' income because these incomes did not accrue to residents in Northern Rhodesia. Similarly, in the sum of outputs calculations, the main difference is in the much greater value attributed to net output of mining on the territorial than on the residential basis, again because of the importance of 'non-resident' companies. Lastly, in the sum of expenditures calculations, the main difference is in the item 'savings, etc.' which in the territorial expenditure includes the investment by these 'non-resident' companies.

Although it is thought to be unusual to observe such a striking difference between the residents' and territorial income, this brief look at Deane's work should illustrate two important points. First, there may be a difference. In the Northern Rhodesian case it was because of UK investment in the economy: more generally, as Deane herself says, such differences may arise 'for a dependent economy where the economic boundaries coincide less closely with national boundaries, and where economic resources can only be exploited with the substantial aid of factors of production drawn from outside its own geographical boundaries' (p. 60) – and, as we have suggested in Chapter 1 and will elaborate in detail later, this dependence characterises the Scottish economy as 'satellite' to that of the UK. Secondly, once it is decided which concept to measure, it is possible at least in principle to produce measures of that concept by all three methods and arrive at the same total; that is, we should in principle get the same answer whether we sum incomes, or outputs, or expenditures, provided the calculations are done on a consistent basis.

Which concept of national income one should measure depends on the purpose to which the measure is to be put. For example, if our concern was to assess the well-being of the inhabitants of a country, then residents' income or expenditure would seem the natural measure; if we were interested in assessing the output potential of a country, then territorial output would be the most appropriate measure. Since in this book we are concerned both with enjoyment of incomes and with output potential, we should ideally wish to present for Scotland tables for each year from 1954 corresponding in form to Table 2.1. In fact, however, the evidence we can present is much more fragmentary, and cannot distinguish adequately between the concepts of residents' income and territorial income.

The most fundamental problem is that some of the information we need is just not collected for regions, rather than for national economies. For example, cross-border flows of purchases of goods and services and of payments for factor services are usually not measured for regions of a country, because there is no institutional need to measure them for customs and excise purposes, and so regional balance of payment accounts cannot be constructed. Similarly, the extent of net savings in a region will not normally be measured unless some kind of flow funds account is compiled for the region, and there are normally inadequate data to construct flow of funds accounts if there is not an independent banking and financial system. But without information about 'rest of the world' transactions or about the extent of net savings, it is not possible to check against each other accounts compiled as the sum of incomes or of outputs and the sum of expenditures. Further, such information as is available is in some cases collected on a residents' basis (like regional income-tax statistics) and in some cases a territorial basis (like regional output statistics derived from the Census of Production), and there are in some respects insuperable problems in trying accurately to identify the practical extent of the differences implied by the two concepts, again because there is no institutional need to keep an accurate tally of how many people live in one region and work in another, or of what tourists from one region of a country spend when they come visiting another region. The obtainable data thus do not conform very tidily to the conceptual distinctions but that does not mean that it is not important to be clear what we are trying to measure.

Income and Output

Suppose, as is the case in most of this book, that our interest is in territorial income. Then national income is a measure of the economic activity within the frontiers of the area under consideration. We can, as Table 2.1 shows, look on this by adding together the different kinds of income received as a result of economic activity within the frontiers of the area. In Table 2.1, income is distinguished according to who received it. It is the convention in more modern presentation to distinguish income into categories of source of income, that is, income from employment, income from self-employment, income from rent, etc. Table 2.2 presents estimates of Scottish income for the years 1954–79 calculated in this way. Because of data deficiencies, it is not completely consistent, and particularly for the earlier years it is probably

Table 2.2   *Scottish national income 1954–79 (sum of incomes),*

A *Absolute income, £ million*		1954	1955	1956
Income from employment		946	1,027	1,112
Income from self-employment		165	170	178
Gross trading profits and surpluses	}	318	342	344
Rent				
Gross domestic product (at factor cost)[1]		1,429	1,539	1,644
B *Scottish income per head as % of UK income per head*[2]				
Income from employment		91.5	91.0	90.6
Income from self-employment		104.1	102.1	103.9
Gross trading surpluses	}	83.4	82.7	80.5
Rent				
Gross domestic product (at factor cost)		90.4	90.9	90.0

A *Absolute income, £ million*		1967	1968	1969
Income from employment		1,980	2,126	2,272
Income from self-employment		266	282	315
Gross trading profits and surpluses	}	551	623	663
Rent		176	194	216
Gross domestic product (at factor cost)		2,957	3,170	3,401
B *Scottish income per head as % of UK income per head*				
Income from employment		87.7	88.4	88.6
Income from self-employment		98.9	97.0	99.3
Gross trading surpluses	}	96.2	100.6	100.9
Rent		95.7	95.4	94.5
Gross domestic product (at factor cost)		89.2	89.3	91.0

[1]The figures for gross domestic product in Scotland in 1960–79 contain an adjustment for stock appreciation not specified in the table.

[2]The figures for the sources of income in the UK for 1958–69 are adjusted for stock appreciation. The total gross domestic product figures for the UK are also corrected for residual error.

closer to residents' than to territorial income, but it represents as coherent a picture as can reasonably be presented. We outline how the table was compiled, and indicate some of its major discontinuities, in pp. 191-6. We should mention here, however, our debt to the pioneering work of Campbell (1955) and that of McCrone (1965) whose figures we have used for the earliest part of this table.

The absolute figures presented for the various types of income in Table 2.2 are set out at current prices – that is, there is no correction for inflation. To help us to place the evidence in context, we have calculated Scottish income per head of Scottish population under each heading as a percentage of the corresponding UK income per head of UK population, and these figures are shown in the lower part of Table 2.2, where, of course, a figure of 100 says that Scottish income per head in this category exactly equals UK income per head, a figure of over 100 that Scottish income per head is greater than the UK average, and a figure of under 100 that Scottish income per head is less than the UK average.

A glance at Table 2.2 reveals that, while Scottish income per head as measured in this way did not differ very markedly from UK income per head (as on most items the percentage is within the range 95-105), there are nevertheless some important dissimilarities and there appear to be some interesting time patterns. We shall here simply mention the differences, put them together later in this chapter with the evidence from other methods of measuring income, and in Chapter 4 we will look in some depth at how they might have emerged and what they imply about the performance of the Scottish economy.

Income from employment in Scotland was consistently below the UK level. We shall in Chapter 3 say a little about the behaviour of wages in Scotland and there we will confirm that the impression given in Table 2.2, of a steady rise in Scottish income from employment relative to the UK from about 1964, reflects wage levels and that it is not a consequence of changing activity rates. This rise, however, followed a period of equally steady relative decline in Scotland from 1954 to 1964, and it was not until 1972-3 that income per head from employment in Scotland as a proportion of the UK reached its 1954 level. In terms of income from employment, which as the top half of Table 2.2 shows is much the most important source of income, Scotland was doing noticeably worse than the UK throughout the period 1954-79, and was slipping further behind the UK for the first ten years or so of that period. Income from self-employment in Scotland was consistently at a little above the UK level per head. This is, as we shall see in Table 2.3, a consequence of the greater importance in Scotland of farming, one of the main areas of self-employment. Rent is a little difficult to measure, because of the necessity to impute a figure for rent of owner-occupied premises, but the picture that emerges from Table 2.2 is that profit (gross trading surplus) and rent together were low in Scotland at the beginning of our period but from 1971 were usually exceeding UK levels, largely thanks to relatively high profit figures. Perhaps the most important information in Table 2.2 is its measure of Scottish income (gross domestic product): as income from employment is so important to the total, it is not surprising that the behaviour of gross domestic product per head in Scotland is similar to that of income from employment, running consistently below UK levels and declining from 1954 to 1961, climbing steadily to 1973, and behaving a little erratically thereafter.

Adding together the income generated as a result of economic activity within an area is not the only way of measuring the territorial income of that area. It is also possible to add together the value of the outputs made in that area. Provided that the outputs are valued at factor cost – that is, at cost of production, free from distortions of indirect taxes or subsidies – and that suitable care is taken to count each value only once, adding together the value of outputs should produce the same result as adding together incomes generated as a result of making that output. This is, of course, because each part of the value of output represents an income to whoever provided the resources – labour, capital equipment, etc. – to make that output; or, looking from the other end, each income is earned out of some contribution to the value of output.

In principle then, the absolute figures in the top half of Table 2.3, which presents income measured as sum of outputs for Scotland for the years 1954 to 1979, should total to the same figures for gross domestic product as those we have presented in Table 2.2, because Table 2.2 looks at a total of activity in terms of type of income, and Table 2.3 looks at the same total in terms of the industry in which the income is earned. In the Appendix, when we discuss the sources and methods used to construct Table 2.3 (see pp. 191-6), we make it clear that the evidence used for this table differs from that used for Table 2.2: and because the calculations are done in two different ways, each of which contains some degree of error, the totals cannot be expected exactly to coincide. When the same source is used, the totals have been balanced – so the data for 1954–7, which are for both tables taken unaltered from McCrone (1965), coincide, as do the estimates for 1971–9, again because the same official source is used for both tables.

As the absolute figures in the top half of Table 2.3 are calculated at current prices, they are difficult to interpret without correction for inflation (which is done later, in Table 2.5), and so our preliminary examination of the evidence here will again focus on the second half of the table, which presents the percentage share of Scottish output contributed by each industry with, in brackets, the share that the corresponding industry in the UK has of UK output.

current prices

1957	1958	1959	1960	1961	1962	1963	1964	1965	1966
112	113	109	113	124	124	126	128	136	149
72	68	65	62	78	78	69	77	75	74
628	639	656	708	651	648	702	779	844	910
97	104	108	125	153	165	176	197	207	226
43	44	47	49	58	64	70	78	85	92
173	152	150	177	178	186	199	215	228	240
204	187	198	208	215	223	232	252	267	279
35	32	34	38	46	49	51	50	54	56
48	55	61	64	74	77	83	91	103	116
110	117	113	117	120	130	138	149	159	170
74	80	87	96	105	113	122	129	141	159
157	149	156	186	208	221	248	251	257	304
1,753	1,740	1,784	1,943	1,998	2,070	2,213	2,373	2,533	2,749

6.4	6.5	6.1	5.8	6.2	6.0	5.7	5.4	5.4	5.4
(4.5)	(4.3)	(4.1)	(4.0)	(3.9)	(3.9)	(3.7)	(3.4)	(3.3)	(3.2)
4.1	3.9	3.6	3.2	3.9	3.8	3.1	3.2	3.0	2.7
(3.7)	(3.5)	(3.3)	(3.0)	(2.9)	(3.0)	(2.8)	(2.5)	(2.3)	(2.1)
35.8	36.7	36.8	36.4	32.6	31.3	31.7	32.8	33.3	33.1
(35.8)	(34.9)	(35.5)	(36.5)	(35.2)	(34.2)	(34.1)	(33.7)	(34.0)	(33.2)
5.5	6.0	6.1	6.4	7.7	8.0	8.0	8.3	8.2	8.2
(5.9)	(5.9)	(5.8)	(6.0)	(6.2)	(6.4)	(6.5)	(6.9)	(6.9)	(6.8)
2.5	2.5	2.6	2.5	2.9	3.1	3.2	3.3	3.4	3.3
(2.5)	(2.6)	(2.7)	(2.7)	(2.8)	(2.9)	(3.1)	(3.1)	(3.2)	(3.2)
9.9	8.7	8.4	9.1	8.9	9.0	9.0	9.1	9.0	8.7
(8.5)	(8.0)	(8.0)	(8.6)	(8.4)	(8.4)	(8.6)	(8.4)	(8.4)	(8.4)
11.6	10.8	11.1	10.7	10.8	10.8	10.5	10.6	10.5	10.1
(12.4)	(12.2)	(12.1)	(12.2)	(11.9)	(11.9)	(11.8)	(11.4)	(11.5)	(11.3)
2.0	1.8	1.9	2.0	2.3	2.4	2.3	2.1	2.1	2.0
(2.6)	(2.7)	(3.0)	(3.0)	(3.2)	(3.4)	(3.5)	(6.5)	(6.7)	(6.6)
6.3	6.7	6.3	6.0	6.0	6.3	6.2	6.3	6.3	6.2
(6.0)	(6.1)	(6.0)	(5.9)	(5.7)	(5.8)	(5.8)	(5.7)	(5.8)	(6.0)
4.2	4.6	4.9	4.9	5.3	5.5	5.5	5.4	5.6	5.8
(3.6)	(3.7)	(3.9)	(4.0)	(4.0)	(4.3)	(4.4)	(4.3)	(4.6)	(4.7)
9.0	8.6	8.7	9.6	10.4	10.7	11.2	10.6	10.1	11.1
(10.5)	(10.9)	(11.1)	(11.3)	(12.1)	(12.1)	(12.4)	(11.8)	(11.7)	(12.0)

Table 2.3   *Scottish national income, 1954–79 (sum of outputs),*

A *Absolute output (£ million)*	1967	1968	1969
Agriculture, forestry and fishing	144	160	175
Mining and quarrying	76	60	62
Manufacturing	915	952	1,066
Construction	236	271	292
Gas, electricity and water	102	108	111
Transport and communication	244	261	292
Distributive trades	284	308	315
Insurance, banking and finance	66	76	87
Ownership of dwellings	129	146	171
Public administration and defence	184	195	211
Public health and education services	173	186	201
Other services	330	357	369
Gross domestic product at factor cost[1]	2,869	3,070	3,312

B *The structure of GDP in Scotland (the UK)*			
Agriculture, forestry and fishing	5.0	5.2	5.3
	(3.2)	(3.0)	(3.0)
Mining and quarrying[2]	2.6	2.0	1.9
	(2.1)	(1.8)	(1.5)
Manufacturing	31.9	31.0	32.2
	(32.0)	(32.0)	(33.0)
Construction	8.2	8.8	8.8
	(6.8)	(6.9)	(6.8)
Gas, electricity and water	3.6	3.5	3.4
	(3.3)	(3.5)	(3.5)
Transport and communication	8.5	8.5	8.8
	(8.1)	(8.4)	(8.6)
Distributive trades	9.9	10.0	9.5
	(11.2)	(10.8)	(10.6)
Insurance, banking and finance[3]	2.3	2.5	2.6
	(6.9)	(7.3)	(6.8)
Public administration and defence	6.4	6.4	6.4
	(6.1)	(6.1)	(6.6)
Public health and education services	6.0	6.1	6.1
	(4.8)	(4.9)	(5.3)
Other services[3]	11.5	11.6	11.1
	(12.3)	(12.5)	(12.8)

[1]The figures for 1961–70 contain an adjustment for stock appreciation not specified in the table.

[2]Excluding petroleum and natural gas.

current prices (cont'd.)

1970	1971	1972	1973	1974	1975	1976	1977	1978	1979
191	222	240	300	312	380	481	501	473	510
67	62	72	78	106	159	184	221	238	312
1,183	1,297	1,417	1,682	1,846	2,312	2,701	3,074	3,654	3,950
294	355	420	550	658	814	926	944	1,062	1,202
129	149	163	186	215	258	356	382	437	451
327	353	400	474	571	716	878	927	1,080	1,231
366	456	524	608	652	837	935	1,110	1,288	1,414
98	132	156	171	159	220	275	301	357	451
195	205	214	254	312	377	440	488	533	601
237	273	322	363	454	632	764	793	919	1,052
230	274	345	372	485	722	810	875	972	1,101
389	509	577	730	804	1,010	1,248	1,418	1,686	2,024
3,693	4,294	4,852	5,768	6,575	8,438	9,998	11,034	12,699	14,299

1970	1971	1972	1973	1974	1975	1976	1977	1978	1979
5.2	5.3	5.0	5.2	4.8	4.5	4.8	4.5	3.7	3.6
(2.9)	(2.9)	(2.8)	(3.1)	(2.8)	(2.7)	(2.7)	(2.6)	(2.5)	(2.3)
1.8	1.5	1.5	1.4	1.6	1.9	1.8	2.0	1.9	2.2
(1.4)	(1.3)	(1.3)	(1.3)	(1.4)	(1.6)	(1.5)	(1.6)	(1.5)	(1.6)
32.0	31.0	29.2	29.2	28.1	27.4	27.0	27.9	28.8	27.6
(32.9)	(31.8)	(31.2)	(30.9)	(29.0)	(28.6)	(28.0)	(28.8)	(28.9)	(27.9)
8.0	8.5	8.7	9.5	10.0	9.7	9.3	8.6	8.4	8.4
(7.0)	(6.9)	(7.7)	(8.3)	(8.1)	(7.1)	(6.7)	(6.3)	(6.3)	(6.3)
3.5	3.6	3.4	3.2	3.3	3.1	3.6	3.5	3.4	3.2
(3.2)	(3.2)	(3.2)	(3.0)	(3.1)	(3.1)	(3.3)	(3.3)	(3.1)	(2.9)
8.9	8.4	8.3	8.2	8.7	8.5	8.8	8.4	8.5	8.6
(8.6)	(8.3)	(8.4)	(8.4)	(8.7)	(8.6)	(8.7)	(8.2)	(8.3)	(8.4)
9.9	10.9	10.8	10.5	9.9	9.9	9.4	10.1	10.1	9.9
(10.6)	(10.8)	(11.1)	(11.0)	(10.4)	(10.6)	(10.0)	(10.2)	(10.6)	(10.5)
2.7	3.2	3.2	3.0	2.4	2.6	2.8	2.7	2.8	3.2
(7.1)	(7.3)	(7.8)	(8.7)	(8.4)	(7.5)	(8.2)	(8.3)	(8.3)	(9.1)
6.4	6.5	6.6	6.3	6.9	7.5	7.6	7.2	7.2	7.4
(6.8)	(7.1)	(7.2)	(6.9)	(7.4)	(7.9)	(7.6)	(7.3)	(7.0)	(7.2)
6.2	6.5	7.1	6.5	7.4	8.6	8.1	7.9	7.7	7.7
(5.4)	(5.6)	(6.0)	(5.8)	(6.5)	(7.7)	(7.3)	(6.9)	(6.7)	(6.7)
10.5	9.8	11.9	12.7	12.2	12.0	12.5	12.9	13.3	14.2
(13.0)	(11.9)	(12.4)	(13.0)	(12.5)	(12.3)	(12.3)	(12.5)	(12.8)	(13.6)

[3]Some services included in 'Other services in the UK' from 1954 to 1963 are included in 'Insurance, banking and finance' from 1964 onwards.

In Chapter 1, we presented an overview of the industrial pattern of economic activity in Scotland in terms of employment, and we argued there that the Scottish economy had adapted much more slowly in the early part of this century to changing patterns of demand than had the UK economy. Table 2.3 gives a very different impression. Obviously, we cannot identify how far the industries in which Scotland is now more specialised than the UK are the potential source of growth for the future, but the sheer alterations of structure of output are really quite striking, even in terms of the very broad categories analysed in the table. The share of manufacturing in Scottish output has fallen from over 35 per cent in 1954 to under 28 per cent in 1979, and the decline took place rather earlier in Scotland than in the UK. Output from agriculture, forestry and fishing and from mining and quarrying has also fallen steadily in relative importance in both economies, though the fall there has been a little slower in Scotland. Construction and the public utilities (gas, electricity and water) have grown in importance in both economies but faster in Scotland than in the UK. Measurement problems make comparisons about the individual service industries a little tricky, but a clear pattern of overall growth at about the same rate in both economies emerges, most clearly exemplified perhaps by the 'other services' group.

What these changes can be taken to imply for the health of the economy is a matter of some dispute. Some would support the view advanced most forcefully by Bacon and Eltis (1976), that the decline in importance of the manufacturing sector, or perhaps of the sector which produces tangible goods (which also embraces agriculture and mining and quarrying and construction) is a symptom of decline in an economy because other industries can thrive only if there is a substantial surplus of physical goods and services which can be made available to pay people employed in these other industries. So, for example, a crude version of this argument would be that workers in service industries are regarded as consuming the surplus generated by workers in manufacturing and not themselves able to give any surplus to those in manufacturing.

Critics of this argument would say that it rests on too simplistic a concept of what is economically useful, because the activities of workers in the service industries add to the total of goods and services in the community, and whether the output is tangible or not is irrelevant. The matter is, however, more complicated when in general the output of the manufacturing sector is sold at a market price and the output of the service sector is available 'free', because then there is no check on whether the output of services is at what is perceived by consumers to be the right level. There is a further complexity in the argument when it is recognised that output in manufacturing industries is typically made by the use of sophisticated machinery, so that output per worker can be high and can be raised by technical progress, whereas output in service industries is frequently generated with very little use of capital equipment and consequently with low output per worker and little prospect of rises in output per worker. So an economy with a declining manufacturing sector and a growing service sector might be changing its output in a manner not really desired by its consumers and in such a way as to reduce its potential for growth in output per head.

Against this line of argument it can be claimed that the decline in manufacturing and growth in services is part of the development process of an economy, rather on the pattern suggested by Rostow (1963). Rostow generalised the experience of developed economies to conclude that they have typically gone through a series of stages in their development process, one such stage being a decline in agriculture and an expansion in manufacturing. Rostow suggested that the most mature economies he could observe were perhaps in the process of starting a similar switch, from manufacturing into services. If this is so, then the structural change we can see in Table 2.3 for both Scotland and the UK is simply a move into a new stage of development.

For better or for worse, the structural changes have been marked. Later in this chapter, we will look at the behaviour of output in manufacturing in Scotland in a little more detail, and return then to what these changes imply for the health of the economy. In Chapter 4, we will look more closely at the evidence about the service sector.

Expenditure

The last of three methods of measuring income is to add together expenditures. Table 2.4 presents the results of such an exercise for Scotland, for the period 1961–79. A shorter period has been used for this table mainly because the basic data are not available for the earlier years. Again, the Appendix describes the sources and methods used (see pp. 191–6).

Whereas the sum of outputs and sum of incomes methods had to give the same total because we were looking at the same transactions from two different standpoints, in the case of the sum of expenditures method the total we reach is in principle different from that reached by the other two methods, and would require an adjustment to bring it into line with them. In the presentation in Table 2.1, the totals are made to match by the item called 'saving, etc.'. In the more modern presentation, as for example in the UK national income accounts in *Blue Book*, the totals are shown to balance through trade flows, in essence as follows:

Table 2.4 *Scottish Expenditure, 1961–79, current prices*

A Absolute expenditure, £ million

	1961	1962	1963	1964	1965	1966	1967	1968	1969	1970
Consumers' expenditure	1,594	1,688	1,729	1,951	2,066	2,180	2,251	2,394	2,568	2,796
General government final consumption	464	493	519	550	587	645	708	755	801	900
Gross domestic fixed capital formation	439	446	479	522	587	648	712	867	919	985
Value of physical increase in stocks and work in progress	50	4	44	218	99	68	61	104	99	32
Gross domestic expenditure at market prices	2,547	2,631	2,771	3,241	3,339	3,541	3,732	4,120	4,387	4,713
Taxes on expenditure	−354	−378	−390	−438	−481	−563	−605	−670	−755	−819
Subsidies	116	113	110	111	115	123	151	201	223	226
Gross domestic expenditure at factor cost	2,309	2,366	2,491	2,914	2,973	3,101	3,278	3,651	3,855	4,120

A Absolute expenditure, £ million

	1971	1972	1973	1974	1975	1976	1977	1978	1979
Consumers' expenditure	3,035	3,384	3,909	4,605	5,620	6,513	7,503	8,632	9,510
General government final consumption	1,041	1,181	1,348	1,734	2,256	2,712	3,218	3,441	3,974
Gross domestic fixed capital formation	970	1,079	1,321	1,680	2,193	2,529	2,747	3,174	3,655
Value of physical increase in stocks and work in progress	30	−2	33	73	−44	−10	35	−4	40
Gross domestic expenditure at market prices	5,076	5,642	6,611	8,092	10,025	11,744	13,503	15,243	17,179
Taxes on expenditure	−847	−872	−967	−1,100	−1,330	−1,582	−1,937	−2,119	−2,651
Subsidies	237	239	265	426	542	582	500	525	605
Gross domestic expenditure at factor cost	4,466	5,009	5,909	7,418	9,237	10,744	12,066	13,649	15,133

Table 2.4 *Scottish Expenditure, 1961–79, current prices (cont'd.)*

B *Percentage analysis of expenditure in Scotland (the UK), and expenditure per head in Scotland (the UK)*

	1961	1962	1963	1964	1965	1966	1967	1968	1969
Consumers' expenditure	69.0	71.3	69.4	67.0	69.5	70.3	68.7	65.6	66.6
	(73.2)	(74.6)	(74.4)	(72.1)	(72.7)	(73.2)	(72.1)	(72.5)	(74.1)
General government final consumption	20.1	20.8	20.8	17.8	19.7	20.8	21.6	20.7	20.8
	(18.7)	(19.2)	(19.0)	(18.3)	(19.0)	(19.6)	(20.4)	(20.2)	(20.3)
Gross capital formation (including stocks)	21.2	19.0	21.0	25.4	23.1	23.1	23.6	26.6	26.4
	(20.5)	(19.0)	(19.4)	(22.7)	(22.2)	(21.8)	(22.2)	(22.9)	(23.2)
Gross domestic expenditure at market prices	110.3	111.2	111.2	111.2	112.3	114.2	113.8	112.8	113.8
	(112.5)	(112.9)	(112.8)	(113.1)	(113.9)	(114.6)	(114.7)	(115.6)	(117.6)
Taxes on expenditure	−15.3	−16.0	−15.7	−15.0	−16.2	−18.2	−18.5	−18.4	−19.6
	(−14.9)	(−15.3)	(−14.8)	(−14.9)	(−15.7)	(−16.3)	(−16.9)	(−17.9)	(−19.7)
Subsidies	5.0	4.8	4.4	3.8	3.9	4.0	4.6	5.5	5.8
	(2.4)	(2.4)	(2.1)	(1.7)	(1.8)	(1.7)	(2.3)	(2.4)	(2.1)
Gross domestic expenditure at factor cost	100.0	100.0	99.9	100.0	100.0	100.0	99.9	99.9	100.0
	(110.0)	(100.0)	(100.1)	(99.9)	(100.0)	(100.0)	(100.1)	(100.1)	(100.0)
Gross domestic expenditure per head at factor cost (£)	445	455	479	559	572	596	631	702	740
	(461)	(476)	(505)	(553)	(582)	(610)	(646)	(690)	(714)

Table 2.4 Scottish Expenditure, 1961–79, current prices (cont'd.)

B Percentage analysis of expenditure in Scotland (the UK), and expenditure per head in Scotland (the UK)

	1970	1971	1972	1973	1974	1975	1976	1977	1978	1979
Consumers' expenditure	67.9 (73.7)	68.0 (73.1)	67.6 (72.5)	66.2 (69.1)	62.1 (66.7)	60.8 (67.2)	60.6 (66.3)	62.2 (68.3)	63.2 (69.1)	62.8 (70.4)
General government final consumption	21.8 (20.8)	23.3 (21.1)	23.6 (21.1)	22.8 (20.2)	23.4 (21.1)	24.4 (23.9)	25.3 (23.7)	26.7 (23.2)	25.2 (23.0)	26.3 (23.1)
Gross capital formation (including stocks)	24.7 (22.9)	22.4 (21.9)	21.5 (21.0)	22.9 (23.7)	23.6 (22.9)	23.3 (19.7)	23.4 (21.6)	23.1 (22.0)	23.2 (21.5)	24.4 (22.2)
Gross domestic expenditure at market prices	114.4 (117.5)	113.7 (116.1)	112.6 (114.6)	111.9 (113.1)	109.1 (110.7)	108.5 (110.8)	109.3 (111.6)	111.9 (113.5)	111.7 (113.7)	113.5 (115.6)
Taxes on expenditure	−19.9 (−19.5)	−19.0 (−18.1)	−17.4 (−16.7)	−16.4 (−15.3)	−14.8 (−14.5)	−14.4 (−14.7)	−14.7 (−14.6)	−16.1 (−16.1)	−15.5 (−16.2)	−17.5 (−18.2)
Subsidies	5.5 (2.0)	5.3 (1.9)	4.8 (2.1)	4.5 (2.2)	5.8 (3.8)	5.9 (3.8)	5.4 (3.1)	4.1 (2.6)	3.8 (2.5)	4.0 (2.6)
Gross domestic expenditure at factor cost	100.0 (100.0)	100.0 (99.9)	100.0 (100.0)	100.0 (100.0)	100.1 (100.0)	100.0 (99.9)	100.0 (100.1)	99.9 (100.0)	100.0 (100.0)	100.0 (100.0)
Gross domestic expenditure per head at factor cost (£)	790 (778)	856 (875)	961 (993)	1,134 (1,183)	1,422 (1,411)	1,774 (1,723)	2,064 (2,023)	2,322 (2,255)	2,630 (2,569)	2,929 (2,968)

total expenditure
plus exports
minus imports
equals total output.

The reasoning is essentially simple. The total of expenditure looks at the total of purchases made by consumers, investors and government within the territory. These purchases will usually include the purchase of some goods not made within the territory – in the case of Scotland, imports from outside the UK, such as Japanese cars, and also imports from the rest of the UK, such as English apples. Since these goods were not made in Scotland, there was no contribution to Scottish output from their production, and no income was earned in Scotland from their production, and so they must be deducted from Scottish expenditure to arrive at Scottish output or Scottish income. At the same time, there were some goods made in Scotland but entering consumption either in the rest of the UK or in some other part of the world – such as Scotch whisky sold in London or in the USA – and since these goods were made in Scotland they contribute to Scottish output and to Scottish income and therefore should be added to the expenditure total to bring it into consistency with the output and income total. If we were able to measure Scottish imports and exports, all we would need to do is add an appropriate tail-piece to Table 2.4 to produce totals consistent with those in Table 2.2 and 2.3, in the same way as, in Table 2.1, the three measures of national income are equated. As we have already mentioned, however, we cannot measure Scottish imports and exports, because the figures simply are not collected, and although there is evidence for 1973 (and there will shortly be similar evidence for 1979) from a special survey (the Scottish Input-Output Project, 1978), it is difficult to use that evidence with any confidence to make firm statements about trade flows. We will, however, offer a few comments in Chapter 6 about what the input-output evidence appears to tell us about trade flows, and later in this chapter we will suggest what can be inferred about trade flows from a comparison of Table 2.4 with Tables 2.2 and 2.3.

The other method of attempting to reconcile the sum of expenditures with the sum of incomes or outputs is the one used in Table 2.1, to argue that the difference between expenditure and income has to be saving (if income exceeds expenditure) or dissaving (if expenditure exceeds income), this saving arising from the net effect of the transactions of individuals, companies and government. Unfortunately, pursuing this line of thought does not help in practice, because to measure the extent of this saving we would need to have access to financial information in the form of flow-of-funds accounts, and as we have already mentioned these too are lacking for Scotland. For a discussion of what *can* be deduced about the flow of funds when there is an input-output table, see Bulmer-Thomas (1978).

Although for these reasons Table 2.4 cannot be fully related to Tables 2.2 and 2.3, we think it is of considerable interest in its own right. Despite the fact that in Table 2.4 there are no figures for exports, it represents the complete statement of the sources of domestic demand within Scotland, and can thus be used to identify whither Scottish producers should look to sell their goods and services in Scotland. Again, it is most useful in exploring matters in greater depth to concentrate not on the first part of the table, which is at current prices (the same information will appear at constant prices in Table 2.7), but on the second part of the table, where each kind of expenditure is measured as a percentage of the total, and the figures in brackets show the percentage which each item in the UK forms of the corresponding UK total.

All but one of the individual items in Table 2.4 merit discussion in detail. The exception is stock appreciation – in principle, this item of expenditure is an interesting indicator of cyclical behaviour (stocks of finished goods and work in progress bear the first brunt when sales are different from expectations, being run down at the start of a boom and built up at the start of a recession), but in practice it is extremely difficult to measure stock appreciation satisfactorily, and so the figures for stock appreciation in Table 2.4 should be treated with great caution.

As the table demonstrates, the most important single component of expenditure, both in Scotland and in the UK, is consumers' expenditure. Since conventional economic theory relates consumers' expenditure to personal income, and since we have seen from Table 2.2 that income per head was in Scotland persistently below UK levels, it is perhaps not surprising that consumers' expenditure represented a noticeably lower proportion of total expenditure in Scotland than its share in the UK, but of course for that to be so there must have been some other parts of total expenditure which were relatively big in Scotland. A glance at Table 2.4 shows that in every year government current expenditure (general government final consumption) was more important in expenditure in Scotland than in the UK generally, and that in nearly every year investment was also relatively higher in Scotland. As total expenditure per head of population was (with some variations which we discuss below) very similar in the two economies, the implication is that this shortfall in consumers' expenditure per head in Scotland was almost exactly balanced by the large amounts, by UK standards, of government and investment expenditure per head. Although the composition of the adjustment to convert transactions from valuation at market prices (that is, valuation at what final purchasers pay) to valuation at factor cost (that is, at cost of production) was systematically different between Scotland and the UK, subsidies being persistently more important in Scotland, mainly because of the relatively large share of output coming from agriculture and because of the relatively large amount of local authority housing, the net effect of the factor cost adjustment was fairly similar in the two economies, although it usually served to diminish Scottish expenditure a little less than UK expenditure. (It should be noted that the statistics used to compile Table 2.4B are not completely consistent in their treatment of indirect taxes and subsidies, as the UK figures include all taxes levied on imports, and these are only partly included in the corresponding Scottish figures.)

The most surprising feature of Table 2.4, in the light of our earlier discussion, is the clear evidence it gives of expenditure per head in Scotland being in aggregate, though not in detailed composition, similar to that in the UK. Indeed, there is a fairly systematic pattern in the relative sums, with Scottish expenditure per head being less than the UK average more or less consistently from 1961 to 1967, above the UK average in 1968 to 1970, below the UK level again in 1971 to 1973, and back above the UK level in 1974–8. In the more recent years, the connection between the relative size of Scottish expenditure and the political complexion of the UK government has been very noticeable: a Conservative government came into office in mid 1970 and was succeeded in early 1974 by a Labour government, which in turn fell to a Conservative government in early 1979. As we shall see later in this book, the role of government in the Scottish economy has been pervasive, both in direct matters represented in Table 2.4 as general government final consumption and in ways which have tended to promote gross capital formation, partly through the placing of government contracts and partly by the stimulation through subsidies and tax allowances and non-financial inducements of private sector investment. This has been, as we will show, partly automatic and partly the conscious operation of regional policy. In recent years, Conservative governments have tended to be more cautious about public expenditure generally and regional policy in particular than Labour governments, and it is accordingly hard to escape the conclusion that party-political processes are relevant to the understanding of Table 2.4.

Real Income

The evidence we have discussed so far in this chapter is of income at current prices – 1974 income at 1974 prices, 1970 income at 1970 prices, etc. For many purposes it is more illuminating to consider income statistics at constant prices – that is, with all items valued at the price levels prevailing in one year – because in that way we can identify changes in the real volume of goods and services. So income at constant prices is the basis from which we can calculate growth rates, as used later in this book.

We have therefore recalculated the basic information in Tables 2.3 and 2.4 at constant prices. We have used 1975 as the base year for the constant price recalculations, because 1975 is the base year used for the official statistics for the UK in *Blue Book* and so presenting the Scottish statistics to the same base facilitates comparison. It should be noted at the outset, however, that the constant prices calculations are inevitably based on rather inadequate information. There is very little comprehensive information about Scottish price levels. There have been some studies of prices of particular consumer items in Scottish towns, and there is fairly firm evidence about prices of some commodities, but in general the price indices used have to be based either on very indirect proxies or on UK price indices. When we had reason to believe on *a priori* grounds that Scottish prices probably behave notably differently from UK prices – for structural reasons, as in output in agriculture, forestry and fishing, where the structure of output in Scotland is different from that in the UK, for other reasons such as in housing, where for reasons of different building standards and differences in the proportions of rented accommodation, Scottish prices are known to be influenced by special factors – we found or devised what we believe to be a suitably Scottish price index, but otherwise we have used UK prices information where there was no obvious alternative. We indicate our sources in the Appendix (see pp. 191–6).

We have not recalculated the analysis of sources of income (in Table 2.2) at constant prices, as we have not used such evidence anywhere later in this book. We do, however, deal later with the sum of outputs evidence and Table 2.5 presents the information in the first part of Table 2.3 re-estimated at constant (1975) prices.

As Table 2.5 shows, at constant prices total output in Scotland rose from some £5,800 million in 1954 to £8,900 million in 1979 – an increase of some 55 per cent over the 25 years, or growth at a compound rate of a little over 1 per cent per annum. In real terms, manufacturing output reached its peak in 1973. In most services output grew slowly, albeit rather irregularly, throughout the period. So far, the conclusions that emerge are, not surprisingly, similar to those we could draw from Table 2.3. Table 2.6 does, however, contribute new evidence, by disaggregating manufacturing output at constant prices into output from individual industries. This, again, is evidence which we use in later chapters. In this case, we present the evidence initially at constant rather than at current prices because, somewhat paradoxically, a constant prices series is closer to the way that the information is originally published. Evidence about output in manufacturing industries in Scotland is available from returns collected as part of the Census of Production.

The Census was originally conducted at roughly five–year intervals – thus, in the period we have been considering in this chapter, there were full Censuses of Production in 1954, 1958, 1963 and 1968. There were some sample Census enquiries in the intervening years but details of these are not published for regions. From 1970, there has been an annual Census of Production. The Census of Production collects details for the relevant industries (manufacturing; mining and quarrying; construction; and gas, electricity and water), and the evidence is published at current prices. Well before the Census details are published, however, information from the Census is used to update the Scottish index of industrial production, which as its name implies is an index of output at constant prices for each major industry covered by the Census.

As explained in the official account of the latest version of this index (*Scottish Economic Bulletin* No. 19), the index is constructed by in most cases using UK price changes but with a weighting of industries reflecting the Scottish pattern of industrial output in the base year (1975). When – as in Chapter 4 – we want to use a long and continuous run of evidence, we have constructed an artificial index of industrial production by a simple chain-linking of three Scottish series (one published to a 1975 base, one to a 1970 base and one to a 1963 base): this is procedurally a little unsatisfactory, because it is technically illegitimate to link indices with different weightings in this way, but is the only practicable method open to us. Table 2.6 sets out the results of a rather more rigorous treatment, when we have concentrated on Census of Production years and the figures we quote are the current price estimates drawn from the Census of Production, revalued to 1975 prices. Exigencies of the data, particularly problems of reclassification in the Standard Industrial Classification, have led us to have to group together some industries but the information in Table 2.6 is still sufficiently disaggregated for some interesting information to emerge.

The most striking feature shown by Table 2.6 is the very rapid growth in real output in electrical engineering: in this technologically advanced sector of the economy, output quadrupled between 1963 and 1978. We shall look later in this book at the part played by government and by multi-national companies in the growth of this industry, but at present simply note its existence and the implication that Scotland is well placed to enter the microelectronics era, with its own 'Silicon Valley'. The restructuring we discussed earlier in the chapter is evident from Table 2.6 in the form of the decline in importance of metal manufacture and of shipbuilding and vehicles and the fairly static output of the textiles, leather and clothing group

Table 2.5   *Scottish national income, 1954–79 (sum of outputs), at constant 1975 prices*
£ million

	1954	1955	1956
Agriculture, forestry and fishing	257	236	262
Mining and quarrying	275	265	260
Manufacturing	1,364	1,325	1,359
Construction	484	501	517
Gas, electricity and water	84	90	92
Transport and communication	536	536	463
Distributive trades	628	649	607
Insurance, banking and finance	133	128	96
Ownership of dwellings	280	281	263
Public administration and defence	688	672	594
Public health and education services	467	469	411
Other services	645	671	602
Stock appreciation			
Gross domestic product at factor cost	5,841	5,823	5,526

	1967	1968	1969
Agriculture, forestry and fishing	305	315	324
Mining and quarrying	184	165	153
Manufacturing	1,942	2,042	2,177
Construction	797	882	899
Gas, electricity and water	174	182	199
Transport and communication	535	536	577
Distributive trades	709	747	742
Insurance, banking and finance	160	160	173
Ownership of dwellings	357	379	404
Public administration and defence	549	544	530
Public health and education services	548	564	563
Other services	798	798	862
Stock appreciation	− 24	− 20	− 71
Gross domestic product at factor cost	7,034	7,294	7,532

Source: Calculated from Table 2.3.

1957	1958	1959	1960	1961	1962	1963	1964	1965	1966
259	235	245	252	253	255	259	272	283	292
254	234	228	215	210	207	205	200	195	184
1,383	1,437	1,469	1,578	1,593	1,595	1,627	1,810	1,901	1,941
534	509	551	568	636	636	645	704	712	764
94	96	99	107	113	124	132	141	153	166
493	450	444	516	473	471	480	517	519	532
649	592	628	642	648	647	661	697	706	711
102	96	107	110	126	128	131	129	132	136
282	272	285	282	312	302	303	305	326	342
580	565	522	510	499	513	526	524	528	528
409	436	439	454	476	484	485	491	498	524
633	612	617	714	718	747	779	767	742	805
				− 30	− 59	− 7	− 56	− 53	− 58
5,672	5,533	5,634	5,948	6,027	6,168	6,226	6,501	6,642	6,867

1970	1971	1972	1973	1974	1975	1976	1977	1978	1979
343	344	357	369	414	380	319	390	374	367
148	159	140	157	142	159	154	146	149	151
2,266	2,224	2,266	2,451	2,428	2,312	2,319	2,312	2,317	2,337
798	773	814	863	781	814	790	822	814	749
212	209	232	263	258	258	268	281	289	310
614	623	650	715	718	716	727	738	764	789
802	877	915	927	837	837	836	878	928	893
182	222	229	211	179	220	220	213	231	238
414	401	373	381	371	377	377	369	361	369
537	527	575	598	600	632	687	655	688	683
584	617	668	663	690	722	759	767	825	826
760	792	1,008	1,069	1,004	1,010	1,104	1,116	1,207	1,193
− 25									
7,635	7,768	8,227	8,667	8,472	8,438	8,560	8,687	8,947	8,905

Table 2.6 Scottish gross domestic product in manufacturing at constant (1975) prices, 1963, 1968 and 1970–8, £ million

	1963	1968	1970	1971	1972	1973	1974	1975	1976	1977	1978
Food, drink and tobacco	270	361	407	426	440	463	487	468	473	473	491
Coal and petroleum products	131	168	173	190	215	230	247	211	247	243	243
Chemicals and allied industries	145	169	175	154	153	168	156	139	129	129	129
Metal manufacture / Mechanical engineering	257	351	440	379	346	370	374	407	391	374	334
Instrument engineering / Electrical engineering	53	81	132	136	146	172	193	172	187	193	218
Shipbuilding and marine engineering / Vehicles	171	215	214	210	191	201	189	193	164	166	152
Metal goods n.e.s / Textiles	66	75	83	83	97	103	108	104	90	86	82
Leather, leather goods and fur / Clothing and footwear	213	232	239	246	253	278	248	232	244	258	253
Bricks, pottery, glass, cement etc.	57	77	83	80	85	88	80	75	74	70	72
Timber, furniture, etc.	42	57	75	75	81	95	82	79	85	76	79
Paper, printing and publishing	183	204	208	196	194	205	196	172	175	179	186
Other manufacturing industries	39	52	56	58	63	75	66	61	66	69	74

Table 2.7 *Scottish expenditure, 1961–79, constant (1975) prices, £ million*

	1961	1962	1963	1964	1965	1966	1967	1968	1969	1970
Consumers' expenditure	4,148	4,206	4,240	4,583	4,662	4,720	4,718	4,832	4,821	4,949
General government final consumption	1,642	1,678	1,706	1,727	1,725	1,789	1,876	1,891	1,886	1,912
Gross domestic fixed capital formation	1,663	1,557	1,599	1,647	1,723	1,836	1,965	2,310	2,332	2,310
Value of physical increase in stocks and work in progress	126	12	107	526	229	151	106	210	176	61
Gross domestic expenditure at market prices	7,579	7,453	7,652	8,483	8,339	8,496	8,665	9,243	9,215	9,232
Factor cost adjustment	−518	−527	−541	−606	−608	−740	−740	−687	−710	−767
Gross domestic expenditure at factor cost	7,061	6,926	7,111	7,877	7,731	7,756	7,925	8,556	8,505	8,465

Table 2.7 *Scottish expenditure, 1961–79, constant (1975) prices (£ million) (cont'd.)*

	1971	1972	1973	1974	1975	1976	1977	1978	1979
Consumers' expenditure	4,936	5,027	5,474	5,541	5,620	5,517	5,558	5,894	6,127
General government final consumption	2,007	2,072	2,161	2,272	2,256	2,351	2,526	2,446	2,477
Gross domestic fixed capital formation	2,113	2,012	2,048	1,986	2,193	2,239	2,176	2,228	2,230
Value of physical increase in stocks and work in progress	53	−3	57	81	−44	−7	−25	−3	24
Gross domestic expenditure at market prices	9,109	9,198	9,740	9,880	10,025	10,100	10,285	10,565	10,948
Factor cost adjustment	−699	−747	−798	−770	−788	−824	−950	−1,004	−981
Gross domestic expenditure at factor cost	8,410	8,451	8,942	9,110	9,237	9,276	9,335	9,561	9,967

and of paper, printing and publishing. As we shall see in Chapter 3, labour productivity has been rising fairly steadily in Scottish manufacturing, so that in terms of employment the restructuring within manufacturing towards electrical engineering and from manufacturing to service industries, that we can see in Tables 2.5 and 2.6, is even more marked.

Table 2.7 looks at expenditure at constant (1975) prices from 1961 to 1979. It bears witness to distinct spurts in the growth of real expenditure: expenditure rose sharply between 1963 and 1964 and then settled, rose again between 1967 and 1968 and again settled, and then rose fairly steadily from 1974 to the end of the period. As might be expected, in view of its importance in the total, consumers' expenditure is responsible for some of this behaviour. About half of the rise between 1963 and 1964 was in consumers' expenditure, the rest coming from investment, and consumers' expenditure has risen fairly strongly from about 1973 onwards, particularly in 1973, 1978 and 1979. The rise in total expenditure between 1967 and 1968 is mainly due to a very sharp increase in investment, especially in fixed capital equipment (buildings, machinery, vehicles, etc.). Indeed, the figure for gross domestic fixed capital formation in 1968 is the highest for that variable in the whole series. Government expenditure rose slowly but fairly steadily throughout the whole period – only between 1977 and 1978 did it drop by more than £10 million between successive years, and the average rise over the period was a little over £40 million per annum, all measured at 1975 prices. Stocks, as we would expect from our earlier discussion, appeared to be very volatile, but relatively unimportant in the totals except that for 1964.

In aggregate, expenditure rose from some £7,100 million in 1961 to £10,000 million in 1979, at 1975 prices, a rise of some 41 per cent over the nineteen years, or growth at a compound rate of about 1.8 per cent. So between 1961 and 1979 at least, expenditure in Scotland was growing about half as fast again as output. We consider in the next section what this implies about the performance of the Scottish economy.

Overview

We conclude this chapter by offering a preliminary discussion of what the evidence we have presented is really telling us about the Scottish economy and its prospects. Our discussion at this stage has to be preliminary, because many of the themes introduced in this chapter will be explored in depth in the rest of this book, so that all we can do at the moment is introduce two of the more important issues.

As we have suggested earlier in this chapter, we can look on total output in the Scottish economy – whether measured by the sum of incomes or calculated as the sum of value added in each industry – as indicating the total of goods and services made available in the economy by its own efforts. The sum of expenditures, on the other hand, is an indicator of the total demand for goods and services. As we have already said, the difference between the two measures can be presented as 'net savings, etc.' (as in Deane's presentation summarised in Table 2.1) or in more modern terminology as the difference between exports and imports, because gross domestic product $\equiv$ gross domestic expenditure + exports − imports. It therefore follows that the difference between gross domestic product and gross domestic expenditure, if both were accurately measured, would enable us to estimate a figure for 'exports minus imports'.

There are so many margins for error in the measurement of Scottish national income that very little significance can be attributed to the (relatively small) difference between gross domestic product and gross domestic expenditure for any year, or even for a few years taken together, but since straightforward arithmetic applied to Tables 2.2, 2.3 and 2.4 leads to the conclusion that there was always an excess of expenditure over product (however product is measured), and since calculation from Tables 2.5 and 2.7 puts that excess at between £225 million and £1,380 million at 1975 prices, averaging at £885 million, we can conclude that it looks as if at least over the period 1961 to 1979 Scottish expenditure did usually exceed Scottish output, and that accordingly Scotland was in some sense importing more than she exported.

To identify what meaning we are to put on this apparent 'balance of payments deficit', or indeed what form it took, is a somewhat complex matter, which can be illuminated by a brief excursion into macro-economic theory. In trying to understand the process of the determi-nation of national income, it is helpful to distinguish three kinds of flows: self-balancing circular flows, injections and leakages. For practical purposes, the only self-balancing flow we need to consider is consumption of home-produced goods and services – if residents in an economy spend some of the income they receive, directly or indirectly from the provision of factor services to firms, on the purchase of goods and services made in the economy, their consumption expendi-ture goes back to the firms that made the goods and services and thus enables those firms to go on hiring factor services and hence giving income to consumers. So consumer expenditure on home-produced goods and services simply recycles income back and forth between the firms and households, and if all income were spent on home-produced consumer goods the level of income in the economy would be unchanging.

Injections into this circular flow of income between firms and households are types of expenditure which represent demand for goods and services from outside the home consumption market. One such injection is sales overseas – exports. Another such injection is the purchase by government of goods and services. The third type of injection is investment, where firms decide to increase their fixed capital equipment or their stocks.

Corresponding to these injections are three kinds of leakages, withdrawals from the circular flow because they represent the disposal of income to purposes other than the purchase of home-produced goods and services. The three kinds of leakage are imports, taxation, and saving. For the economy to be in equilibrium (and we can never observe it to be out of equilibrium, because if planned demand is greater than supply, stocks will be run down, and if planned demand is less than supply stocks will be accumulated), total injections into the circular flow must equal total leakages from it, and so the total of exports, government expenditure and investment must equal the total of imports, taxation and savings. Therefore, if imports exceed exports, as the evidence we have examined suggests is true for Scotland, then government expenditure and investment must together have exceeded the total of taxation and savings. If investment were to have exceeded savings, that would imply that the excess of Scottish expenditure over income was financed by transfers of (mainly private) capital to Scotland, which would entail a corresponding interest flow the other way. If government expenditure were to have exceeded government receipts from taxation, that would imply that the excess of Scottish expenditure over income was financed by the UK taxpayer.

As we have already indicated, there are no flow of funds accounts for Scotland, so we cannot bring any direct empirical evidence to bear on this question of how the deficit was financed. There has, however, been a little work done for Scotland on the construction of hypothetical government budgets for selected years. These studies have included that by McCrone (1969) for 1967 and a calculation of our own (Lythe, 1977) for 1973. Although it is recognised that there is a wide margin of error in such exercises, what work has been done seems to suggest that part of the excess of expenditure over income was indeed financed out of UK taxation. But to identify the extent of financing in that way, and of financing by private capital flows, requires reconciliation of the input-output based work of Bulmer-Thomas (1978) with studies conducted on other evidence, and such reconciliation is difficult to effect with confidence until the results of the second input-output study for Scotland are available. Recent work by Short and Nicholas (1981) will prove very valuable in this reconciliation.

However the apparent deficit was financed, it nevertheless remains true that a deficit in a region's transactions with other parts of a country has quite different implications from a deficit in a country's transactions with the rest of the world. A deficit in international trading leads to predictable pressures on the exchange rate or on reserves, and in practice countries can identify that a deficit exists and make a decision as to how far they will try to ride it out and how far they must try to correct it. Since imports usually respond to income changes, rising as income rises, whilst exports have no very clear connection with income, one method which countries may adopt to eliminate a balance of payments deficit is to reduce home demand, thereby cutting imports but leaving exports more or less unaffected. It can be argued that for a region an excess of imports over exports is especially dangerous, because since the existence of the deficit is never recognised (because trade is not measured) the processes which automatically finance the deficit might lead to some undetected structural weakness in the economy – for example, if the deficit is financed by government expenditure the region is vulnerable if the government then decides for reasons of national macroeconomic policy to reduce its planned expenditure, because that will have a disproportionate effect on the region in question. In such cases, a policy which a government chooses to pursue for some reason quite unconnected to regional policy may accidentally have completely unexpected regional consequences. So while an excess of expenditure over income causes no perceptible immediate embarrassment to a region, it may store up long-term problems.

The second theme we want to highlight at this stage is again a topic we have mentioned several times earlier in this chapter, the extent of the restructuring of the economy which the evidence has identified. There are two facets to restructuring – the expansion of the new and the contraction of the old. In discussing the expansion of the new, we have already alluded to the shift towards service industries generally and within manufacturing towards electrical engineering. If, as current thinking suggests, the likely growth industries of the future are microelectronics and other high technology industries, the restructuring has left Scotland well placed, with a strong electrical engineering industry and with a large number of institutions offering higher education.

Let us turn, however, to the other aspect of restructuring, the contraction of the old. What this has meant is the actual decline (in constant price terms) or virtual stagnation of output over a long period in certain industries, notable mining and quarrying; metal manufacture; and shipbuilding and vehicles. Such decline or stagnation of output over a long period when technology can be expected to have improved the efficiency of inputs has to be associated with a sharper decline in the use of inputs. Unless this decline in contracting industries is exactly balanced by the growth in the use of inputs by the expanding industries, we would expect to see the effects in the form of redundant inputs. As far as capital equipment is concerned, measurement problems make it very difficult to identify the degree of excess capacity, but the capacity utilisation index we use in Chapter 4 and present quantitatively in the Appendix (see Table A3, p. 208) tells a clear story of mounting excess capacity throughout the 1970s. Excess capacity in the labour market manifests itself in unemployment or emigration or both, and in Tables 1.3 and 1.2 we have briefly reviewed the evidence on these matters. To come properly to grips with the analysis of the effects of restructuring, however, we must look at the evidence about the use of inputs at a more disaggregated level, and that is the theme of our next chapter.

3

Outputs and Inputs in Scotland 1961–78

Introduction

In Chapter 2, we looked at Scottish output, to see how it had changed over time and to comment in a preliminary way on the growth performance of the Scottish economy. We can, however, make only limited observations about the interpretation to put on this growth until we examine with what resources the growth has been achieved. Output is made by combining different inputs. The logical way to proceed, then, would be to examine the quantity and quality of the various inputs with a view to identifying how efficiently they have been used.

Such exercises have been conducted for many western economies by E. F. Denison – see, for example, Denison's chapter in Caves *et al.* (1968). Denison's procedure is to identify changes in the amounts of the various inputs – labour, capital, land – and in their quality – for example, the educational standards of labour – and then compare the growth contribution from these sources with the total growth of output. That yields a (positive) 'residual', which Denison seeks to analyse in terms of economies of scale, improvements in the allocation of resources, technical change, etc. A bold attempt to apply Denison's techniques to Scotland was made by Johnston *et al.* (1970), but this exercise foundered on measurement problems: whilst it is possible with reasonable certainty to say something about the quantity of labour, there are more or less acute measurement problems for all other inputs. In this chapter, therefore, while we shall say something about other inputs, our attention will be primarily devoted to the quantity and the productivity of labour.

Employment and Labour Productivity in Scotland

The Scottish working force can be enumerated by adding together two officially published series, that for employees in employment and that for the self-employed and employers, both of which are published in the Department of Employment *Gazette*. As we show in the Appendix, there are some difficulties, in the form of discontinuities and gaps in the data, and we outline in the Appendix how we have overcome these problems. Table 3.1 presents our series for the total Scottish working force from 1961 to 1978. There are three comments we would make about the series. First, we have not attempted to consider employment in the armed forces: details of the numbers in the armed forces in Scotland are no longer officially published, presumably for security reasons. Second, we have identified in the table employment in individual manufacturing industries only for those years for which we have reasonably reliable output data – that is, only for the Census of Production years of 1963, 1968 and 1970 onwards. Third, and most importantly, we think the table brings out an important fact. Frequently, discussion of labour productivity is based on dividing output by employees in employment. The table shows how distorting that can be. In agriculture, forestry and fishing, employees in employment account typically for only 60–70 per cent of total employment, whereas in manufacturing as a whole employees in employment are 98–99 per cent of total employment. Similarly, within the service sector self-employment varies considerably in importance, from accounting for some 15 per cent of the workforce in distributive trades to being negligible in insurance, banking and finance and in public administration and defence.

Once we have a series for the workforce, we can use that to calculate output per worker. Table 3.2 has been constructed by dividing the output figures in Tables 2.3 (output at current prices) and 2.5 (output at constant, 1975, prices) by the working force totals in Table 3.1. Thus, part A of Table 3.2 presents output per worker in Scotland at current prices, and part B presents output per worker in Scotland at constant (1975) prices. In Table 3.2 manufacturing is treated as a whole. Table 3.3 divides manufacturing into its component industries and presents output per worker in each Census of Production year at constant (1975) prices. It is calculated from Tables 2.6 and 3.1.

The most obvious fact conveyed in Tables 3.2 and 3.3 is the wide variation across industries in output per worker. In 1961, output per worker in distributive trades, at £664 in current prices, was only just over a third of output per worker in gas, electricity and water. By 1978, the miscellaneous group of other services had the lowest output per worker in current prices, and output per worker there was under a third of that in gas, electricity and water. Within manufacturing, the industry with the highest output per worker at constant prices (coal, chemical and allied products) had well over double the output per worker in shipbuilding, marine engineering and vehicles. Inter-industry

Table 3.1 Scottish working force (excluding armed forces) ('000)

	1961	1962	1963	1964	1965	1966	1967	1968	1969	1970	1971	1972	1973	1974	1975	1976	1977	1978
Agriculture, forestry and fishing																		
Employees in employment	93	91	89	84	78	73	66	64	61	59	55	54	52	50	49	49	49	48.3
Self-employed (inc. employers)	48.5	46.3	44.2	42.1	39.9	38.2	37.4	36.8	35.2	33.9	32.7	32.2	32.7	32.2	31.5	31.5	31.5	31.5
Total employment	141.5	137.3	133.2	126.1	117.9	111.2	103.4	100.8	96.2	92.9	87.7	86.2	84.7	82.2	80.5	80.5	80.5	79.8
Mining and quarrying																		
Employees in employment	85	78	69	64	61	56	53	45	42	39	39	37	35	34	36	35	36	39.3
Self-employed (inc. employers)	0.1	0.1	–	–	–	–	0.1	0.1	0.1	0.1	0.1	0.1	0.1	0.1	0.1	0.1	0.1	0.1
Total employment	85.1	78.1	69.0	64.0	61.0	56.0	53.1	45.1	42.1	39.1	39.1	37.1	35.1	34.1	36.1	35.1	36.1	39.4
Food, drink and tobacco																		
Employees in employment			91					94	99	99	97	95	95	99	92	91	92	90.6
Self-employed (inc. employers)			0.7					0.8	0.9	0.9	0.9	0.9	0.9	0.9	0.9	0.9	0.9	0.9
Total employment			91.7					94.8	99.9	99.9	97.9	95.9	95.9	99.9	92.9	91.9	92.9	91.5
Coal and petroleum products																		
Employees in employment			3					3	2.7	2.7	3	3	3	3	3	3	3	2.8
Self-employed (inc. employers)			–					0.1	0.1	0.1	0.1	0.1	0.1	0.1	0.1	0.1	0.1	0.1
Total employment			3.0					3.1	2.8	2.8	3.1	3.1	3.1	3.1	3.1	3.1	3.1	2.9
Chemical and allied industries																		
Employees in employment			29					31	31	31	28	26	27	28	28	29	31	32.3
Self-employed (inc. employers)			0.1					0.1	0.1	0.1	0.1	0.1	0.1	0.1	0.1	0.1	0.1	0.1
Total employment			29.1					31.1	31.1	31.1	28.1	26.1	27.1	28.1	28.1	29.1	31.1	32.4
Metal manufacture																		
Employees in employment			50					47	47	47	46	43	44	43	44	39	40	36.8
Self-employed (inc. employers)			0.1					–	–	–	0.1	0.1	0.1	0.1	0.1	0.1	0.1	0.1
Total employment			50.1					47.0	47.0	47.0	46.1	43.1	44.1	43.1	44.1	39.1	40.1	36.9
Mechanical engineering																		
Employees in employment			111					108	109	109	96	85	87	94	96	92	88	86.8
Self-employed (inc. employers)			0.2					0.4	0.5	0.5	0.5	0.6	0.6	0.6	0.6	0.6	0.6	0.6
Total employment			111.2					108.4	109.5	109.5	96.5	85.6	87.6	94.6	96.6	92.6	88.6	87.4
Instrument engineering																		
Employees in employment			13					15	15	18	19	18	17	18	18	16	16	15.9
Self-employed (inc. employers)			–					–	–	–	–	0.1	0.1	0.1	0.1	0.1	0.1	0.1
Total employment			13.0					15.0	15.0	18.0	19.0	18.1	17.1	18.1	18.1	16.1	16.1	16.0

Electrical engineering											
Employees in employment	38	48	53	50	50	52	60	51	49	50	48.0
Self-employed (inc. employers)	0.1	0.1	0.2	0.2	0.1	0.1	0.1	0.1	0.1	0.1	0.1
Total employment	38.1	48.1	53.2	50.2	50.1	52.1	60.1	51.1	49.1	50.1	48.1
Shipbuilding and marine engineering											
Employees in employment	49	46	45	45	44	44	43	43	42	40	40.7
Self-employed (inc. employers)	0.1	0.2	0.2	0.2	0.2	0.2	0.2	0.2	0.2	0.2	0.2
Total employment	49.1	46.2	45.2	45.2	44.2	44.2	43.2	43.2	42.2	40.2	40.9
Vehicles											
Employees in employment	41	38	41	37	35	38	40	36	32	34	35.5
Self-employed (inc. employers)	0.1	0.1	0.1	0.1	0.2	0.2	0.2	0.1	0.1	0.1	0.1
Total employment	41.1	38.1	41.1	37.1	35.2	38.2	40.2	36.1	32.1	34.1	35.6
Metal goods not elsewhere specified											
Employees in employment	29	30	31	30	29	30	32	29	27	28	28.5
Self-employed (inc. employers)	1.0	0.8	0.8	0.9	0.9	0.9	0.9	0.9	0.9	0.9	0.9
Total employment	30.0	30.8	31.8	30.9	29.9	30.9	32.9	29.9	27.9	28.9	29.4
Textiles											
Employees in employment	88	86	80	72	71	71	69	59	57	59	55.3
Self-employed (inc. employers)	1.2	1.2	1.3	1.4	1.3	1.3	1.3	1.3	1.3	1.3	1.3
Total employment	89.2	87.2	81.3	73.4	72.3	72.3	70.3	60.3	58.3	60.3	56.6
Leather, leather goods and fur											
Employees	3	3	34	36	38	37	38	35	33	35	25
Self-employed (inc. employers)	0.2	0.1	0.2	0.2	0.2	0.2	0.2	0.2	0.2	0.2	0.2
Total employment	3.2	3.1	34.2	36.2	38.2	37.2	38.2	35.2	33.2	35.2	25.2
Clothing and footwear											
Employees in employment	26	30	30	—	—	—	—	—	—	—	31.9
Self-employed (inc. employers)	0.5	0.5	0.5	0.5	0.5	0.5	0.5	0.5	0.5	0.5	0.5
Total employment	26.5	30.5	30.5	—	—	—	—	—	—	—	33.4
Bricks, pottery, glass, cement											
Employees in employment	23	23	24	22	21	21	20	19	17	17	17
Self-employed (inc. employers)	0.2	0.2	0.2	0.2	0.2	0.2	0.2	0.2	0.2	0.2	0.2
Total employment	23.2	23.2	24.2	22.2	21.2	21.2	20.2	19.2	17.2	17.2	17.2

Table 3.1 *Scottish working force (excluding armed forces) ('000) (cont'd.)*

	1961	1962	1963	1964	1965	1966	1967	1968	1969	1970	1971	1972	1973	1974	1975	1976	1977	1978
Timber, furniture, etc.																		
Employees in employment			23					26		24	23	23	24	23	21	20	20	19.6
Self-employed (inc. employers)			2.5					2.6		2.8	2.9	2.9	2.9	2.9	2.8	2.8	2.8	2.8
Total employment			25.5					28.6		26.8	25.9	25.9	26.9	25.9	23.9	22.8	22.8	22.4
Paper, printing and publishing																		
Employees in employment			55					56		55	52	50	50	50	48	44	44	43.8
Self-employed (inc. employers)			0.4					0.5		0.5	0.5	0.5	0.5	0.5	0.5	0.5	0.5	0.5
Total employment			55.4					56.5		55.5	52.5	50.5	50.5	50.5	48.5	44.5	44.5	43.8
Other manufacturing																		
Employees in employment			15					17		17	16	16	17	18	16	16	16	16.1
Self-employed (inc. employers)			0.1					0.1		0.1	0.1	0.1	0.1	0.1	0.1	0.1	0.1	0.1
Total employment			15.1					17.1		17.1	16.1	16.1	17.1	18.1	16.1	16.1	16.1	16.2
Total manufacturing																		
Employees in employment	717	704	687	688	725	726	702	701	714	710	669	643	657	676	637	608	615	603.6
Self-employed (inc. employers)	7.4	7.4	7.5	7.5	7.6	7.6	7.8	8.0	8.4	8.6	8.8	8.7	8.8	8.7	8.5	8.5	8.5	8.5
Total employment	724.4	711.4	694.5	695.5	732.6	733.6	709.8	709.0	722.4	718.6	677.8	651.7	665.8	684.7	645.5	616.5	623.5	612.1
Construction																		
Employees in employment	163	165	169	176	180	187	186	187	182	173	159	157	173	170	173	171	164	160
Self-employed (inc. employers)	9.5	9.4	9.4	9.3	9.3	9.0	9.5	10.1	10.5	11.1	11.9	11.7	11.9	11.7	11.5	11.5	11.5	11.5
Total employment	172.5	174.4	178.4	185.3	189.3	196.0	195.5	197.1	192.5	184.1	170.9	168.7	184.9	181.7	184.5	182.5	175.5	171.5
Gas, electricity and water																		
Employees in employment	31	31	32	33	34	35	34	33	33	31	31	29	29	28	26	29	28	28.4
Self-employed (inc. employers)	–	–	–	–	–	–	–	–	–	–	–	–	–	–	–	–	–	–
Total employment	31.0	31.0	32.0	33.0	34.0	35.0	34.0	33.0	33.0	31.0	31.0	29.0	29.0	28.0	26.0	29.0	28.0	28.4
Transport and communication																		
Employees in employment	176	177	173	168	165	160	157	153	148	146	143	138	139	139	140	137	134	135.2
Self-employed (inc. employers)	4.2	4.1	4.0	4.0	3.9	3.8	4.1	4.3	4.6	4.8	5.1	5.0	5.1	5.0	4.9	4.9	4.9	4.9
Total employment	180.2	181.1	177.0	172.0	168.9	163.8	161.1	157.3	152.6	150.8	148.1	143.0	144.1	144.0	144.9	141.9	138.9	140.1
Distributive trades																		
Employees in employment	275	286	283	286	283	280	270	264	260	255	238	237	243	242	241	237	239	239
Self-employed (inc. employers)	49.0	47.1	45.3	43.4	40.2	38.8	38.9	39.2	37.4	37.9	37.9	37.4	37.9	37.4	36.5	36.5	36.5	36.5
Total employment	324.0	333.1	328.3	329.4	323.2	318.8	308.9	303.2	298.4	291.9	275.9	274.4	280.9	279.4	277.5	273.5	275.5	275.5

	44	45	46	47	48	49	50	53	56	59	65	66	68	72	75	76	78	77.9
Insurance, banking, etc.																		
Employees in employment	–	–	–	–	–	–	–	–	–	–	–	–	–	–	–	–	–	–
Self-employment (inc. employers)	–	–	–	–	–	–	–	–	–	–	–	–	–	–	–	–	–	–
Total employment	44.0	45.0	46.0	47.0	48.0	49.0	50.0	53.0	56.0	59.0	65.0	66.0	68.0	72.0	75.0	76.0	78.0	77.9
Professional and scientific services																		
Employees in employment	377	393	400	417	424	438	439	446	459	466	288	301	311	323	329	352	349	350.9
Self-employed (inc. employers)	42.2	41.7	41.0	40.4	39.7	37.6	39.2	40.5	40.8	41.6	42.6	42.0	42.6	42.0	41.1	41.1	41.1	41.1
Total employment	419.2	434.7	441.0	457.4	463.7	475.6	478.2	486.5	499.8	507.6	515.6	532.0	555.6	569.0	581.1	620.1	624.1	632.4
Miscellaneous services																		
Employees in employment	–	–	–	–	–	–	–	–	–	–	185	189	202	204	211	227	234	240.5
Self-employed (inc. employers)	–	–	–	–	–	–	–	–	–	–	–	–	–	–	–	–	–	–
Total employment	–	–	–	–	–	–	–	–	–	–	185.0	189.0	202.2	204.0	211.0	227.0	234.0	240.5
Public administration and defence																		
Employees in employment	108	115	121	117	117	117	124	124	121	123	131	137	141	145	158	150	146	144.2
Self-employed (inc. employers)	–	–	–	–	–	–	–	–	–	–	–	–	–	–	–	–	–	–
Total employment	108.0	115.0	121.0	117.0	117.0	117.0	124.0	124.0	121.0	123.0	131.0	137.0	141.0	145.0	158.0	150.0	146.0	144.2
Total																		
Employees in employment	2069	2085	2069	2080	2115	2121	2080	2070	2076	2061	2003	1989	2050	2084	2076	2071	2071	2067.2
Self-employed (inc. employers)	160.8	156.1	151.4	151.4	140.6	135.0	137.0	139.0	138.0	137.0	139.0	137.0	139.0	137.0	134.0	134.0	134.0	134.0
Total employment	2,229.8	2,241.1	2,220.4	2,231.4	2,255.6	2,256.0	2,217.0	2,209.0	2,214.0	2,198.0	2,142.0	2,126.0	2,189.0	2,221.0	2,210.0	2,205.0	2,205.0	2,201.2

Table 3.2 Output per worker in Scotland

A Output per worker, £, current prices

	1961	1962	1963	1964	1965	1966	1967	1968	1969	1970
Agriculture, forestry and fishing	876.3	903.1	945.9	1,015.1	1,153.5	1,339.9	1,392.6	1,587.3	1,819.1	2,056.0
Mining and quarrying	916.6	998.7	1,000.0	1,203.1	1,229.5	1,321.4	1,431.3	1,330.4	1,472.7	1,713.6
Manufacturing	898.7	910.9	1,010.8	1,120.1	1,152.1	1,240.5	1,289.1	1,342.7	1,475.6	1,646.3
Construction	887.0	946.1	986.5	1,063.1	1,093.5	1,153.1	1,207.2	1,374.9	1,516.9	1,597.0
Gas, electricity and water	1,871.0	2,064.5	2,187.5	2,363.6	2,500.0	2,628.5	3,000.0	3,272.7	3,363.6	4,161.3
Transport and communication	987.8	1,027.1	1,124.3	1,250.0	1,349.9	1,465.2	1,514.6	1,659.2	1,913.5	2,168.4
Distributive trades	663.6	669.5	706.7	765.0	826.1	875.2	919.4	1,015.8	1,055.6	1,253.9
Insurance, banking and finance	1,045.5	1,088.9	1,108.7	1,063.8	1,125.0	1,142.9	1,320.0	1,434.0	1,553.6	1,661.0
Other services (excluding public administration and defence)	746.7	768.3	839.0	830.8	858.3	973.5	1,051.9	1,116.1	1,140.5	1,219.5
Gross domestic product per worker	896.0	923.7	996.7	1,063.5	1,123.0	1,218.5	1,294.1	1,389.8	1,495.9	1,680.2

B Output per worker, £, constant (1975) prices

	1961	1962	1963	1964	1965	1966	1967	1968	1969	1970
Agriculture, forestry and fishing	1,788.0	1,857.2	1,944.4	2,157.0	2,400.3	2,625.9	2,949.7	3,125.0	3,368.0	3,692.1
Mining and quarrying	2,467.7	2,650.4	2,971.0	3,125.0	3,196.7	3,285.7	3,465.2	3,658.5	3,643.2	3,785.2
Manufacturing	2,199.1	2,242.1	2,342.7	2,602.4	2,594.9	2,645.9	2,736.0	2,880.1	3,013.6	3,153.4
Construction	3,687.0	3,646.8	3,615.5	3,799.2	3,761.2	3,898.0	4,076.7	4,474.9	4,670.1	4,334.6
Gas, electricity and water	3,645.2	4,000.0	4,125.0	4,272.7	4,500.0	4,742.9	5,117.6	5,515.2	6,030.3	6,838.7
Transport and communication	2,624.9	2,600.0	2,711.9	3,005.8	3,072.8	3,247.9	3,320.9	3,407.5	3,781.1	4,071.6
Distributive trades	2,000.0	1,942.4	2,013.4	2,116.0	2,184.4	2,224.0	2,295.0	2,463.7	2,486.6	2,747.5
Insurance, banking and finance	2,863.6	2,844.4	2,847.8	2,744.7	2,750.0	2,775.5	3,200.0	3,018.9	3,089.3	3,084.7
Other services (excluding public administration and defence)	2,848.3	2,831.8	2,866.2	2,750.3	2,674.1	2,794.4	2,814.7	2,799.6	2,851.1	2,647.8
Gross domestic product per worker	2,702.9	2,752.2	2,804.0	2,913.4	2,944.7	3,043.9	3,172.8	3,301.9	3,402.0	3,473.6

Table 3.2 *Output per worker in Scotland (cont'd.)*

A *Output per worker, £, current prices*

	1971	1972	1973	1974	1975	1976	1977	1978
Agriculture, forestry and fishing	2,531.4	2,784.2	3,541.9	3,793.6	4,720.5	5,975.2	6,223.6	6,391.0
Mining and quarrying	1,585.7	1,940.7	2,222.2	3,108.5	4,404.4	5,242.2	6,121.9	6,040.6
Manufacturing	1,913.5	2,174.3	2,526.3	2,696.1	3,581.7	4,381.2	4,930.2	5,969.6
Construction	2,077.2	2,489.6	2,974.6	3,621.4	4,411.9	5,074.0	5,378.9	6,192.4
Gas, electricity and water	4,806.5	5,620.7	6,413.8	7,678.6	9,923.1	12,275.9	13,642.9	15,387.3
Transport and communication	2,383.5	2,797.2	3,289.4	3,965.3	4,941.3	6,187.5	6,673.9	7,708.8
Distributive trades	1,652.8	1,909.6	2,164.5	2,333.6	3,016.2	3,418.6	4,029.0	4,675.1
Insurance, banking and finance	2,030.8	2,363.6	2,514.7	2,208.3	2,933.3	3,618.4	3,859.0	4,582.8
Other services (excluding public administration and defence)	1,518.6	1,733.1	1,983.4	2,265.4	2,980.6	3,318.8	3,674.1	4,203.0
Gross domestic product per worker	2,004.7	2,282.2	2,635.0	2,960.4	3,818.1	4,534.2	5,004.1	5,769.1

B *Output per worker, £, constant (1975) prices*

	1971	1972	1973	1974	1975	1976	1977	1978
Agriculture, forestry and fishing	3,922.5	4,141.5	4,356.6	5,036.3	4,720.5	3,962.7	4,844.7	4,686.7
Mining and quarrying	4,066.5	3,773.6	4,472.9	4,164.2	4,404.4	4,387.5	4,044.3	3,785.7
Manufacturing	3,281.2	3,477.1	3,681.3	3,546.1	3,581.7	3,761.6	3,708.1	3,785.3
Construction	4,523.1	4,825.1	5,115.6	4,298.3	4,411.9	4,328.8	4,683.8	4,746.4
Gas, electricity and water	6,741.9	8,000.0	9,069.0	9,214.3	9,923.1	9,241.4	10,035.7	10,176.0
Transport and communication	4,206.6	4,545.5	4,961.8	4,986.1	4,941.3	5,123.3	5,313.2	5,453.2
Distributive trades	3,178.7	3,334.5	3,300.1	2,995.7	3,016.2	3,056.7	3,186.9	3,368.4
Insurance, banking and finance	3,415.4	3,469.7	3,102.9	2,486.1	2,933.3	2,894.7	2,730.8	2,965.3
Other services (excluding public administration and defence)	2,782.7	3,150.4	3,117.4	2,977.2	2,980.6	3,004.4	3,017.1	3,213.2
Gross domestic product per worker	3,626.5	3,869.7	3,959.3	3,792.0	3,818.1	3,882.1	3,939.7	4,064.6

Table 3.3 *Output per worker in manufacturing, Scotland, at constant (1975) prices*

	1963	1968	1970	1971	1972	1973	1974	1975	1976	1977	1978
Food, drink and tobacco	2,944.4	3,808.0	4,074.1	4,351.4	4,588.1	4,827.9	4,874.9	5,037.7	5,146.9	5,091.5	5,366.1
Coal and petroleum products	4,081.0	4,912.3	5,103.2	6,089.7	7,363.0	7,615.9	7,916.7	6,762.8	7,670.8	7,105.3	6,883.9
Chemicals and allied industries ⎱ Metal manufacture	2,894.2	3,595.7	3,723.4	3,340.6	3,549.9	3,809.5	3,619.5	3,151.9	3,299.2	3,217.0	3,495.9
Mechanical engineering ⎱ Instrument engineering	2,069.2	2,844.4	3,451.0	3,281.4	3,336.5	3,533.9	3,318.5	3,548.4	3,597.1	3,572.1	3,230.1
Electrical engineering ⎱ Shipbuilding and marine engineering	1,391.1	1,684.0	2,481.2	2,709.2	2,914.2	3,301.3	3,211.3	3,365.9	3,808.6	3,852.3	4,532.2
Vehicles	1,895.8	2,550.4	2,479.7	2,551.6	2,531.5	2,439.3	2,266.2	2,433.8	2,149.4	2,234.2	1,986.9
Metal goods n.e.s ⎱ Textiles	2,200.0	2,435.1	2,610.1	2,686.1	3,244.1	3,333.3	3,282.7	3,478.3	3,225.8	2,975.8	2,789.1
Leather, leather goods and fur ⎱ Clothing and footwear	1,791.4	1,920.5	2,078.3	2,275.7	2,321.1	2,504.5	2,296.3	2,416.7	2,652.2	2,687.5	2,729.2
Bricks, pottery, glass, cement etc.	2,456.9	3,319.0	3,429.8	3,603.6	4,0009.4	4,150.9	3,960.4	3,906.3	4,302.3	4,069.8	4,186.0
Timber, furniture, etc.	1,647.1	1,993.0	2,798.5	2,895.8	3,127.4	3,531.6	3,166.0	3,319.3	3,728.1	3,333.3	3,526.8
Paper, printing and publishing	3,303.2	3,610.6	3,747.7	3,733.3	3,841.6	4,059.4	3,881.2	3,546.4	3,932.6	4,022.5	4,246.6
Other manufacturing industries	2,582.8	3,040.9	3,274.9	3,602.5	3,913.0	4,386.0	3,646.4	3,788.8	4,099.3	4,285.7	4,567.0

differences in output per head are, however, to be expected, because of differences in the labour-intensity of production, and it is on that account more illuminating to consider how output per worker has changed over time. To focus the evidence, we consider in Table 3.4 and 3.5 the changes in output per worker at constant prices over the whole period and over sub-periods within it. The sub-periods, which we shall use again in Chapter 4, are chosen to try to reflect conventional thinking about the vicissitudes of regional policy towards manufacturing industry, but we do not argue in any way for their exactness as conveying with precision the timing of the impact of major changes in policy. For the purposes of this chapter, the sub-periods are no more than an arbitrary device to make the year-to-year changes more comprehensible.

Table 3.4   *Annual percentage change in output per worker in Scotland, at constant (1975) prices*

	% 1961– 78	% 1961–3	% 1963–8	% 1968– 71	% 1971–5	% 1975–8
Agriculture, forestry and fishing	9.5	4.4	12.1	8.5	5.1	−0.2
Mining and quarrying	3.1	10.2	4.6	3.7	2.1	−4.7
All manufacturing industries	4.2	3.3	4.6	4.6	2.3	1.9
Construction	1.7	−0.1	4.8	0.4	−0.6	2.5
Gas, electricity and water	10.5	6.6	6.7	7.4	11.8	0.9
Transport and communication	6.3	1.7	5.1	7.8	4.4	3.5
Distributive trades	4.0	0.3	4.5	9.7	−1.3	3.9
Insurance, banking and finance	0.2	−0.3	1.2	4.4	−3.5	0.4
Other services (excluding public administration and defence)	0.8	0.3	−0.5	−0.0	2.3	2.6
Gross domestic product per worker	3.0	1.9	3.6	3.3	1.3	2.2

What the tables show is that the only industries in which output per worker (calculated as a simple average percentage change) grew on average over the whole period by more than 5 per cent per annum were agriculture, forestry and fishing (output per head in which, as could be expected, experienced a very uneven pattern of growth), gas, electricity and water (output per head in which grew strongly until towards the end of the period), transport and communication (which had a sharp rise in output per head in 1963–71), food, drink and tobacco (where the growth in output per head was strongest at the beginning of the period), electrical engineering (where output per head

Table 3.5   *Annual percentage change in output per worker in manufacturing industries in Scotland, at constant (1975) prices*

	1963–78	1963–8	1968–71	1971–5	1975–8
Food, drink and tobacco	5.5	5.9	4.8	3.9	2.2
Coal and chemical products	4.6	4.1	8.0	2.8	0.6 .
Metal manufacturing	1.4	4.9	– 2.4	– 1.4	3.6
Mechanical and instrument engineering	3.7	7.5	5.1	2.0	– 3.0
Electrical engineering	15.1	4.2	20.3	6.1	11.6
Shipbuilding and vehicles	0.3	3.7	0.0	– 1.2	– 6.1
Metal goods n.e.s	1.8	2.1	3.4	7.4	– 6.6
Textiles, leather and clothing	3.5	1.4	6.2	1.6	4.3
Bricks, pottery, glass and cement	4.7	7.0	2.9	2.1	2.4
Timber and furniture	7.6	4.2	15.1	3.7	2.1
Paper, printing and publishing	1.9	1.9	1.1	– 1.3	6.6
Other manufacturing industries	5.1	3.6	6.2	1.3	6.9

grew very fast, especially in 1968–71 and 1975–8), timber and furniture (where the high average growth rate is the result of a very fast rise in output per head in 1968–71), and the miscellaneous group 'other manufacturing' (where there were marked rises in output per worker in 1968–1971 and 1975–8). Overall, output per worker grew by only 3 per cent on average and that was attributable to relatively fast growth in 1963–71 and some recovery in 1975–8.

While it might reasonably be expected that output per worker would rise only fairly slowly on average and rather unevenly in individual industries (where the impact of major technical developments should tend to cause spurts in output per worker followed and preceded by relative stability), it is difficult to find any comforting rationale for declines in output per worker (except in agriculture, forestry and fishing, where the forces of nature are so important). Many of the declines in output per head documented in Tables 3.4 and 3.5 are probably the result of changes in the composition of an industry – for example, the difference in the performances of shipbuilding and marine engineering in Scotland from that in vehicles must account for some of the rather strange patterns exhibited by the shipbuilding and vehicle group – but the implication must be that changes in composition have sometimes led to an increase of specialisation in Scotland in the industry with the *lower* output per worker, and while there are circumstances in which that would be economically sound, it is not evident that these circumstances prevail here. We will return to this topic later in this chapter.

So far, we have used the change in output per worker as a basis for discussing the productivity of labour in Scotland. There is another straightforward method we can use to identify signs of success and of failure, that of comparing output per worker in Scotland with output per worker elsewhere. The most direct comparison that can be made here is between output per worker in Scotland and that in the UK. To calculate output per worker in the UK, we had to construct figures for the UK working force (these are presented in Table 3.6) and then, from official statistics for the UK in the annual *Blue Book*, calculate output per worker in all industries (Table 3.7, which is at current prices) and in the manufacturing industries (Table 3.8, which is at constant, 1975, prices). Combining the information in Table 3.7 with that in Table 3.2, and that in Table 3.8 with that in Table 3.3, output per worker in Scotland can be presented as a percentage of that in the UK: this is done in Table 3.9 for all industries for 1961–78 and in Table 3.10 for the manufacturing industries for Census of Production years. Table 3.9 is calculated at current prices: by avoiding the use of constant price statistics it is possible to circumvent some of the problems arising from the absence of a reliable Scottish price index. Table 3.10 is, however, presented at constant prices because the basic data behind it, both for Scotland and for the UK, come from indices of industrial production and thus recasting that data into current price terms might involve unnecessary distortions. In both tables, the object is to compare Scotland with the UK by using what appears to be the more reliable information.

As Table 3.9 shows, whilst gross domestic product per worker in Scotland was always below that of the UK, over the whole period 1961–78 the gap narrowed fairly steadily. Output per worker in Scotland was consistently above that in the UK in agriculture, forestry and fishing (where at least part of the explanation may lie in the difference in the composition of the industry between Scotland and the UK – it appears that forestry and fishing are much more important in the industry total in Scotland than in the UK), gas, electricity and water (where output per head in Scotland appears to have dropped below that of the UK in 1969 but was otherwise clearly greater), coal, chemicals and allied industries (where differences in the composition of the industry are again important), bricks, pottery, glass, cement, etc. (which is a relatively small industry in Scotland, and composed differently from the UK average) and (except in 1968) the heterogeneous 'other manufacturing' group. A strong improvement in Scottish relative output per head over the period is evident for agriculture, forestry and fishing; construction; transport and communications; 'other services'; manufacturing as a whole and, within manufacturing: food, drink and tobacco; electrical engineering; and timber and furniture. It should be noted that the apparently disastrous

Table 3.6 UK working force ('000)

	1961	1962	1963	1964	1965	1966	1967	1968	1969	1970	1971	1972	1973	1974	1975	1976	1977	1978
Agriculture, forestry and fishing																		
Employees in employment	712	687	691	657	605	582	542	519	492	468	432		434	417	401	395	388	382
Self-employed (inc. employers)	388	379	368	357	347	334	341	334	324	316	302		281	286	267	267	267	267
Total employment	1,100	1,066	1,059	1,014	952	916	883	853	816	784	734		715	683	668	662	655	649
Mining and quarrying																		
Employees in employment	727	705	676	649	617	569	545	481	437	410	396	379	363	349	352	348	350	353
Self-employed (inc. employers)	1	1	1	1	1	1	1	1	1	1	1	1	1	1	1	–	–	–
Total employment	728	706	677	650	618	570	546	482	438	411	397	380	364	350	353	348	350	353
Food, drink and tobacco																		
Employees in employment			793					792		772	770	756	754	766	726	714	711	704
Self-employed (inc. employers)			6					7		8	7	8	7	6	5	5	5	5
Total employment			799					799		780	779	764	761	772	731	719	716	709
Coal and petroleum products																		
Employees in employment			46					44		48	44	42	41	40	40	38	37	40
Self-employed (inc. employers)			1					2		–	–	1	–	–	–	–	–	–
Total employment			47					46		48	44	43	41	40	40	38	37	40
Chemical and allied industries																		
Employees in employment			437					425		443	438	426	427	435	430	423	436	440
Self-employed (inc. employers)			1					1		1	1	1	1	1	1	1	1	1
Total employment			438					426		444	439	427	428	436	431	424	437	441
Metal manufacture																		
Employees in employment			601					585		594	557	516	518	507	501	459	483	459
Self-employed (inc. employers)			1					1		1	1	1	1	1	1	1	1	1
Total employment			602					586		595	558	517	519	508	502	460	484	460
Mechanical engineering																		
Employees in employment			1,013					1,057		1,105	1,051	975	967	976	960	929	925	933
Self-employed (inc. employers)			6					8		10	11	10	9	9	9	9	9	9
Total employment			1,019					1,065		1,115	1,062	985	976	985	969	938	934	942
Instrument engineering																		
Employees in employment			161					161		163	166	157	161	161	156	150	150	150
Self-employed (inc. employers)			3					2		2	2	2	2	2	2	2	2	2
Total employment			164					163		165	168	159	163	163	158	152	152	152

Electrical engineering											
Employees in employment	771	824	827	812	792	808	843	781	739	753	758
Self-employed (inc. employers)	1	3	4	4	3	3	3	2	2	2	2
Total employment	772	827	831	816	795	811	846	783	741	755	760
Shipbuilding and marine engineering											
Employees in employment	220	195	190	193	186	187	185	184	185	182	182
Self-employed (inc. employers)	1	1	2	1	2	1	1	2	2	2	2
Total employment	221	196	192	194	188	188	186	186	187	184	184
Vehicles											
Employees in employment	863	813	840	816	784	797	792	756	744	750	753
Self-employed (inc. employers)	2	2	2	2	1	1	1	1	1	1	1
Total employment	865	815	842	818	785	798	793	757	745	751	754
Metal goods n.e.s.											
Employees in employment	555	585	596	576	557	567	581	546	522	535	542
Self-employed (inc. employers)	12	13	14	15	13	13	14	14	14	14	14
Total employment	567	598	610	591	570	580	595	560	536	549	556
Textiles											
Employees in employment	776	690	678	622		594	585	529	513	512	490
Self-employed (inc. employers)	7	6	5	5		4	5	4	4	4	4
Total employment	783	696	683	627		598	590	533	517	516	494
Leather, leather goods and fur											
Employees in employment	57	52	49	47	45	45	43	42	40	41	38
Self-employed (inc. employers)	2	2	3	2	2	2	3	3	3	3	3
Total employment	59	54	52	49	47	47	46	45	43	44	41
Clothing and footwear											
Employees in employment	526	474	455	455	440	440	427	402	381	388	378
Self-employed (inc. employers)	19	19	18	16	17	17	17	15	15	15	15
Total employment	545	493	473	471	457	457	444	417	396	404	393
Bricks, pottery, glass and cement											
Employees in employment	326	327	318	307	305	305	301	276	264	264	265
Self-employed (inc. employers)	3	4	4	4	4	4	4	2	2	2	2
Total employment	329	331	322	311	309	309	305	278	266	266	267

Table 3.6 UK working force ('000) (cont'd.)

	1961	1962	1963	1964	1965	1966	1967	1968	1969	1970	1971	1972	1973	1974	1975	1976	1977	1978
Timber, furniture, etc.																		
Employees in employment			278					294		271	269		292	283	264	264	257	256
Self-employed (inc. employers)			24					30		37	37		48	43	46	46	46	46
Total employment			302					324		308	306		340	326	310	310	304	302
Paper, printing and publishing																		
Employees in employment			604					613		626	596		574	589	565	542	537	540
Self-employed (inc. employers)			8					9		9	9		9	8	10	10	10	10
Total employment			612					622		635	605		583	597	575	552	547	550
Other manufacturing																		
Employees in employment			296					330		345	339		352	358	330	330	331	329
Self-employed (inc. employers)			4					4		4	4		3	3	3	3	3	3
Total employment			300					334		349	343		355	361	333	333	334	332
Total manufacturing																		
Employees in employment	8,535	8,456	8,322	8,450	8,561	8,584	8,319	8,240	8,353	8,339	8,056		7,828	7,871	7,488	7,246	7,292	7,357
Self-employed (inc. employers)	97	99	101	103	105	107	108	113	121	123	123		125	123	121	121	121	121
Total employment	8,632	8,555	8,423	8,553	8,666	8,691	8,427	8,353	8,474	8,462	8,179		7,953	7,994	7,609	7,367	7,413	7,378
Construction																		
Employees in employment	1,482	1,517	1,545	1,583	1,621	1,645	1,556	1,520	1,459	1,335	1,262		1,380	1,328	1,313	1,308	1,270	1,264
Self-employed (inc. employers)	173	183	192	202	212	222	252	276	299	314	332		443	438	386	386	386	386
Total employment	1,655	1,700	1,737	1,785	1,833	1,867	1,808	1,796	1,758	1,649	1,594		1,823	1,766	1,699	1,694	1,656	1,650
Gas, electricity and water																		
Employees in employment	389	396	406	412	419	432	434	422	406	391	377	356	344	347	353	353	347	340
Self-employed (inc. employers)	–	–	–	–	–	–	–	–	–	–	–	–	–	–	–	–	–	–
Total employment	389	396	406	412	419	432	434	422	406	391	377	356	344	347	353	353	347	340
Transport and communication																		
Employees in employment	1,678	1,689	1,670	1,656	1,648	1,623	1,617	1,597	1,561	1,573	1,568		1,525	1,506	1,518	1,475	1,468	1,483
Self-employed (inc. employers)	46	46	47	47	47	47	52	55	63	68	31		71	78	83	83	83	83
Total employment	1,724	1,735	1,717	1,703	1,695	1,670	1,669	1,652	1,624	1,641	1,639		1,595	1,584	1,601	1,558	1,551	1,566
Distributive trades																		
Employees in employment	2,767	2,830	2,863	2,884	2,909	2,921	2,795	2,770	2,711	2,676	2,610		2,744	2,761	2,763	2,723	2,753	2,780
Self-employed (inc. employers)	537	523	510	496	481	468	472	464	471	478	478		452	444	434	434	434	434
Total employment	3,304	3,353	3,373	3,379	3,390	3,389	3,267	3,234	3,182	3,154	3,088		3,196	3,205	3,197	3,167	3,187	3,214

Insurance, banking and finance

Employees in employment	685	716	744	782	803	819	827	858	893	956	976		1,058	1,116	1,103	1,103	1,145	1,200
Self-employed (inc. employers)	32	32	32	32	32	32	36	39	43	47	49		50	52	52	52	52	52
Total employment	717	748	776	814	835	851	863	897	936	1,003	1,025		1,108	1,168	1,155	1,155	1,197	1,252

Professional and scientific services

Employees in employment	2,723	2,217	2,288	2,379	2,478	2,590	2,704	2,774	2,849	2,897	2,989		3,250	3,374	3,556	3,655	3,647	3,680
Self-employed (inc. employers)	175	174	172	170	168	166	179	176	184	189	190		185	195	208	208	208	208
Total employment	2,298	2,391	2,460	2,549	2,646	2,756	2,883	2,950	3,033	3,086	3,179		3,435	3,569	3,764	3,863	3,855	3,888

Miscellaneous services

Employees in employment	1,821	1,897	1,915	2,205	2,046	2,068	1,999	1,986	1,994	1,948	1,946	2,040	2,153	2,151	2,202	2,299	2,343	2,414
Self-employed (inc. employers)	301	301	302	303	304	305	321	329	347	366	363	354	339	328	339	339	339	339
Total employment	2,122	2,298	2,217	2,508	2,530	2,373	2,320	2,315	2,341	2,314	2,309	2,394	2,492	2,479	2,541	2,638	2,682	2,753

Public administration and defence

Employees in employment	1,310	1,338	1,385	1,355	1,374	1,422	1,471	1,484	1,465	1,480	1,509	1,551	1,583	1,596	1,646	1,627	1,615	1,605
Self-employed (inc. employers)	—	—	—	—	—	—	—	—	—	—	—	—	—	—	—	—	—	—
Total employment	1,310	1,338	1,385	1,355	1,374	1,422	1,471	1,484	1,465	1,480	1,509	1,551	1,583	1,596	1,646	1,627	1,615	1,605

Total

Employees in employment	22,228	22,447	22,505	22,812	23,081	23,255	22,809	22,650	22,620	22,471	22,122		22,662	22,790	22,707	22,539	22,619	22,757
Self-employed (inc. employers)	1,750	1,738	1,725	1,710	1,696	1,681	1,762	1,786	1,853	1,902	1,909		1,947	1,925	1,886	1,886	1,886	1,886
Total employment	23,978	24,185	24,230	24,522	24,777	24,936	24,571	24,436	24,473	24,373	24,031		24,609	24,715	24,593	24,425	24,505	24,653

Sources: Employees in employment, *Department of Employment Gazette*, October 1975 for 1961–70; *British Labour Statistics, 1972–6* for 1971–6; *Department of Employment Gazette*, March 1980 for 1977 and March 1981 for 1978. Self-employed, *Department of Employment Gazette*, December 1976 for 1961–74, June 1977 for 1975 (scaled up to UK by adding the Northern Ireland statistics in the December 1976 figures). 1975 figures repeated without further adjustment for 1976–8.

Table 3.7 Output per worker in the UK 1961–78, current prices

	£ 1961	£ 1962	£ 1963	£ 1964	£ 1965	£ 1966	£ 1967	£ 1968	£ 1969	£ 1970	£ 1971	£ 1972	£ 1973	£ 1974	£ 1975	£ 1976	£ 1977	£ 1978
Agriculture, forestry and fishing	873.6	926.8	929.2	982.2	1,078.8	1,158.3	1,232.5	1,304.8	1,468.1	1,614.8	1,955.0	2,191.8	2,753.8	3,042.5	3,729.0	4,593.7	5,042.7	5,457.6
Mining and quarrying[1]	973.9	1,055.2	1,107.8	1,144.6	1,147.2	1,249.1	1,316.8	1,433.6	1,401.8	1,486.6	1,644.8	1,944.7	2,239.0	3,060.0	4,383.5	4,945.4	5,611.4	6,189.8
Manufacturing	984.3	1,007.0	1,082.4	1,152.2	1,225.9	1,266.0	1,357.5	1,436.1	1,545.2	1,749.5	1,920.5	2,208.0	2,494.3	2,702.2	3,533.7	4,228.9	4,905.3	5,657.9
Construction	904.5	954.7	994.2	1,124.4	1,174.6	1,210.5	1,320.8	1,435.4	1,538.1	1,849.6	2,143.7	2,554.4	2,925.4	3,395.2	3,953.5	4,398.5	4,789.9	5,493.3
Gas, electricity and water	1,732.6	1,866.2	2,056.7	2,223.3	2,401.0	2,474.5	2,642.9	3,068.7	3,416.3	3,542.2	4,169.8	4,918.5	5,558.1	6,562.0	8,277.6	10,475.9	12,002.9	13,364.7
Transport and communication	1,173.4	1,219.0	1,332.6	1,434.5	1,551.0	1,666.5	1,701.0	1,914.0	2,104.7	2,287.6	2,469.2	2,887.9	3,385.3	4,096.6	5,059.3	6,213.1	6,677.0	7,652.0
Distributive trades	869.2	898.3	941.0	983.4	1,063.4	1,108.3	1,198.3	1,256.0	1,324.0	1,459.4	1,723.1	1,984.5	2,217.5	2,419.3	3,116.4	3,513.1	4,048.0	4,749.5
Insurance, banking and finance[2]	1,087.9	1,151.1	1,194.6	2,326.8	2,505.4	2,565.2	2,790.3	3,037.9	2,885.1	3,087.7	3,540.5	4,158.2	5,022.6	5,335.6	6,136.8	7,895.2	8,774.4	9,534.4
Other services (excl. public administration and defence)	881.0	879.7	963.0	934.3	1,016.4	1,080.7	1,154.7	1,242.4	1,335.1	1,486.7	1,578.7	1,785.6	2,035.8	2,341.9	2,968.3	3,341.8	3,754.0	4,243.9
Gross domestic product per worker	1,007.5	1,042.9	1,104.8	1,193.0	1,260.7	1,329.0	1,442.7	1,533.6	1,619.5	1,786.1	2,057.4	2,301.5	2,611.2	3,010.9	3,820.4	4,554.6	5,146.3	5,861.4

[1] Excluding petroleum and natural gas.
[2] There is a major discontinuity in the gross domestic product figures for this industry between 1963 and 1964.

Table 3.8 *Output per worker in manufacturing in the UK, at constant (1975) prices*

	£ 1963	£ 1968	£ 1970	£ 1971	£ 1972	£ 1973	£ 1974	£ 1975	£ 1976	£ 1977	£ 1978
Food, drink and tobacco	3,131	3,668	3,837	3,866	4,133	4,300	4,210	4,338	4,530	4,606	4,750
Coal and petroleum products	8,809	11,783	13,479	15,182	15,419	17,366	17,100	14,750	16,421	16,378	14,950
Chemical and allied industries	2,849	4,153	4,432	4,581	4,984	5,554	5,667	5,237	5,962	5,986	5,989
Metal manufacture	3,302	3,799	3,818	3,717	4,014	4,378	4,100	3,624	4,021	3,890	4,052
Mechanical engineering	2,323	2,860	2,970	3,040	3,147	3,457	3,570	3,582	3,519	3,494	3,404
Instrument engineering	1,384	2,080	2,388	2,429	2,528	2,663	2,847	2,975	2,987	3,053	3,257
Electrical engineering	1,915	2,305	2,517	2,603	2,804	3,129	3,095	3,199	3,329	3,408	3,563
Shipbuilding and marine engineering	2,127	2,638	2,828	2,763	2,585	2,617	2,742	2,774	2,615	2,620	2,424
Vehicles	2,743	3,234	3,042	3,139	3,391	3,456	3,343	3,215	3,242	3,309	3,231
Metal goods n.e.s	2,735	3,072	3,062	2,949	3,125	3,314	3,192	3,109	3,216	3,291	3,200
Textiles	1,642	2,274	2,388	2,616	2,787	2,963	2,715	2,839	3,014	2,959	3,040
Leather, leather goods and fur	2,136	2,389	2,385	2,592	2,633	2,660	2,500	2,600	2,791	2,591	2,756
Clothing and footwear	1,339	1,639	1,679	1,777	1,827	1,991	2,011	2,137	2,184	2,277	2,389
Bricks, pottery, glass, cement etc.	2,398	3,003	2,975	3,338	3,643	3,926	3,751	3,838	4,038	3,996	4,052
Timber, furniture etc.	2,454	2,932	2,896	3,003	3,172	3,479	3,098	3,171	3,277	3,135	3,301
Paper, printing and publishing	2,979	3,477	3,540	3,615	3,920	4,322	4,207	3,788	4,043	4,256	4,324
Other manufacturing industries	2,350	3,156	3,155	3,204	3,360	3,620	3,446	3,498	3,802	4,000	4,142

Table 3.9 *Output per worker in Scotland as a percentage of output per worker in the UK, current prices*

	1961	1962	1963	1964	1965	1966	1967	1968	1969	1970	1971	1972	1973	1974	1975	1976	1977	1978
Agriculture, forestry and fishing	100.3	97.4	101.8	103.4	106.9	115.7	111.2	121.7	123.9	127.3	129.5	127.0	128.6	124.8	126.6	130.1	123.4	117.1
Mining and quarrying[1]	94.1	94.7	90.3	105.1	107.2	105.8	108.7	92.8	105.1	115.3	96.4	99.8	99.3	101.6	100.5	106.0	109.1	97.6
Manufacturing	91.3	90.5	93.4	97.2	94.0	98.0	95.0	93.5	95.5	94.1	99.6	98.5	101.3	99.8	101.4	103.6	100.5	105.5
Construction	98.1	99.1	99.2	94.6	93.1	95.3	91.4	95.8	98.6	86.3	96.9	97.5	101.7	106.7	111.6	115.4	112.3	112.7
Gas, electricity and water	108.0	110.6	106.4	106.3	104.1	106.2	113.5	106.7	98.5	117.5	115.3	114.3	115.4	115.5	119.9	117.2	113.7	115.1
Transport and communication	84.2	84.3	84.4	87.1	87.0	87.9	89.0	86.7	90.9	94.8	96.5	96.9	97.2	96.8	97.7	99.6	100.0	100.7
Distributive trades	76.9	74.5	75.1	77.8	77.7	79.0	76.7	80.9	79.7	85.9	95.9	96.2	97.6	96.5	96.8	97.3	99.5	98.4
Insurance, banking and finance[2]	96.1	94.6	92.8	45.7	44.9	44.6	47.3	47.2	53.8	53.8	57.4	56.8	50.1	41.4	47.8	45.8	44.0	48.1
Other services (excl. public administration and defence)	84.8	87.3	87.1	88.9	84.5	90.1	91.1	89.8	85.4	82.0	96.2	97.1	97.4	96.7	100.4	99.3	97.9	99.0
Gross domestic product per worker	88.9	88.6	90.2	89.2	89.0	91.7	91.0	90.6	92.4	94.1	97.4	99.1	100.9	98.2	99.9	99.6	97.2	98.4

1, 2See corresponding notes to Table 3.7.

Table 3.10 *Output per worker in Scotland, as a percentage of output per worker in the UK in manufacturing industries, at constant (1975) prices*

	1963	1968	1970	1971	1972	1973	1974	1975	1976	1977	1978
Food, drink and tobacco	94.0	103.8	106.2	112.6	111.6	112.3	115.8	116.1	113.6	110.5	113.0
Coal and petroleum products	119.1	100.3	104.2	109.8	124.0	115.6	119.4	111.9	112.4	104.5	102.2
Chemicals and allied industries	87.6	94.6	97.5	89.9	88.4	87.0	88.3	87.0	82.0	82.7	86.3
Metal manufacture	94.4	103.2	119.2	111.0	109.0	105.7	95.7	98.1	107.3	104.1	95.5
Mechanical engineering	72.6	73.1	98.6	104.1	103.9	105.5	103.8	105.2	114.4	113.0	127.2
Instrument engineering	72.4	81.8	82.6	83.2	77.8	74.0	70.2	77.8	68.8	70.4	64.6
Electrical engineering	80.4	79.3	85.2	91.1	103.8	100.6	102.8	111.9	100.3	90.4	87.2
Shipbuilding and marine engineering	116.0	94.7	98.5	100.2	97.6	98.3	95.0	95.4	99.7	101.2	99.2
Vehicles	102.5	110.5	115.3	108.0	110.1	105.7	105.6	101.8	106.5	101.8	103.3
Metal goods n.e.s.	67.1	68.0	96.6	96.4	98.6	101.5	102.2	104.7	113.8	106.3	106.8
Textiles	110.9	103.8	105.9	103.3	98.0	93.9	92.3	93.6	97.3	94.5	98.2
Leather, leather goods and fur	109.9	96.4	103.8	112.4	116.5	121.2	105.8	108.3	107.8	107.1	110.3
Clothing and footwear											
Bricks, pottery, glass, cement, etc.											
Timber, furniture, etc.											
Paper, printing and publishing											
Other manufacturing industries											

performance shown in Table 3.9 for insurance, banking and finance is at least partly misleading: as explained in the notes in Table 3.7, there is a major discontinuity in the UK output series for the industry between 1963 and 1964 (that discontinuity also affects 'other services', but much less importantly), and so the series for insurance, banking and finance in Table 3.9 should really be interpreted as starting in 1964: even then, output per worker in the industry looks poor in Scotland, but there are major problems in measuring output in the industry and also important differences in the composition of the industry between Scotland and the rest of the UK.

On the whole, Tables 3.9 and 3.10 can be interpreted as showing that output per worker in Scotland, while starting low, was improving quite rapidly by UK standards, but the improvement was rather erratic both in relative terms and, as Tables 3.4 and 3.5 show, in absolute terms. Before we can go further in interpreting the evidence, we will find it useful briefly to review how in principle labour productivity is expected to behave and what other factors are relevant.

The Determinants of Labour Productivity

In considering what might really lie behind the evidence on output per head that we have outlined, the first and most obvious consideration is that there are several inputs, not just labour, involved in the making of outputs. Most outputs required labour, capital equipment (such as buildings and machines) and raw materials in their production. Further, for most output there will be labour of many different kinds – operatives, administrators, clerical workers, storemen, etc. – and capital and materials could well be equally diverse. If however, we follow the economist's usual device of simplification, we can pretend for illustrative purposes that each kind of input really is homogeneous, and to keep our presentation within the bounds of a two-dimensional diagram we can pretend that there are only two inputs that are relevant – for example, labour and capital.

Now consider one particular level of output. If technology is such that there is only one way of making the output, so that, for example, one worker tends one loom, then finding output per worker is a matter of simple arithmetic. If, however, there are several ways of making output, so that, for example, we could have one worker tending one loom or two workers tending three looms between them, there is a choice of techniques to make, and that choice will determine output per head.

In Figure 3.1, quantities of labour and of capital are on the axes. The line OA represents combinations in the ratio of 1 unit of capital to 1 unit of labour – and so can represent the technique of 1 worker per loom. The line OB represents combinations in the ratio of 3 units of capital to 2 units of labour, and so can represent the technique of 2 workers tc 3 looms. Suppose that at point C 10 units of output are made by the technique of line OA, and at point D 10 units of output are made by the technique of line OB. Now, on the technique on line OA, these 10 units of output are made by 3 units of labour, so that output per head is $3^1/_3$ units, and on the technique on line OE, 10 units of output are made by less than 3 units of labour – say 2½ units, and so on that technique output per head is 4 units. As the simplified diagram suggests, one important determinant of output per head is the degree of labour-intensity of production (that is, the ratio of labour to other inputs employed), and the more labour-intensive production is (for example, 1 unit of labour to 1 unit of capital rather than 1 unit of labour to 1½ units of capital) the lower will output per head be. So one important factor determining the level of output per head will be the labour-intensity of production.

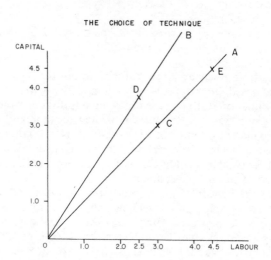

Figure 3.1   *Outputs and inputs*

The second important factor can also be illustrated by Figure 3.1. Consider the technique of 1 worker per loom – i.e., that on the line OA. We know that at point C 10 units of output are made. What will the output at point E be? We have no *a priori* reason to assume that just because at point E we have 1½ times the input of labour and 1½ times the input of capital that are used at point C, we will get 1½ times the output – i.e., 15 units. There might, for example, be economies of scale, such that when we expand the quantity of inputs, output expands more than proportionately. If so, then at point E we will have a higher output per head than at point C. So output per head can well depend on the scale of production.

All this discussion of Figure 3.1 is predicated on the simplifying assumptions we made to construct it. There is no great difficulty in principle in allowing the analysis to become multi-dimensional, to take account of more than two kinds of input and to take account of the multiplicity of types there are of each input, but there are important measurement problems in relating such an analysis to the available evidence. It should also be remembered that in Figure 3.1 we are portraying a uniform, homogeneous product, because there will be a separate diagram for each product, unless by chance we get two physically different products with an identical menu of techniques of production.

What this section has shown so far is that output per head can be influenced by:

the range of techniques available,
the choice of techniques,
the presence of non-proportional returns to scale, and
heterogeneity in the output or input units.

There is a fifth influence that we can add to our list. If a new set of technological possibilities appears, we will modify Figure 3.1 either by drawing new lines on it, to represent new mixes of labour and capital, or by shifting points, if for example on the new technology 10 units of output can be made by 2 units of capital and 2 units of labour. So our last influence is technical progress. Let us consider the possible relevance of these five considerations to the Scotland/UK comparisons we made earlier in this chapter.

In some of the literature about international trade, and especially trade between developing and developed economies, much is made of a technology gap between countries, where this gap represents ignorance by the inhabitants of one country of the range of technology available to the more advanced country – an ignorance created perhaps by patenting arrangements, or simply by variations in educational standards. Although there are some circumstances in which such a technology gap might exist between Scotland and the rest of the UK, and thus account for differences in output per head, these circumstances seem sufficiently unlikely to exist at all, and if they do exist to persist for any length of time, that we can reject this explanation as implausible.

There is a little, but only a little, more likelihood that the choice of technique is relevant. According to standard 'neo-classical' economic theory, the technique will be chosen in such a way that the producer makes his predetermined level of output at as low cost as possible. To find what is the least cost method, he has to discover what is the cost to him of the various inputs. In our simple diagram with only two inputs, if he wants to make 10 units of output he can do so at point C, with 3 units of capital and 3 units of labour, or at point D, when he has 3¾ units of capital and 2½ units of labour. Which method is cheaper obviously depends on the relative prices of capital and labour – if by using half a unit less of labour he saves more than it cost him to use an extra three-quarters of a unit of capital, the producer should opt for point D and so for the technique it represents, and we can similarly specify the conditions in which he would choose point C and in which he would be indifferent between the two. So for the technology chosen to be systematically different in Scotland from that chosen in the rest of the UK, there should be some systematic differences in the relative cost of inputs.

We can fairly quickly dismiss systematic differences in the cost of capital. The real measure of the cost of capital in a business has probably been expressed as an interest cost – either a rate of interest or rate of dividend the firm has to pay, on borrowed or equity capital, or an implicit rate of interest on financial assets which the firm chooses to use for the purchase of investment goods rather than for other purposes. It is of course not true that all firms face the same interest rate – the actual interest they have to pay will be systematically related to what risk lending to them is thought to be, which in turn depends on the size of the firm, on its past history, and on various other considerations specific to the firm and perhaps specific also to the investment project. Similarly the implicit interest rate represented by opportunities foregone depends on exactly what those opportunities are. But while there is some reason for believing that the interest rate can vary from firm to firm, since there is more or less a uniform market for finance throughout the UK there is no reason to think that there will be any very systematic difference between the cost of capital to Scottish firms and its cost to firms elsewhere in the UK.

As far as raw materials are concerned, there is really too little evidence to present any definite view, but it seems likely that raw-material prices at point of production are pretty well uniform throughout the UK, and that any systematic differences in raw-material prices experienced by firms would reflect transport costs. High transport costs are one of the phenomena to be associated with a peripheral location, but it is not evident from observation that Scottish manufacturers are noticeably worse placed in that respect than those situated elsewhere in the UK. To account for output per worker which starts below the UK level and more or less steadily increases towards it, we would have to suppose that raw material costs started relatively high in Scotland (so that a more labour-intensive, less material-intensive method was used there) but that the gap between Scottish and UK raw materials prices has diminished. There is however some plausibility in this proposition and we will return to it shortly when we consider transport costs. The last relevant kind of input is labour and it is here that in principle there is most room for difference in price between the regions of the UK, because of the immobility of labour. Discussion here is facilitated by the availability of reasonably good evidence about earnings and hours worked.

Information about UK earnings has been collected for some time by the Department of Employment and its predecessors, and some details for Scotland have been available for years since 1960. Particulars of the weekly earnings of adult male manual workers in most but not all industries are available for October in each year. The average figures for Scotland, in total (current prices) and as a percentage of the corresponding UK figures, are set out in part A of Table 3.11. More detail, about hours worked, about all industries and about all categories of workers including male manual, are available from the New Earnings Survey, starting from 1970. The survey is conducted only for Great Britain (GB), so that comparisons in section B of Table 3.11 are between Scotland and GB, but for this purpose the difference between GB and the UK is slight (earnings in Northern Ireland are usually a little below the GB average, so the GB average is therefore fractionally higher than the UK average in most cases). The major drawback of the New Earnings Survey as a source is that it is constructed by asking for information about a sample of the working population, and the sample is sufficiently small that some of the detailed industry figures for Scotland are not published: but these problems do not affect the evidence quoted in Table 3.11.

If the differences between output per worker in Scotland and the UK average were to be explained by the wage level alone, what we would expect to find is that Scottish wages levels are relatively low (so that relatively more labour-intensive methods are adopted in Scotland, thus lowering output per worker), and that wages in Scotland have been rising towards the UK average over our period (so that the gap in output per worker narrows). This is exactly what Table 3.11 demonstrates, and so it might appear that here we have found the explanation of the behaviour of Scottish labour productivity. It can, however, be shown that this argument confuses cause and effect.

In a careful analysis of the evidence we have presented in Table 3.11, the Scottish Office writers of the *Scottish Economic Bulletin*, no. 15 (Summer, 1978) sought to explain the really rather remarkable rise in Scottish average earnings relatively to the UK in the 1970s. A little of the rise in relative earnings in Scotland was attributable to a rise in relative overtime working. The changes in the industrial structure of employment in Scotland should have *decreased* relative Scottish earnings a little at least for male manual workers in manufacturing.

Table 3.11 *Average weekly earnings (including overtime) in Scotland*

A *Adult male manual workers, manufacturing and certain other industries[1]*

	£	Scotland as % of UK		£	Scotland as % of UK
1960[2]	12.92	91.6	1970	27.04	96.4
1961	14.25	92.9	1971	29.88	96.6
1962	14.71	92.7	1972	34.93	97.5
1963	15.49	92.5	1973	40.35	98.6
1964	16.92	93.4	1974	48.37	99.5
1965	18.45	94.2	1975	60.71	101.9
1966	19.58	96.5	1976	67.88	101.4
1967	20.77	97.2	1977	73.53	100.9
1968	22.30	97.0	1978	83.96	100.6
1969	24.10	97.1	1979	95.46	98.4

[1]The industries covered are manufacturing, mining and quarrying (except coal mining), construction, gas, electricity and water, transport and communication (except railways and sea transport), certain miscellaneous services, and public administration.
[2]April figure for 1960. October figures for all other years.

B *New Earnings Survey data, all categories of workers, all industries, Scotland as % of GB*

	Male manual	Male non-manual	Female manual	Female non-manual
1970	95.9	94.4	97.8	93.4
1971	96.9	95.1	97.4	95.4
1972	96.6	95.9	98.2	94.6
1973	97.4	97.3	99.0	95.9
1974	98.4	95.2	99.2	94.4
1975	101.8	98.1	100.0	95.4
1976	101.7	99.0	100.0	96.3
1977	101.4	99.0	100.0	95.2
1978	100.9	99.1	101.6	95.8
1979	100.7	100.0	98.4	95.5
1980	100.5	98.8	97.5	94.6

Source: Updated and modified from *Scottish Economic Bulletin*, nos. 8 (Summer 1975) and 15 (Summer 1978).

Changes in the occupational structure of employment (that is, in the extent to which members of the workforce within each broad group are lower- or higher-paid employees in that group) might have contributed

fractionally to the relative improvement in average earnings in
Scotland. Even allowing for the impact of North Sea oil developments
in certain regions and industries (a topic we will consider in Chapter 6),
the pressure of demand for labour seems to have had only a very slight
impact on relative earnings in Scotland.

The Scottish Office analysis concludes therefore by suggesting that
the relative improvement in earnings in Scotland reflects (and so is presumably caused by, though the analysis never explicitly says so) the
productivity improvement:

> the increase in earnings in Scotland relative to the UK as a whole
> appears to have been accompanied by a more rapid growth in
> overall labour productivity in Scotland, and the same pattern is
> partly evident at industry level. The relative increase in Scottish
> earnings does not appear to have been accompanied by significant
> increase in relative wage costs (*Scottish Economic Bulletin*, no. 15
> (Summer 1978), p. 19).

If we accept this argument, and it is so meticulously documented that
it is difficult to resist, then we must assume that changes in wages have
mainly followed, rather than preceded, changes in labour productivity. From that we must conclude that, of the various input prices we
have considered, the only empirically plausible change in prices which
might help to account for the level and change in labour productivity
we have examined is that in transport costs affecting the delivered
price of raw materials.

There are, however, three more kinds of influence on output per
head which we have not considered – the effect of non-proportionate
returns to scale, the effects of heterogeneity in output or in inputs, and
technical progress. We will treat them together because of the
difficulty of disentangling one from the other in practice. Some forms
of technical progress, by increasing the output attainable from a given
mix of inputs, are in practice difficult to distinguish from economies of
scale (unless output is then decreased again). Other forms of technical
progress are 'embodied' in capital equipment designed specifically for
a particular process, and in that case capital equipment can be distinguished into 'vintages' when each 'vintage' has its own technical
characteristics reflecting what was the most advanced or the most
'efficient' form of technology when it was made, so that capital is *not*
homogeneous.

Studies for other economies suggest that it is in the group of
influences we are about to examine that we should expect to find the
key to the behaviour of labour productivity. For example, in his
classic work on labour productivity in UK manufacturing over the
period 1924–50, after expressing due caution about his evidence Salter
(1966) concluded,

The analysis has suggested that, to explain the data (on increased labour productivity), primary emphasis must be placed on technical progress and economies of scale. These are causes of labour productivity which extend their influences to all factors and so can account for the behaviour of costs. Increases in the personal efficiency of labour and factor substitution cannot explain the data by themselves although, in the case of factor substitution at least, it is possible (and indeed likely) that an important contribution has been made to the observed increases in productivity (Salter, 1966, p. 144).

The basic source for detailed studies of the differences in labour productivity in any manufacturing industry in the UK is the Census of Production. Census statistics have been used in this way by McCrone (1965), Brown (1969) and Blake (1976 and 1981). McCrone's exercise is of interest for our purposes simply because it was he who drew attention to the existence of regional differences in the UK in output per employee in manufacturing, but he did not offer any very sophisticated analysis.

Brown used the 1954 Census data for regression analysis of net output per head in each Census industry and region. He expressed net output per head in each Census industry and region as a percentage of the (unweighted) average for that industry in all regions, and regressed the resultant percentage on the proportion of the industry situated in the region, the average size of establishment in that region, and dummy variables. He concluded that there was evidence of significant positive effect on net output per head of having a high proportion of the industry in the region and of having a larger plant size. Even allowing for these factors, however, Brown found a general tendency for net output per head in Scotland (and in Northern Ireland and Wales) to be low in comparison with that in the Midlands and the south-east of England.

Blake analysed the 1968 Census data of net output per head. He found that overall net output per head in manufacturing in Scotland was almost exactly 95 per cent of the UK level, but that the individual industries had net output per head in Scotland between half and twice the UK level. To establish the basic cause of the lower output per head in Scotland, he used alternative hypothetical economies, one in which the labour force had the same structure as that of Scotland in 1968 but with UK levels of net output per head in each industry, and the other with the 1968 Scottish net output per head in each industry but a UK structure of employment. The first hypothetical economy had a net output per head of 102 per cent of the UK level, and the second of 94 per cent of the UK level, so the structure of manufacturing employment was slightly in Scotland's favour in 1968 and the lower net output per head is due to relatively low net output per head within industries.

Blake then proceeded to consider how far this gap in net output per head was attributable to heterogeneity in the capital equipment in Scotland and how far to heterogeneity in the type of product. The conclusion of his 1976 paper was that heterogeneity of capital equipment – the 'vintages' embodied in the capital stock – *was* important in the explanation, as regression analysis using rather indirect proxies isolated it as an important factor in most cases. In his 1981 study, Blake returned to the question of the dispersion of labour productivity, using the 1973 Census of Production, and relating labour productivity to size of plant (as measured by employment) and the output per £ of goods and service absorbed (that is, output *less* value added at that stage of production, or output minus brought-in components).

The first explanatory variable was significant, with the right sign, in 21 industries of the 70 available for analysis, and the second in 55 industries. The second explanatory variable was significant for 19 of the 21 industries for which the first variable was significant. The second variable therefore looked much more useful as an explanation, but posed questions of interpretation itself – did it reflect the degree of backwards integration of production (which would affect the proportion of inputs bought in) or the specification of the product? The evidence seemed to point to specification of the product – as Blake concludes, 'Tighter manning levels, improved work flow, lower rejection rates, more automation of products, all contribute to higher productivity. Nevertheless the quasi-rents earned by superior quality and designs are crucial. It is what we make that matters at least as much as the way in which it is made' (Blake, 1981, p. 6).

When we consider the productivity of labour in industries other than manufacturing, we meet up with important measurement as well as conceptual problems. As we have explained in Chapter 2, the output statistics we are using are a more or less faithful measure of the value of physical product when there is an identifiable physical product, which means for manufacturing, for agriculture, forestry and fishing, for mining and quarrying, for construction and for gas, electricity and water. For all the service industries, there is no physical product we can meaningfully measure – the tonnage of hair swept up from barbers' and hairdressers' floors, for example, would not give us a sensible measure of the output of the hairdressing industry – and so output is measured as the sum of value of inputs. As service industries are usually very labour-intensive, this means that expenditure on labour is a high proportion of what is measured as the output of the industry, and so while we can measure labour productivity and comment on its change over time or in relation to some other economy, what we are really measuring is earnings levels. So the casual problem that we have discussed in dealing with the relationship between earnings and productivity in manufacturing becomes for service industries a chicken-and-egg problem because we cannot use differences in timing or in incidence between industries to distinguish cause from effect.

The Efficiency of Scottish Production

Our discussion so far has reflected the difficulty most economists feel in arriving at a clear explanation of productivity levels. We can measure Scottish labour productivity – more or less, we can discuss some of the simple explanations for its changes relatively to the UK level, and we can conclude that, although there are some cases when a simple explanation fits, in general labour productivity differences must reflect differences in product which official definitions of industries are too crude to identify. But to say that changes in labour productivity are mainly caused by changes in product is not to conclude that the economist cannot comment on the efficiency of production. Even if he cannot say with any certainty what the better product mix might be, he can offer some observations on how resources might be used more efficiently.

The efficiency of use of resources is a crucial issue not just in economic theory but in the practical economic fortunes of a country. As we write this, many economists would say that the practical key present issue for the British, and for the Scottish, economy, is not how to achieve high output per unit of labour but simply how to employ all the labour available, but the Government's argument is that unemployment is the inevitable consequence of low productivity (coupled with high wages) and that its outcome will be to raise productivity. In happier times, high and growing labour productivity is the only route to high and growing income per head.

For an economy very dependent on trade, with its immediate and more distant neighbours, even parity of cost of production at the factory is not necessarily enough to ensure competitive equality: there is also the question of transport costs. It has long been accepted that one of the reasons why the regions of the UK which are furthest from south-east England (and now from the main economic powers of Continental Europe) are the least prosperous is transport costs: the extra cost of taking raw material and bought-in components to the peripheral regions, and the extra cost of taking finished products from the regions to the main markets of the more prosperous areas.

The importance of transport costs in manufacturing in Scotland was analysed in an interesting discussion in *Scottish Economic Bulletin*, no. 22 (Spring 1981). The source of evidence was once again the Census of Production, this time that of 1974. As the authors of the article properly stress, there are some problems of interpretation; particularly, the conclusions drawn rest on the assumptions that firms quote to customers a price that includes delivery costs, and that firms that operate transport fleets of their own do so to distribute output rather than to collect inputs. On these assumptions, in both Scotland and the UK transport costs from factory to market were fairly low – representings 6½–7 per cent of gross value added and 2–2½ per cent of gross output, and transport costs were on average fractionally *lower* in Scotland than in the UK. As the authors of the article are well aware, it is dangerous to base too much on the evidence for one year, but as they demonstrate an unpublished student thesis using a broadly similar methodology on the 1963 Census returns suggested that transport costs in Scotland were only marginally greater than those in the UK. With due official caution, the *Scottish Economic Bulletin* article concludes by emphasising the wide divergence in transport costs between industries:

> individual firms may well face severe transport cost problems depending on the location of their competitors, particular markets and other factors. Conversely many firms, particularly those with high value to weight products may not be disadvantaged by a Scottish location. It is also necessary to emphasise the wide variation in transport circumstances of different parts of Scotland (*Scottish Economic Bulletin*, no. 22 (Spring 1981), p. 35)

but the conclusion that transport costs do not militate against Scottish output in manufacturing as a whole is very interesting. It is regrettable that the method used in this article cannot be adapted to study the costs of inward transport of materials used in production, but in the absence of such information we must conclude that transport costs are probably unimportant in total and in any case not noticeably different between Scotland and the rest of the UK.

Since the peripherality of Scotland does not appear to have any readily measurable costs and particularly since there is no obvious reason to argue that these costs have worsened, the rise in the relative labour productivity of the Scottish economy, whatever its cause, is the reason for some optimism about its future. But to compare Scotland with the UK average is to use an unexacting standard: the UK and the US have competed since the early 1950s for the unenviable position of being the slowest-growing developed western economy, and, as Jones (1976) demonstrated, value-added per man-hour in manufacturing in the UK had by 1974 fallen even below that of Italy (which had in 1955 been only two-thirds of the UK level) and, having in 1955 been only a little below that in Germany, France, Belgium and the Netherlands, the UK figure was by 1974 only around half their average. The fact remains, however, that output per worker in the Scottish economy has been improving, both absolutely and relatively to the UK average. Whether this is associable mainly with something inherent in the Scottish economy or with external policy forces is a matter to which we turn our attention in the next chapter.

4

Scottish Economic Performance, 1954–78

Introduction

This chapter will focus on Scottish growth performance since 1954. We first give a general picture of the growth of the Scottish economy as revealed by Scottish GDP estimates in constant (1975) prices and compare the Scottish economic performance at sectoral and industry levels with that of the UK. Then we examine further these output aggregates in terms of the technique known as 'growth standardisation'. Basically, the growth standardisation technique enables us to examine the relationship between actual and 'expected' time-series by industry and by sector. To arrive at a series of 'expected output', the technique was to take as base Scottish value added in 1963 and apply to this the UK annual growth rates to extrapolate backward and forward from 1963. It is argued that such technique, although useful, provides only a first step insight into the identification of the possible regional and other policy effects.

Scottish Growth Performance, 1954–78

From the constant (1975) prices estimates of Scottish GDP presented in Chapter 2 average annual growth rates by industry and sector can be calculated for various arbitrarily divided sub-periods as well as for the entire period of 1954–78. These growth rates can be compared to those for the UK calculated in the same way by using the official index numbers of output at constant factor cost. We have arbitrarily divided the whole study period into three to five year periods. These sub-periods are 1954–8, 1958–63, 1963–8, 1968–71, 1971–5 and 1975–8. We also consider 1971–8 as a rather longer sub-period.

Table 4.1 gives the UK GDP in constant (1975) prices for the entire period of 1954–78. The methodology for arriving at the corresponding

Scottish series is described in Chapter 2. As can be appreciated, the Scottish series is arrived at from data, of varying degrees of reliability and precision, and relies fairly heavily on the Scottish Index of Industrial Production. Hence, it must be taken as rather rough and ready, but nonetheless providing a long-term picture of Scottish economy, perhaps for the first time. It must be admitted however that it is a picture whose consistency and accuracy of detail could be considerably improved. From Tables 2.5 and 4.1, growth rates for Scotland and for the UK for the various sub-periods and the entire period have been calculated and this evidence is presented in Table 4.2. To take the entire period of 1954–78 first, it can be seen that the total GDP growth rates in Scotland and the UK are very similar, with the UK GDP growth rate marginally faster than in Scotland. At sectoral level, Scottish growth rate was lower than the corresponding UK rate in the primary sector and in the services. The Scottish growth rate was higher than the corresponding UK rate in public utilities and the two rates were identical in manufacturing. At industry level, Scottish growth rate was higher than the corresponding UK rate in construction and in gas, electricity and water.

For the period 1954–8, average GDP growth in the UK was much higher than that for Scotland, where GDP was lower in 1958 than in 1954. At the sectoral level, the decline in Scottish output was most severe in the primary sector, followed by services. In manufacturing and public utilities too, the average Scottish growth rate was below that of the UK. For the period 1958–63 there was some improvement in the Scottish GDP growth rate, which coincided with the UK. At sectoral level the decline in primary sector was much smaller than that for the earlier period. However, at industry level, the Scottish growth rate in agriculture, forestry and fishing lagged behind that of the° UK and mining and quarrying continued to experience greater decline in Scotland than in the UK as a whole. In manufacturing, although there was some improvement in the overall growth rate for Scotland, this still lagged behind that for the UK. At the industry level, Scottish growth rate was higher than that for the UK, in food, drink and tobacco; electrical engineering; metal goods not elsewhere specified; textiles etc.; bricks, pottery, etc.; and paper, printing etc. The overall growth rate for public utilities was higher than that for the UK overall and for gas, electricity and water within the sector.

The next two sub-periods mark a different phase of Scottish economic performance. When the Scottish economy showed more distinct signs of revival in nearly all the economic sectors for the period 1963–8, average Scottish GDP growth rate was higher than that for the UK for the first time due to growth rates higher than the corresponding UK growth rate in primary; manufacturing; and public utilities sectors. At the industry level, Scottish growth rate was higher

Table 4.1   UK Gross domestic product by industry 1954–79, constant (1975) prices, £ million

Industry SIC order 1968	1954	1955	1956	1957	1958	1959	1960	1961	1962	1963	1964	1965	1966
Agriculture, forestry and fishing (I)	1,670.6	1,646.4	1,743.2	1,767.4	1,718.8	1,786.0	1,903.1	1,913.1	1,975.4	2,052.6	2,132.3	2,189.6	2,197.1
Mining and quarrying (II)	2,542.2	2,502.9	2,515.4	2,497.5	2,387.0	2,320.7	2,235.8	2,201.9	2,260.5	2,262.0	2,266.7	2,183.3	2,058.3
Primary sector (I, II)	4,212.9	4,149.3	4,258.6	4,264.9	4,105.8	4,106.7	4,138.9	4,115.9	4,235.9	4,314.6	4,399.0	4,372.9	4,255.4
Food, drink and tobacco (III)	1,985.6	2,036.1	2,083.6	2,116.2	2,175.3	2,248.2	2,311.7	2,384.6	2,429.0	2,501.9	2,559.0	2,619.2	2,695.3
Chemicals, coal and petroleum products (VI, V)	1,019.4	1,068.1	1,138.6	1,193.3	1,235.0	1,355.7	1,493.2	1,526.1	1,560.7	1,661.7	1,828.8	1,951.4	2,066.2
Metal manufacture (VI)	1,741.8	1,887.5	1,917.2	1,942.3	1,762.6	1,840.8	2,135.5	2,010.0	1,899.0	1,988.2	2,255.6	2,355.6	2,219.2
Engineering and allied industries (VII–XII)	6,444.7	7,098.9	7,002.6	7,227.5	7,349.0	7,641.3	8,220.7	8,232.7	8,280.2	8,466.1	9,270.4	9,460.2	9,661.0
Mechanical and instrument engineering (VII, VIII)	2,024.2	2,141.4	2,154.0	2,231.9	2,137.0	2,191.4	2,392.1	2,587.3	2,586.6	2,594.2	2,845.2	3,023.9	3,204.3
Electrical engineering (IX)	897.2	993.4	983.0	1,049.9	1,114.7	1,227.4	1,290.1	1,342.7	1,400.3	1,477.9	1,598.2	1,570.6	1,710.9
Shipbuilding and vehicles (X, XI)	2,169.3	2,456.8	2,391.9	2,466.4	2,655.7	2,784.4	2,909.0	2,746.2	2,790.8	2,842.7	3,033.7	3,004.5	2,985.6
Metal goods n.e.s. (XII)	1,354.0	1,507.3	1,473.7	1,479.3	1,441.5	1,438.1	1,629.6	1,556.4	1,502.4	1,551.2	1,793.2	1,861.1	1,760.1
Textiles, leather, clothing (XIII–XV)	2,200.9	2,176.8	2,154.0	2,139.4	1,959.6	2,090.6	2,186.1	1,453.3	2,079.7	2,142.1	2,265.6	2,339.3	2,333.7
Bricks, pottery, etc. (XVI)	624.9	648.2	639.3	618.9	610.3	647.7	721.3	752.2	765.0	788.5	906.9	916.5	908.0
Timber, furniture, etc. (XVII)	573.9	591.8	572.1	600.5	590.8	674.3	701.9	727.4	712.7	741.2	865.0	872.9	855.2
Paper, printing, etc. (XVIII)	1,399.6	1,509.8	1,489.6	1,521.1	1,570.3	1,642.2	1,801.2	1,772.9	1,768.5	1,823.0	1,990.7	2,032.1	2,086.5
Other manufacturing (XIX)	467.9	514.3	485.5	510.9	499.8	555.7	633.8	630.3	661.7	704.8	814.3	865.6	901.7
All manufacturing (III–XIX)	16,458.7	17,531.5	17,482.5	17,870.1	17,752.6	18,696.5	20,205.3	19,489.4	20,156.4	20,817.6	22,755.9	23,412.7	23,726.7
Construction (XV)	4,847.2	4,854.5	5,121.4	5,114.1	5,091.5	5,373.6	5,655.7	6,092.3	6,146.0	6,132.6	6,657.3	7,073.0	7,207.3
Gas, electricity and water (XXI)	1,122.4	1,181.3	1,235.4	1,282.2	1,338.3	1,373.3	1,478.5	1,545.7	1,668.5	1,750.3	1,840.8	1,323.5	2,045.4
Public utilities (XX, XXI)	5,969.7	6,035.8	6,356.8	6,396.3	6,429.8	6,746.9	7,134.2	7,638.0	7,815.5	7,882.9	8,598.1	8,396.5	9,252.7
Transport and communications (XXII)	4,580.4	4,722.3	4,792.8	4,792.8	4,722.3	4,924.8	5,175.9	5,297.4	5,337.9	5,516.1	5,872.5	5,994.0	6,164.1
Distributive trades (XXIII)	6,251.3	6,535.4	6,630.1	6,914.3	6,914.7	7,302.9	7,631.7	7,781.0	7,831.0	8,090.0	8,408.8	8,657.8	8,757.5
Insurance, banking and finance¹ (XXIV)	1,328.2	1,354.8	1,354.8	1,407.9	1,487.6	1,758.1	1,825.7	1,859.5	1,928.2	2,075.5	2,110.7	2,312.1	2,442.7
Ownership of dwellings	3,496.6	3,596.1	3,746.0	3,745.8	3,796.4	3,908.1	3,963.9	4,075.6	4,131.4	4,187.2	4,243.1	4,410.6	4,522.2
Public health and education services (part of XXV)	3,756.7	3,818.2	4,003.5	4,126.3	4,249.2	4,321.2	4,465.2	4,609.3	4,825.3	4,897.4	5,041.4	5,257.5	5,401.5
Public administration and defence (XXVII)	6,960.4	6,753.3	6,687.7	6,530.5	6,294.5	6,220.2	6,146.1	6,146.1	6,146.1	6,294.2	6,294.2	6,368.3	6,516.4
Other services (rest of XXV, XXVI)	7,967.8	8,075.5	8,075.5	8,183.2	8,289.4	8,634.7	9,095.3	9,325.5	9,440.7	9,786.0	10,361.7	10,361.7	10,476.8
Services (XXII–XXVII)	34,385.5	34,855.6	35,290.4	35,700.8	35,753.7	37,070.0	38,303.8	39,094.5	39,639.5	40,846.0	42,332.4	43,362.0	44,281.2
Gross domestic product at factor cost	61,026.7	62,572.2	63,387.8	64,232.1	64,041.9	66,620.1	69,781.9	70,336.9	71,847.3	73,861.1	78,125.4	79,544.1	81,516.0

Table 4.1 UK Gross domestic product by industry 1954–79, constant (1975) prices, £ million (cont'd.)

Industry SIC order 1968	1967	1968	1969	1970	1971	1972	1973	1974	1975	1976	1977	1978	1979
Agriculture, forestry and fishing (I)	2,269.3	2,266.8	2,261.8	2,398.8	2,525.9	2,608.1	2,690.3	2,747.6	2,491.0	2,311.6	2,638.0	2,822.3	2,747.6
Mining and quarrying (II)	2,042.9	2,039.8	1,908.7	1,834.6	1,834.6	1,544.5	1,698.8	1,387.2	1,543.0	1,941.1	2,896.2	3,587.5	4,547.2
Primary sector (I, II)	4,312.2	4,306.6	4,170.5	4,233.5	4,360.4	4,152.6	4,389.1	4,134.7	4,034.0	4,252.7	5,533.2	6,409.8	7,294.8
Food, drink and tobacco (III)	2,742.9	2,857.0	2,949.0	2,993.4	3,012.4	3,142.5	3,272.5	3,250.3	3,171.0	3,256.6	3,297.8	3,367.6	3,405.6
Chemicals, coal and petroleum products (IV, V)	2,135.3	2,311.1	2,461.7	2,614.2	2,679.5	2,791.5	3,088.2	3,155.2	2,847.0	3,151.5	3,221.8	3,238.9	3,307.1
Metal manufacture (VI)	2,088.2	2,226.5	2,279.2	2,271.9	2,073.7	2,075.5	2,271.9	2,082.8	1,819.0	1,889.9	1,882.7	1,864.5	1,886.3
Engineering and allied industries (VII–XII)	9,671.4	10,282.5	10,827.2	10,769.3	10,607.0	10,663.7	11,517.7	11,658.1	11,137.0	10,858.4	11,704.0	11,072.0	11,010.0
Mechanical and instrument engineering (VII, VIII)	3,225.7	3,386.0	3,574.5	3,705.7	3,636.0	3,501.9	3,808.1	3,980.0	3,941.0	3,754.9	3,726.6	3,702.6	3,688.9
Electrical engineering (IX)	1,823.6	1,906.3	2,056.6	2,091.7	2,124.2	2,229.4	2,537.6	2,617.7	2,505.0	2,467.4	2,572.6	2,707.9	2,845.7
Shipbuilding and vehicles (X, XI)	2,936.7	3,152.5	3,253.2	3,103.9	3,104.0	3,151.3	3,250.0	3,160.9	2,950.0	2,912.5	2,967.6	2,882.2	2,764.0
Metal goods n.e.s. (XII)	1,685.3	1,836.8	1,942.9	1,868.0	1,742.7	1,781.0	1,922.1	1,899.4	1,741.0	1,723.6	1,807.2	1,779.3	1,711.4
Textiles, leather clothing (XII–XV)	2,266.3	2,519.7	2,557.8	2,548.4	2,604.0	2,662.3	2,806.7	2,610.5	2,521.0	2,482.7	2,559.7	2,555.0	2,517.6
Bricks, pottery, etc. (XVI)	940.0	994.4	997.6	958.2	1,038.1	1,110.7	1,213.2	1,143.8	1,067.0	1,074.5	1,062.7	1,081.9	1,080.9
Timber, furniture, etc. (XVII)	881.7	949.6	889.6	891.6	919.1	1,099.0	1,283.6	1,009.5	983.0	1,016.4	952.5	996.8	1,016.4
Paper, printing, etc. (XVIII)	2,080.0	2,162.7	2,232.4	2,247.7	2,186.7	2,308.7	2,519.9	2,515.6	2,178.0	2,232.4	2,328.3	2,378.4	2,441.5
Other manufacturing (XIX)	937.8	1,054.3	1,095.1	1,100.9	1,098.6	1,148.7	1,285.0	1,238.4	1,165.0	1,266.4	1,336.3	1,374.7	1,371.2
All manufacturing (III–XIX)	23,743.7	25,357.8	26,289.9	26,396.3	26,219.1	27,002.6	29,258.7	28,664.3	26,888.0	27,228.9	27,715.8	27,929.9	28,036.7
Construction (XX)	7,496.2	7,684.2	7,623.8	7,482.7	7,610.4	7,751.4	7,939.5	7,106.6	6,717.0	6,623.0	6,602.8	7,052.8	6,858.1
Gas, electricity and water (XXI)	2,121.4	2,249.9	2,363.9	2,457.4	2,550.9	2,735.0	2,901.5	2,898.6	2,922.0	3,006.7	3,129.5	3,220.0	3,410.0
Public utilities (XX, XXI)	9,617.5	9,934.2	9,987.7	9,940.1	10,161.3	10,486.4	10,841.0	10,005.2	9,639.0	9,629.7	9,732.3	10,272.9	10,268.0
Transport and communications (XXII)	6,237.0	6,496.2	6,755.4	7,038.9	7,225.2	7,573.5	8,148.6	8,164.8	8,100.0	8,237.7	8,480.7	8,480.7	8,845.2
Distributive trades (XXIII)	8,857.1	9,136.1	9,215.8	9,425.0	9,574.4	10,052.7	10,640.5	10,291.8	9,963.0	10,042.7	9,953.0	10,491.0	10,730.1
Insurance, banking and finance[1] (XXIV)	2,431.1	2,557.8	2,754.9	2,998.1	3,130.1	3,191.2	3,353.8	3,236.0	3,381.0	3,556.5	3,661.3	3,722.3	4,656.3
Ownership of dwellings	4,633.9	4,801.4	4,913.0	5,024.7	5,136.4	5,248.0	5,359.7	5,471.3	5,583.0	5,694.7	5,806.3	5,918.0	6,029.6
Public health and education services (part of XXV)	5,617.6	5,833.6	5,833.6	5,977.7	6,193.7	6,409.8	6,625.8	6,841.9	7,202.0	7,562.1	7,634.1	7,778.2	7,992.2
Public administration and defence (XXVII)	6,738.5	6,738.5	6,590.4	6,664.5	6,738.5	7,034.7	7,182.8	7,182.8	7,405.0	7,627.1	7,553.1	7,553.1	7,553.1
Other services (rest of XXV, XXVI)	0,476.8	10,592.0	10,707.1	10,937.3	11,282.7	11,858.4	12,088.7	11,628.1	11,513.0	12,088.6	12,434.0	13,124.8	13,124.8
Services (XXII–XXVII)	44,942.0	46,155.6	46,770.2	48,066.2	49,281.0	51,368.3	53,155.4		53,147.0	54,590.8	55,279.6	57,068.2	57,883.9
Gross domestic product at factor cost	82,665.4	85,754.2	87,218.3	88,807.1	90,922.6	93,010.0	97,644.2		93,708.0	95,702.1	98,260.9	101,680.8	103,483.4

[1] Value added in insurance, banking and finance is net of the item 'adjustment for financial services'.

Source: Compiled from the Blue Book (1980) indices of output at constant factor cost.

Table 4.2 Average annual growth rates by industry and sector, Scotland and UK, 1954–78, constant (1975) prices

	1954–8 Scotland	1954–8 UK	1958–63 Scotland	1958–63 UK	1963–8 Scotland	1963–8 UK	1968–71 Scotland	1968–71 UK	1971–8 Scotland	1971–8 UK	1954–78 Scotland	1954–78 UK
Agriculture, forestry and fishing (I)	-2.1	-0.7	2.0	3.9	4.3	2.1	3.1	3.8	1.2	1.7	1.9	2.9
Mining and quarrying (II)	-3.7	-1.5	-2.5	-1.0	-3.9	-2.0	-1.2	-3.3	-0.9	13.6	-1.9	1.7
Primary sector (I, II)	-3.8	-0.6	-0.2	1.0	0.7	0.0	1.6	0.4	0.6	6.7	-0.1	2.2
Food, drink and tobacco (III)	—	2.4	5.7	3.0	6.7	2.8	6.0	1.8	2.2	1.6	—	2.9
Chemicals, coal and petroleum products (IV, V)	—	5.3	6.7	6.9	5.6	7.8	4.4	5.3	4.0	3.0	—	9.1
Metal manufacture (VI)	—	0.3	-0.7	2.6	3.3	2.4	-2.9	-2.3	-2.3	-1.4	—	0.3
Engineering and allied industries (VII–XII)	—	3.5	1.2	3.0	6.4	4.3	4.0	1.0	-0.4	0.6	—	3.0
Mechanical and instrument engineering (VII, VIII)	—	1.4	1.8	4.3	7.3	6.1	2.6	2.4	-1.7	0.3	—	3.4
Electrical engineering (IX)	—	6.1	15.3	6.5	10.6	5.8	22.6	3.8	8.6	3.9	—	7.3
Shipbuilding and vehicles (X, XI)	—	5.6	-2.8	1.4	5.1	2.2	-0.8	-0.5	-3.9	-1.0	—	1.4
Metal goods n.e.s. (XII)	—	1.6	3.6	1.5	2.7	3.7	3.5	-1.7	-0.2	0.3	—	1.3
Textiles, leather, clothing, footwear (XIII–XV)	—	-2.7	1.8	1.9	1.8	3.5	2.0	1.1	0.4	-0.3	—	0.7
Bricks, pottery, etc. (XVI)	—	-0.6	3.7	5.8	7.0	5.2	1.3	1.5	-1.4	0.6	—	3.0
Timber, furniture, etc. (XVIII)	—	0.7	2.1	5.1	7.1	5.6	10.5	-1.1	0.8	1.2	—	3.1
Paper, printing, etc. (XVIII)	—	3.0	5.1	3.2	2.3	3.7	-1.3	0.4	-0.7	1.2	—	2.9
Other manufacturing (XIX)	—	1.7	5.2	8.2	6.7	9.9	3.8	1.4	3.9	3.6	—	8.1
All manufacturing (III–XIX)	1.3	2.0	2.6	3.4	5.1	4.4	3.0	1.1	0.6	0.9	2.9	2.9
Construction (XX)	1.3	1.3	5.3	4.1	7.3	5.1	-4.1	-0.3	0.8	-1.0	2.8	1.9
Gas, electricity and water (XXI)	3.6	4.8	7.5	6.2	7.6	5.7	4.9	4.5	5.5	3.7	10.2	7.8
Public utilities (XX, XXI)	1.6	1.9	5.7	4.5	7.4	5.2	-2.6	0.8	1.8	0.2	3.9	3.0
Services (XXII–XXVII)	-2.6	1.1	2.3	1.8	2.2	2.6	2.3	2.2	3.6	2.3	2.0	2.5
Gross domestic product at factor cost	-1.3	1.3	2.5	2.5	3.4	3.2	1.8	1.6	2.3	1.8	2.2	2.6

than the corresponding UK rate in agriculture, forestry and fishing; food, drink and tobacco; metal manufacture; mechanical and instrument engineering; electrical engineering; shipbuilding and vehicles; bricks, pottery, etc.; and timber, furniture, etc. Overall, for public utilities as a whole and for individual industries within it, the growth rate in Scotland was higher than that for the UK. This pattern of economic performance also continued for the period 1968–71 but in general at a much lower pace. The overall GDP growth rates for both the UK and Scotland were much lower for this period with the Scottish rate just marginally ahead.

At sectoral level, primary and manufacturing sectors continued to show higher than the average growth rates. In public utilities sector, some decline was noticeable. On the other hand, in the services sector, Scottish growth rate was marginally ahead of the UK growth rate. At the industry level, in agriculture, forestry and fishing; food, drink and tobacco; mechanical and instrument engineering; electrical engineering; metal goods not elsewhere specified; textiles, leather, etc.; timber, furniture, etc.; other manufacturing; and gas, electricity and water, the Scottish growth rate was higher than that for the UK. In construction, the Scottish decline was much greater than that for the UK.

The sub-periods 1971–5 and 1975–8 herald some important changes in both Scottish and the UK economic performance – for the period 1971–5, both the Scottish and UK growth rates were lower, with Scottish GDP growth rate a little above that for the UK. The Scottish growth rate was also above that for the UK in primary, manufacturing and public utilities. Within manufacturing, higher than UK average growth rates were limited to fewer industries, namely food, drink and tobacco; chemicals; electrical engineering; and metal goods not elsewhere specified. Construction and gas, electricity and water also had higher than average UK growth rates. For the sub-period 1975–1978, the average growth rates revived both for Scotland and the UK, but mainly due to higher-than-before average growth rates in the services sector, where the Scottish growth rate exceeded that of the UK.

At the sectoral level primary, manufacturing and public utilities showed a greater decline for Scotland than that for the UK. At the industry level, the inordinately high growth rate in mining and quarrying reflects the growth rates in petroleum and gas. But apart from that, chemicals and allied, electrical engineering, metal goods not elsewhere specified and textiles were the industries within manufacturing in which Scottish growth rate was still higher than that for the UK. Taking the entire sub-period of 1971–8, it can be seen that the overall GDP growth rate in Scotland was still ahead of the corresponding UK GDP but for this period the higher-than-average growth rate was primarily due to a higher growth rate than the UK in services. For this period as a whole, the primary, manufacturing and public utilities sectors were already showing signs of severe contraction.

Thus, behind the overall pattern for the entire period of 1954–78 lies a fairly complex pattern of growth performance for the individual sub-periods. By and large it can be concluded that the Scottish economic performance lagged behind that of the UK over the broad period of 1954–63, revived quite markedly over the period 1963–71, with gradual slowing down over the period 1968–71 and 1971–5, followed more or less by a collapse of manufacturing and construction but with a continued revival of the service sector over the difficult period of 1975–8. The period beginning with 1963 also marks the beginning of the era of increased central government intervention in regional economies in more than one way, and in particular marks the phase of an active 'special' regional policy. It is therefore quite tempting to associate directly the marked improved performance in Scottish manufacturing over the period since 1963 to the 'special' regional policy.

The Behaviour of Scottish Output: Growth Standardisation

In this section the time-pattern of Scottish actual and 'expected' output will be examined with a view to identifying the sectors in which the time-pattern of actual output appears to be different from that of the UK, rather than to try and attribute such differences to any particular policy effect. As explained earlier, to arrive at a series of 'expected' output, the technique was to take as base 1963 actual Scottish value in any given industry and apply to it the UK growth rates to extrapolate backward and forward from 1963. The familiar limitations on the conclusions from standardisation techniques apply to this particular application to output data. In particular, the choice of base year was important.

The base year should be a census of production year which should ideally be characteristic of the period in its structure of output within industry groups, in its state of overall cyclical expectations, etc. The choice of 1963 was dictated principally because it was reasonably central in the long-term time-series. It is more difficult to assess how far it has the other necessary attributes. Table 4.3 sets out the series of actual and 'expected' value added in the primary sector. Figures 4.1 and 4.2 plot these values.

Figure 4.1 shows that the actual value added in the primary sector was above the 'expected' level in years before 1963 and for the years between 1963 and 1974 with marked divergence between the two values between 1972 and 1974. From 1974 onwards the two series appear to be converging with a reversal in the pattern between 1975 and 1978. It needs to be pointed out that the series of value added in

Table 4.3   Actual and 'expected' value added in Scotland in the primary sector, 1954–78
Growth standardisation, £ million, constant (1975) prices, 1963 base

		1954	1955	1956	1957	1958	1959	1960	1961	1962	1963	1964	1965	1966
Agriculture, forestry and fishing	A[1]	257	236	262	259	235	245	252	253	255	259	272	283	292
	E[2]	210.8	207.7	220	223	216.9	225.4	240.1	241.4	249.3	259	269.1	276.3	277.2
Mining and quarrying	A	275	265	260	254	234	228	215	210	207	205	200	195	184
	E	230.4	226.8	22	226.3	216.3	210.3	202.6	199.5	204.9	205	205.4	197.9	186.5
Total: primary sector	A	532	501	522	313	469	473	467	463	462	464	472	478	476
	E	441.2	434.5	448	449.3	433.2	435.7	442.7	440.9	454.2	464	474.5	474.2	463.7

		1967	1968	1969	1970	1971	1972	1973	1974	1975	1976	1977	1978
Agriculture, forestry and fishing	A	305	315	324	343	344	357	369	414	380	319	390	374
	E	280.3	286	285.4	302.7	318.7	329.1	339.5	346.7	314.3	291.7	332.9	356.1
Mining and quarrying	A	184	165	153	148	159	140	157	142	159	154	146	149
	E	185.1	184.9	173	166.3	166.3	140	154	125.7	139.8	175.9	262.5	352.1
Total: primary sector	A	489	480	477	491	503	497	526	556	539	473	536	523
	E	465.4	470.9	458.4	469	486	469.1	493.5	472.4	454.1	467.6	595.4	681.2

[1] A = actual
[2] E = 'expected'

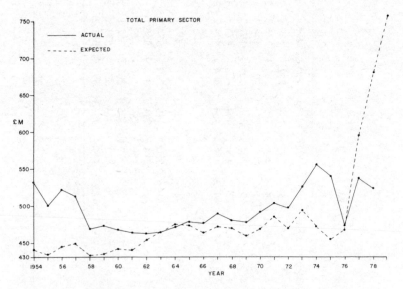

Figure 4.1 *Actual and 'expected' value added in Scotland, primary sector, 1954-79*

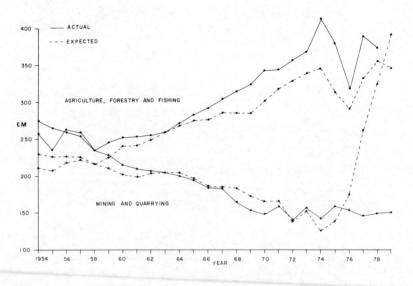

Figure 4.2 *Actual and 'expected' value added in Scotland, agriculture, forestry and fishing, and mining and quarrying, 1954-79*

mining and quarrying for the UK is inclusive of the value added in petroleum and gas which accounts for much of the divergence in the two series for the period since 1978. This is shown by Figure 4.2 which plots these values for individual industries within the primary sector. Scottish actual output in mining was above that of the UK in the period before 1963 but since then the decline in Scottish output (exclusive of petroleum and natural gas) seems to be greater than that for the UK up to 1972 when the two values converge. In agriculture, forestry and fishing, the time pattern of actual value added is consistently higher than that of the 'expected' value added despite a downturn between 1974 and 1976. However, in comparing the two series, it must be remembered that the structure of output within this industry differs quite considerably as between the rest of the UK and Scotland since forestry and fishing are much more important to Scotland than to the rest of the UK.

Table 4.4 sets out the series of 'expected' value added in manufacturing industries. The resultant series of actual and 'expected' value added are plotted in Figures 4.3, 4.4, 4.5 and 4.6. In manufacturing as a whole, Figure 4.3 shows that the actual output was below the 'expected' between 1955–7, was ahead of 'expected' in 1958, the two series converged between 1959 and 1960 but after that the 'expected' output surged ahead of actual in 1960 and then converged by definition in 1963. Since 1963 actual output in Scottish manufacturing remained consistently above the 'expected' with some interesting time-patterns. The divergence between the actual and 'expected' reached a peak in 1966–7 and then again in 1970 and 1972 with both series reaching a trough in 1974. Figures 4.4 and 4.5 give the pattern for manufacturing industries.

In food, drink and tobacco, the actual output was below 'expected' before 1963 but the actual output always exceeded 'expected' from 1963, with the divergence reaching a peak in 1974. In chemical and allied the two series moved very close throughout the period, with 'expected' output slightly ahead of the actual for most part of the study period. In engineering and allied industries, the actual output was only marginally ahead of 'expected' before 1963 with divergence setting in since 1963 reaching a peak in 1966 and 1970 and then again in 1975. In textiles, leather and clothing the time-pattern of actual and 'expected' output is fairly close with actual output marginally ahead of 'expected' between 1958 and 1963 but since 1963 the 'expected' output remained marginally ahead of actual with cyclical troughs in 1967 and 1975 and peaks in 1969, 1973 and 1977. In metal manufacture the actual output exceeded the 'expected' for most part of the period, with a reversal in pattern between 1976 and 1978. In other manufacturing while actual output always exceeded 'expected' before 1963, the reverse was the case between 1963 and 1972 when the two series con-

Table 4.4 *'Expected' value added in manufacturing industries: Scotland, 1954–78*
Growth standardisation, constant (1975) prices, £ million, 1963 base

	1954	1955	1956	1957	1958	1959	1960	1961	1962	1963	1964	1965	1966
Food, drink, tobacco	214.3	219.7	224.8	228.4	234.7	242.6	249.4	257.3	262.1	270	276.2	282.6	290.0
Coal, petroleum and chemical industries	80.4	84.2	89.8	94.1	97.4	106.9	117.7	120.3	123.0	131	144.2	153.8	162.9
Metal manufacture	127.0	137.7	139.8	141.7	128.5	134.2	155.7	146.6	138.5	145	164.5	171.8	161.8
Mechanical and instrument engineering	200.5	212.1	213.4	221.1	211.7	216.1	237.0	256.3	256.2	257	281.9	299.6	317.4
Electrical engineering	32.2	35.6	35.2	37.6	40.0	44.0	46.3	48.1	50.2	53	57.3	56.3	61.3
Shipbuilding and vehicles	130.5	147.8	143.9	148.4	159.7	167.5	175.0	165.2	167.9	171	182.5	180.7	179.6
Metal goods, n.e.s.	57.6	64.1	62.7	62.9	61.3	61.1	69.3	66.2	63.9	66	76.3	79.2	74.9
Textiles, leather, clothing	218.8	216.4	214.2	212.7	194.8	207.9	217.4	213.2	206.8	213	225.3	232.6	232.0
Other manufacturing	244.1	260.4	255.0	257.2	260.4	278.0	304.9	305.4	306.8	321	355.8	367.6	373.4
Total	1,305.4	1,378.1	1,378.8	1,404.1	1,388.5	1,458.3	1,572.8	1,578.6	1,572.4	1,627	1,764.0	1,824.2	1,854.2

Table 4.4 'Expected' value added in manufacturing industries: Scotland, 1954–78 (cont'd.)
Growth standardisation, constant (1975) prices, £ million, 1963 base

	1967	1968	1969	1970	1971	1972	1973	1974	1975	1976	1977	1978
Food, drink, tobacco	296.0	308.3	318.2	323.0	325.1	339.1	353.2	350.8	342.2	351.4	355.9	363.4
Coal, petroleum and chemical industries	168.8	182.2	194.1	206.1	211.2	220.1	243.4	248.7	224.4	248.4	254.0	255.3
Metal manufacture	152.3	162.4	166.2	165.7	151.2	151.4	165.7	151.9	132.7	137.8	137.3	136.0
Mechanical and instrument engineering	319.5	335.5	354.1	367.1	360.2	346.9	377.2	394.3	390.4	372.0	369.2	366.8
Electrical engineering	65.4	8.3	73.7	75.0	76.2	79.9	91.0	93.9	89.8	88.5	92.3	97.1
Shipbuilding and vehicles	176.7	189.6	195.7	186.7	186.7	189.6	195.5	190.1	177.4	175.2	178.5	173.3
Metal goods, n.e.s.	71.7	78.1	82.7	79.5	74.1	75.8	81.8	80.8	74.1	73.3	76.9	75.7
Textiles, leather, clothing	225.3	250.5	254.3	253.4	258.9	264.7	279.1	259.6	250.7	246.9	254.5	254.0
Other manufacturing	378.6	401.1	407.2	406.3	407.4	437.9	484.5	460.9	415.9	429.4	438.5	449.5
Total	1,853.7	1,976.0	2,046.3	2,062.8	2,051.0	2,105.4	2,271.4	2,231.0	2,097.6	2,122.9	2,157.1	2,171.1

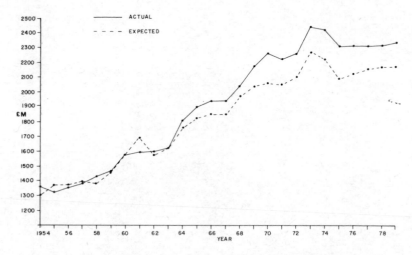

Figure 4.3   *Actual and 'expected' value added in Scotland, all manufacturing, 1954–79*

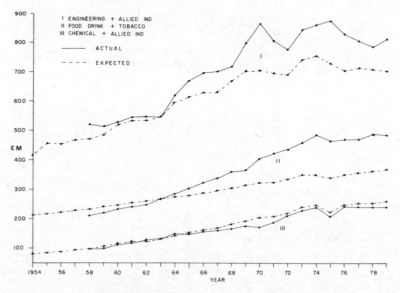

Figure 4.4   *Actual and 'expected' value added in Scotland, engineering and allied industries; food, drink and tobacco; and chemicals and allied industries, 1954–79*

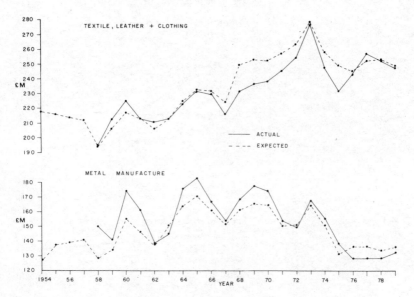

Figure 4.5   *Actual and 'expected' value added in Scotland, textiles, leather and clothing, and metal manufacturing, 1954–79*

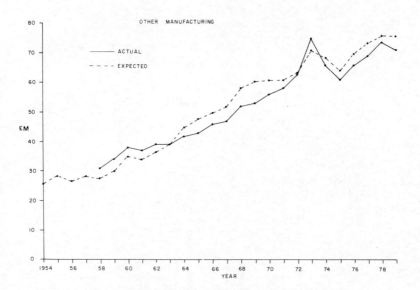

Figure 4.6   *Actual and 'expected' value added in Scotland, other manufacturing, 1954–79*

Table 4.5 *Actual minus 'expected' value added in Scotland in manufacturing and public utilities*
Growth standardisation, constant (1975) prices, £ million

	1954	1955	1956	1957	1958	1959	1960	1961	1962	1963	1964	1965	1966
All manufacturing	58.6	−53.1	−19.9	−21.1	48.3	10.6	5.2	14.2	19.5	0	46.1	76.7	86.6
Engineering and allied	—	—	—	—	48.2	26.1	0.4	13.1	10.7	0	33.0	54.2	64.7
Electrical engineering	—	—	—	—	10.0	−12.0	−12.3	−4.1	1.8	0	4.7	5.7	9.6
Metal goods, n.e.s.	—	—	—	—	−5.3	−1.2	−2.3	0.8	−0.9	0	−3.3	−3.2	0.1
Shipbuilding and vehicles	—	—	—	—	39.2	19.5	2.0	11.8	5.1	0	26.5	34.3	29.4
Mechanical and instrument engineering	—	—	—	—	24.3	19.9	13.0	4.7	4.8	0	5.1	17.4	25.6
Construction	−25.8	−9.6	−21.6	−3.9	−26.5	−14.2	−26.8	−4.8	−10.4	0	−6.7	−31.9	6.0
Gas, electricity, water	−0.6	0.9	−1.2	−2.7	−4.9	−4.6	−4.5	−3.6	−1.8	0	2.2	53.1	11.7
Total public utilities	−26.5	−8.6	−22.6	−6.6	−31.4	−18.7	−1.3	−8.3	−12.2	0	−4.5	21.3	17.7

Table 4.5 Actual minus 'expected' value added in Scotland in manufacturing and public utilities (cont'd.)
Growth standardisation, constant (1975) prices, £ million

	1967	1968	1969	1970	1971	1972	1973	1974	1975	1976	1977	1978
All manufacturing	86.3	65.7	130.7	203.1	172.8	160.6	179.6	197.0	214.3	196.0	155.0	145.7
Engineering and allied	73.7	50.3	95.8	160.7	110.7	87.8	100.5	104.9	144.2	123.0	102.2	73.0
Electrical engineering	14.6	12.6	29.2	57.7	59.8	66.0	81.0	99.1	82.2	98.5	100.7	120.9
Metal goods, n.e.s.	-0.7	-3.1	4.3	3.5	8.8	21.2	21.2	27.2	29.9	16.7	9.1	6.3
Shipbuilding and vehicles	28.3	25.4	13.3	27.3	23.3	1.4	5.5	-1.1	15.5	-11.2	-12.5	-21.4
Mechanical and instrument engineering	31.4	15.5	48.9	72.9	18.8	-0.9	-7.2	-20.3	16.6	19.0	4.8	32.8
Construction	8.6	73.8	97.2	11.0	-27.4	-1.3	28.0	33.6	107.5	93.4	127.5	72.2
Gas, electricity, water	14.0	12.3	20.7	26.7	16.6	25.7	44.2	39.4	37.6	41.0	45.0	46.2
Total public utilities	22.6	86.1	117.9	37.7	-10.8	24.5	72.1	73.0	145.2	134.7	172.5	118.4

verged. Except for 1972-3 the 'expected' output remained above actual between 1974 and 1978.

Thus, the overall pattern for the manufacturing industries seems to be heavily influenced by the performance of engineering and allied industries, particularly in the timing of spurts of actual output above the expected level, but the steady pull of actual output above 'expected' in food, drink and tobacco must also be important in explaining the growth of actual output above 'expected' levels since 1963. These conclusions are brought out in Figure 4.7 and the actual values are set out in Table 4.5. It shows that for all the manufacturing

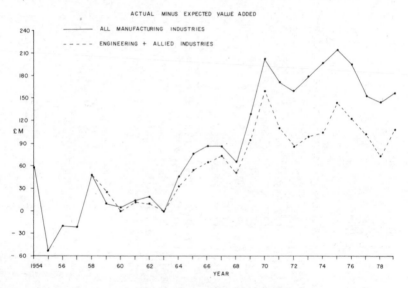

Figure 4.7   *Actual minus 'expected' value added in Scotland, all manufacturing industries, 1954-79*

industries actual minus 'expected' output reached a peak of 48.3 million in 1958, was 0 in 1963 by definition and climbed steadily upwards between 1963 and 1966 to reach £86.6 million (in 1975 prices) in 1966 and £86.3 million in 1967, declined in 1968 and then rose markedly between 1969 and 1970 to reach a total of £203 million, fell in 1971 and 1972, and started to rise in 1973. The actual minus 'expected' output reached another peak in 1975 (£214.3 million) declining thereafter. The engineering group of industries shows an identical pattern except that between 1966 and 1967 there was a slight increase in actual minus 'expected' before starting to drop in 1968.

It is therefore interesting in Figure 4.8 to disaggregate the engineering and allied industries. In electrical engineering, actual output started below 'expected' but grew very fast after 1963 to reach £160.7 million in 1970 and £144.2 million in 1975. In mechanical and instrument engineering the actual output was above 'expected' between 1958 and 1963, but never exceeded £24.3 million. Actual minus 'expected' output climbed upwards after 1963 to reach a peak in 1967 and then again in 1970, but fell relative to 'expected' between 1972 to 1974 with a small revival since then. In shipbuilding and vehicles, actual minus 'expected' output was £39 million to begin with but this difference steadily declined, reached 0 in 1963 by definition, rose to £34 million in 1965 and remained slightly below that up to 1968 and then again for 1970 and 1971, fell in 1969, 1972–4, was positive for 1975 but fell since then relative to 'expected' output. In metal goods not elsewhere specified, the actual output was below 'expected' before 1963 as well as between 1964 and 1968, and was above that 'expected' since then to reach a peak of £30 million in 1975.

The general pattern that emerges from the above analysis is that of an improvement in Scottish growth performance in manufacturing over the period since 1963. This is shown by remarkably consistent movement of Scottish output above the 'expected' level. At the level of individual industries, food, drink and tobacco, and engineering and allied industries are most important in explaining the pattern observed for the manufacturing as a whole. In engineering and allied industries, the pattern of actual minus 'expected' output itself resulted from a complex intereaction of the three industries in the group (electrical engineering; mechanical and instrument engineering; and shipbuilding and vehicles). This spell of steady improvement can be conveniently divided into 1963–6, 1967–70, 1971–5 and 1975–8. It is significant to note that the pattern of actual output as against 'expected' output, and the pattern of actual minus 'expected' output fits well with the data on the movement of firms into Scotland and the Scottish Office analysis which shows a significant improvement over the period 1961–6 in the contribution of 'incomers' to total jobs due to openings. However, it must be stressed that the industry level data examined in this section shows that the improvement in Scottish manufacturing was indeed confined to a few industries, most noticeably food, drink and tobacco, and engineering.

Hence, it can be concluded that Scottish manufacturing seems to be an important sector, where, over the relevant period, there was a significant divergent movement from what could be expected of Scottish output if it had experienced industry by industry the UK growth rate. But this in no way enables us to claim that the whole of this divergence is solely due to 'special' regional policy. For this, a more rigorous regression approach is needed which will be presented in Chapter 5.

Turning now to the remaining sectors, Table 4.6 gives the relevant

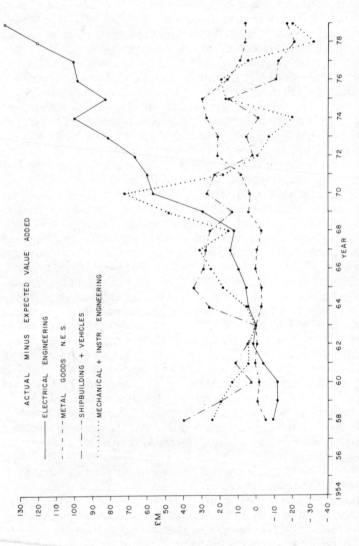

Figure 4.8 Actual minus 'expected' value added in Scotland, electrical engineering, metal goods n.e.s., shipbuilding and mechanical and instrument engineering, 1954–79

Table 4.6   Actual and 'expected' value added in public utilities in Scotland, 1954-78
Growth standardisation, constant (1975) prices, £ million 1963 base

		1954	1955	1956	1957	1958	1959	1960	1961	1962	1963	1964	1965	1966
Construction	A[1]	484	501	517	534	509	551	568	636	636	645	704	712	764
	E[2]	509.8	510.6	538.6	537.9	535.5	565.2	594.8	640.8	646.4	645	710.7	743.9	758
Gas, electricity and water	A	84	90	92	94	96	99	107	113	124	132	141	153	166
	E	84.6	89.1	93.2	96.7	100.9	103.6	111.6	116.6	125.8	132	138.8	99.8	154.3
Total: public utilities	A	568	591	609	628	605	650	675	749	760	777	845	865	930
	E	594.4	599.7	631.8	634.6	636.4	668.8	706.4	757.4	772.2	777	849.5	843.7	912.3

		1967	1968	1969	1970	1971	1972	1973	1974	1975	1976	1977	1978
Construction	A	797	882	899	798	773	814	863	781	814	790	822	814
	E	788.1	808.2	801.8	787.0	800.4	815.3	835.0	747.4	706.5	696.6	694.4	741.8
Gas, electricity and water	A	174	182	199	212	209	232	263	258	258	268	281	289
	E	160	169.7	178.3	185.3	192.4	206.3	218.8	218.6	220.4	226.8	236.0	242.8
Total: public utilities	A	971	1,064	1,098	1,010	982	1,046	1,126	1,039	1,072	1,058	1,103	1,203
	E	948.4	977.9	980.1	972.3	992.8	1,021.6	1,053.8	966.0	926.9	923.4	930.4	984.6

[1] A = actual
[2] E = 'expected'

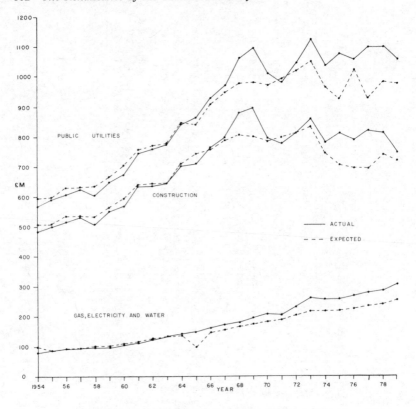

Figure 4.9   *Actual and 'expected' value added in Scotland, public utilities, construction and gas, electricity and water, 1954–79*

figures for the public utilities sector and Figures 4.9 and 4.10 give the plots of actual and 'expected' value added and actual minus 'expected' value added for the sector as a whole and for individual industries. It can be seen from Figure 4.9 that the difference between actual and 'expected' value added for the public utilities group is the almost exact reflection of that of construction; with gas, electricity and water in Scotland having a growth of value added much in line with the UK average. For the public utilities as a whole, then, value added in Scotland showed a faster growth than the UK average from 1965 with some evidence of recession in 1970, 1971, 1974 and 1978. Actual minus 'expected' output, which was negative until 1964 started to rise, reaching a peak of £117.9 million in 1969 and £145.2 million in 1975 and £172.5 million in 1978.

The data on per capita GDFCF in construction show that per capita GDFCF in construction, which stood at over 110 per cent of the UK

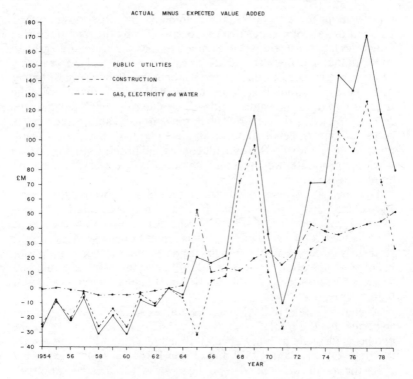

Figure 4.10 *Actual minus 'expected' value added in Scotland, public utilities, construction and gas, electricity and water, 1954-79*

level in 1961, slipped under 80 per cent in 1962; ran at a bit under 100 per cent in 1963-4 and a little under in 1965-7 but rose thereafter, especially in 1970, 1972 and 1973. This pattern therefore compared well with that of output. Regional policy could well be an important factor in explaining the relatively good performance of the Scottish construction industry in Scotland/UK comparisons, but there could also be other factors such as differences between Scotland and the UK in the structure of construction industry and the impact of different building regulations which could also be important.

Services

It has long been conventional wisdom that regional policy which stimulates the manufacturing sector will affect services through multiplier effects. This case has been developed theoretically in terms of the export base model (North, 1955): for discussion of theory see Armstrong and Taylor (1978), pp. 226-34, and Richardson (1969) pp. 247-53). If we take manufacturing as the basic sector (the Scottish input-output Table for 1973, for example, shows that more than 85 per cent of the total exports are accounted for by the manufacturing industries (see Burdekin, 1978, Figure 14)) then the more rapid growth of the manufacturing sector analysed earlier should lead us to expect a growth rate induced in the service sector in Scotland perhaps higher than the corresponding growth rate in the UK (in other words, the time pattern of actual value could well be above the 'expected' over the relevant period). It is therefore important to examine the service sector in greater detail. It must also be admitted that the measurement of value added poses difficult conceptual problems and therefore where appropriate we may turn to look at the relevant data on employment directly.

The analysis of the services sector should also throw light on the Bacon and Eltis argument regarding the structural shift in employment over the period 1961–75. It is therefore convenient to examine the evidence in terms of 'public services' and 'private services'. In the former is grouped public administration and defence and public health and education services. Table 4.7 gives the data on actual and 'expected' value added in public services and Figure 4.11 gives a plot of these values.

It can be seen that the actual value added was below that 'expected' for the total of public services between 1954 and 1962, the two being identical in 1963. Thereafter, actual value added was always less than 'expected' until 1971 and also in 1974. Thus for much of the 1970s the actual value added in public services exceeded the 'expected'. At industry level, in public administration and defence, except between 1954 to 1959, actual value added exceeded 'expected', but thereafter the actual was below 'expected' until 1974 when the two series converged and thereafter the actual value added was always above 'expected'. In public health and education services, actual value added was always greater than 'expected' before 1963 but after 1963 actual was below 'expected' until 1970. From 1971 to 1973 and 1975 to 1978 the actual was marginally ahead of 'expected'.

The evidence presented here in terms of value added in public administration and defence conceals important differences between Scotland and UK in the relative importance of national *vs.* local government in total employment. Table 4.8 gives data for selected years on the number and percentage of local government employees in the total for public administration and defence. It can be seen that local government was more important to Scotland in 1960 and also for much of the 1950s too (see McCrone, 1965, p. 167). For the entire period the relative importance of local government employment continued to grow in Scotland and this pace seems to have accelerated in the 1971–5 period. For the UK as a whole, the increase in local government employment over the 1971–5 period is smaller than in Scotland. Table 4.9 gives the figures of percentage growth.

Table 4.7 Actual and 'expected' value added in 'public services' in Scotland, 1954–78
Growth standardisation, constant (1975) prices, £ million 1963 base

		1954	1955	1956	1957	1958	1959	1960	1961	1962	1963	1964	1965	1966
Public administration and defence	A[1]	688	672	594	580	565	522	510	499	513	526	524	528	528
	E[2]	581.2	564.7	559.2	546	526.3	520.1	514	514	514	526	526	532.2	544.5
Public health and education services	A	467	469	411	409	436	439	454	476	484	485	491	498	524
	E	371.7	377.8	396.2	408.5	420.7	427.9	442.2	456.5	477.9	485	499.2	520.6	534.9
Total	A	1,155	1,141	1,005	989	1,001	1,483	964	975	997	1,011	1,015	1,026	1,052
	E	952.9	942.5	955.4	954.5	947	948	956.2	970.5	991.9	1,011	1,025.2	1,052.8	1,079.4

		1967	1968	1969	1970	1971	1972	1973	1974	1975	1976	1977	1978
Public administration and defence	A	549	544	530	537	527	575	598	600	632	687	655	688
	E	563	563	550.6	556.8	563	587.8	600.1	600.1	618.7	637.3	630.9	630.9
Public health and education services	A	548	564	563	584	617	668	663	690	722	759	767	825
	E	556.4	577.8	577.8	592.1	613.5	634.9	656.3	677.7	713.3	749	756.1	770.7
Total	A	1,097	1,108	1,093	1,121	1,144	1,243	1,261	1,290	1,354	1,446	1,422	1,513
	E	1,119.4	1,140.8	1,128.4	1,148.9	1,176.5	1,222.7	1,256.4	1,277.8	1,332	1,386.3	1,387	1,401.6

[1] A = Actual
[2] E = 'Expected'

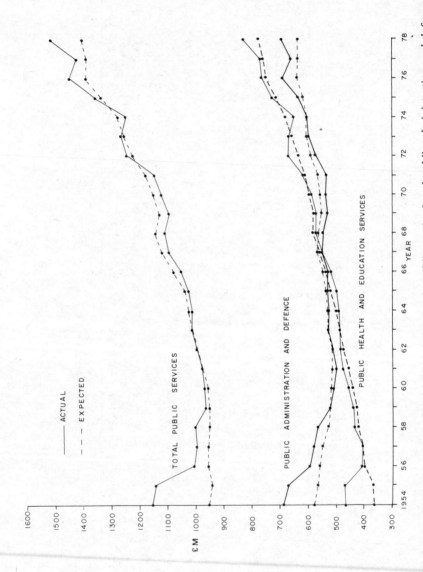

Figure 4.11 Actual and 'expected' value added in Scotland, 'public services' and public administration and defence, 1954–79

Table 4.8 Central and local government[1] in Scotland and the UK, selected years, 1960–75

A Scotland	Thousands of employees									
	1960	1966	1967	1968	1969	1970	1971	1973	1974	1975
National government service	40.7	43.0	46.7	46.0	44.9	44.9	46.0	48.0	48.5	51.9
Local government service	72.1	70.9	73.8	74.6	72.9	76.2	82.1	92.8	96.1	106.4
Total	112.8	113.9	120.5	121.3	117.8	121.1	128.1	140.8	144.6	158.3
Local government as % of total	63.9%	62.2%	61.2%	61.5%	61.9%	62.9%	64.1%	65.9%	66.5%	67.2%

B UK	Thousands of employees							
	1960	1966	1969	1970	1971	1973	1974	1975
National government	534	585	592	573	577	614	610	650
Local government	760	812	851	858	880	969	986	1,005
Total	1,294	1,397	1,443	1,430	1,458	1,583	1,596	1,654
Local government as % of total	58.7%	58.1%	58.9%	60.0%	60.3%	61.2%	61.8%	60.7%

[1]Gives breakdown of employees under public administration and defence exclusive of armed forces.
Sources: Compiled from Scottish Digest of Statistics, 1961, 1966, 1968, Annual Abstract of Statistics, 1961–78, and Scottish Abstract of Statistics, 1971–8.

Table 4.9   *Percentage growth of local government employment in Scotland and UK, 1960–75*

	% Growth in local government employment		
	1960–75	1960–71	1971–5
Scotland	47.5	13.8	29.0
UK	32.2	15.8	17.1

Source: Compiled from Table 4.8.

It can be seen that over the entire period of 1960–75, the growth in local government employment was of the order of 47.5 per cent in Scotland as compared to 32.3 per cent for the UK. In this, the percentage growth was much higher for Scotland over 1971–5, while for the UK the growth for the earlier period was only marginally

Table 4.10   *Employment in industrial and non-industrial sectors in Scotland, 1961–78.*

	(Thousands)			
	1961	1971	1975	1978
Industry[1]				
Mining and quarrying	85.1	39.1	36.1	39.4
Manufacturing	724.4	677.8	645.5	612.1
Construction	172.5	170.9	184.5	171.5
Gas, electricity and water	31.0	31.0	26.0	28.4
	1,013.0	918.8	892.1	851.4
Non-industrial				
Transport and communications	180.2	148.1	144.9	140.1
Distributive trades	324.0	275.9	277.5	275.5
Insurance, banking and finance	44.0	65.0	75.0	77.9
Professional and scientific services	419.2	515.6	540.0	591.3
Public administration and defence	108.0	131.0	158.0	144.2
	1,075.4	1,135.6	1,195.4	1,229.0
Ratio of non-industrial to industrial employment	1.06	1.23	1.34	1.44

| | 1961–75 | 1975–8 |
| % growth in non-industrial employment | 26.4 | 7.5 |

[1]The classification corresponds to Bacon and Eltis (1976).
Source: Compiled from Table 3.1.

below that for 1971-5. Hence, it would appear that the closer movement or lack of divergency in actual and 'expected series' up to 1975 is attributable to two factors: (i) in so far as there is some earning differential between local and central government sectors, the larger weight of local government in Scotland may account for the 'expected' value added series remaining below actual; (ii) during the period 1960-7 differential growth between Scotland and the UK is smaller. Thus the overall evidence throws interesting light on the nature of public services growth in Scotland. Bacon and Eltis (1976) also argued that long-term and far-reaching changes occurred in Britain over the period 1961-75 in terms of the ratio of non-industrial to industrial employment and percentage change in it over the period. Taking their classification, Table 4.10 gives data on employment in industrial and non-industrial sectors from which ratios of non-industrial to industrial employment are calculated. Table 4.11 compares these ratios for Scotland with the UK and other OECD countries.

Table 4.11 *Ratio of non-industrial to industrial employment in Scotland, the UK and the OECD countries*

	1961	*1975*	*% change*
Scotland	1.06	1.34	26.4
USA	1.81	2.31	27.9
UK	0.97	1.37	41.0
France	1.06	1.29	22.15
W. Germany	0.76	1.08	32.8
Italy	0.81	0.91	12.6
Japan	1.37	1.44	4.5

Source: Bacon and Eltis (1976), p. 214.

It can be seen from Table 4.11 that the ratio of non-industrial employment to industrial employment was higher in Scotland than in the UK in 1961, and the Scottish ratio in 1961 compared well with France and other OECD countries, all of which, except Italy, had higher proportions of total employment absorbed in the non-industrial sector in 1961. A comparison of ratios in 1975 shows that by that year the ratio of non-industrial to industrial employment was higher for the UK than for Scotland and this is also reflected in the percentage growth in the UK in non-industrial employment being highest at 41 per cent as compared to all other countries. But the fact remains that even in 1975 the ratio of non-industrial to industrial employment in the UK was lower than in the USA and Japan, but higher than in France, Germany and Italy.

In order to understand the above pattern fully, it is important to

Table 4.12   *Actual and 'expected' value added in Scotland in 'private services'; 1954–78, Growth standardisation Constant (1975) prices, £ million*

		1954	1955	1956	1957
Transport and communications	A[1]	536	536	463	493
	E[2]	398.5	410.8	417	417
Distributive trades	A	628	649	607	649
	E	510.8	534	541.7	565
Insurance, banking and finance[3]	A	133	128	96	102
	E	83.6	85.3	85.3	88.7
Ownership of dwellings	A	280	281	263	282
	E	239.5	246.3	256.6	256.6
Other services	A	645	671	602	633
	E	636	644.6	644.6	653.2
Total 'private' services	A	2,222	2,265	2,031	2,159
	E	1,864.4	1,921	1,945.2	1,980.5

		1967	1968	1969	1970
Transport and communications	A	535	536	577	614
	E	542.7	565.3	587.8	612.5
Distributive trades	A	709	747	742	802
	E	723.7	747	753	770.1
Insurance, banking and finance[3]	A	160	160	173	182
	E	153.4	161.1	173.5	188.8
Ownership of dwellings	A	357	379	404	414
	E	335.5	347.6	355.8	372.2
Other services	A	798	798	862	760
	E	834	842.3	851.6	869.5
Total 'private' services	A	2,559	2,620	2,758	2,772
	E	2,589.3	2,663.3	2,721.7	2,813.1

[1] A = Actual.
[2] E = Expected.

1958	1959	1960	1961	1962	1963	1964	1965	1966
450	444	516	473	471	480	517	519	532
410.9	428.5	450.4	461	464.5	480	511	521.6	536.4
591	628	642	648	647	661	677	706	711
564.9	596.7	623.5	635.8	639.9	661	687	707.4	715.5
96	107	110	126	128	131	129	132	136
93.7	110.8	115.1	117.3	121.6	131	133.2	145.9	154.1
272	285	282	312	302	303	305	326	342
260.1	267.8	271.6	294.9	298.9	303	307	319.2	327.3
612	617	714	718	747	779	767	742	805
661.8	689.4	726.2	742.3	751.5	779	825	825	834
2,021	2,081	2,264	2,277	2,295	2,354	2,415	2,425	2,526
1,991.4	2,093.2	2,186.8	2,251.3	2,276.4	2,354	2,463.2	2,519.1	2,567.3

1971	1972	1973	1974	1975	1976	1977	1978
623	656	715	718	716	727	738	764
628.7	659	709.1	710.5	704.8	697.8	716.8	738
877	915	927	837	837	836	878	928
782.3	821.4	869.4	840.9	814.0	820.5	813.2	857.2
222	229	211	179	220	220	213	231
197.1	200.9	211.5	204.1	222.8	234.4	241.6	245.6
401	373	381	371	377	377	369	361
380.5	389	396	404	412.1	420.3	428.7	436.8
792	1,008	1,069	1,004	1,010	1,104	1,116	1,207
896.4	942.1	960	923.5	914.3	960	987.4	1,041.7
2,915	3,181	3,303	3,109	3,160	3,264	3,314	3,491
2,885	3,012.4	3,146	3,083	3,068	3,133	3,187.7	3,319.3

[3]The value added figures for insurance, banking and finance are net (i.e., after deducting the item adjustment for financial services).

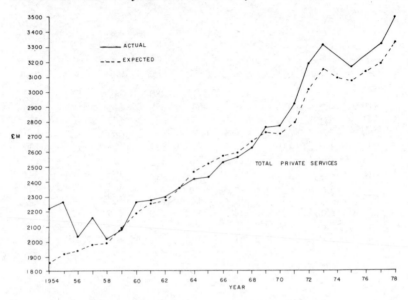

Figure 4.12   *Actual and 'expected' value added in Scotland, 'private services',
1954–79*

examine the actual and 'expected' value added series in 'private
services'. These data are given in Table 4.12 and Figures 4.12 and 4.13
plot these values.

To examine the industry level time-pattern first, in transport and
communications, actual value added was above 'expected' up to 1969
but for the most part since that time, the actual has been above the
'expected'. In the distributive trades, actual always exceeded 'expected'
until 1963 when the two were equal by definition; from 1963 'expected'
was marginally ahead of actual until 1968 when the two values converged, and for much of the 1970s the actual value added has been
above that 'expected'. In insurance, banking and finance, the actual
value added was below 'expected' for most of the period up to 1966
after which for the most part the actual marginally exceeded the
'expected' value added. In ownership of dwellings, for the most part of
the period up to 1971 the actual value added exceeded the 'expected',
while the reverse has been the case since 1971. In 'other services',
actual value added exceeded 'expected' up to 1963 when the two were
equal; from 1964 till 1975 the 'expected' always exceeded the actual
value added, while the reverse pattern occurred between 1976 and
1978.

For the total of 'private services' then, the pattern is the result of a
complex interaction of various industries. The actual value added

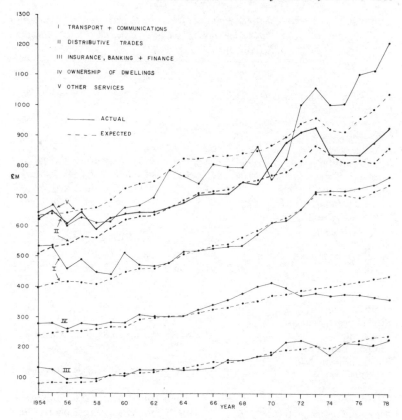

Figure 4.13 *Actual and 'expected' value added in Scotland, transport and communication; distributive trades; insurance, banking and finance; ownership of dwellings; and other services, 1954–79*

remained above 'expected' between 1954 and 1958 with a reversal in pattern up to 1963 when the two values were identical. From 1964 till 1975 the 'expected' value added remained consistently below the actual. Between 1976 and 1978 the actual value added exceeded the 'expected'. Thus, for the 'private' services there is no evidence to suggest that the upturn in the manufacturing sector since 1963 led to any significant upsurge. For most service industries some upsurge in growth rates relative to the UK noticeable between 1975 and 1978. However, an important element in this period could be growth of earnings and some catching up of earnings differentials between Scotland and the UK for various industries.

Scottish Office evidence on trends in earnings in Scotland (*Scottish Economic Bulletin*, no. 15, 1978) is summarised in Table 4.13.

Table 4.13   *Average hourly earnings (including the effect of overtime)
of male manual workers[1] in Scotland, as a percentage
of the UK average 1970-7*

	1970	1971	1972	1973	1974	1975	1976	1977
Food, drink and tobacco	98.7	96.2	99.7	96.2	98.3	95.8	96.8	94.9
Coal and petroleum products	100.4	97.4	96.4	99.3	102.0	103.3	101.8	98.1
Chemicals and allied industries	102.6	100.6	98.2	100.9	97.7	98.1	98.9	101.4
Metal manufacture	97.2	92.9	100.3	97.7	101.2	101.4	100.3	100.2
Mechanical engineering	104.4	104.6	106.5	106.4	106.3	108.5	109.7	106.7
Instrument engineering	92.2	94.3	102.7	101.2	102.6	105.9	103.7	100.7
Electrical engineering	101.7	100.8	98.6	100.6	98.4	98.1	101.9	99.4
Shipbuilding and marine engineering	101.5	100.7	98.2	100.2	102.0	103.9	104.5	104.3
Vehicles	96.6	100.0	96.5	99.6	102.1	100.6	94.9	95.1
Metal goods (n.e.s.)	99.1	98.5	99.4	98.6	100.5	103.5	101.9	100.5
Textiles	92.7	94.1	95.9	95.5	95.2	98.6	96.9	94.8
Leather, leather goods and fur	100.7	97.0	105.3	97.9	99.3	105.1	97.6	97.6
Clothing and footwear	96.3	94.0	97.6	93.8	96.9	93.9	99.4	95.0
Bricks, pottery, glass, cement, etc.	94.7	94.2	95.3	96.0	96.8	100.2	99.2	100.2
Timber, furniture, etc.	95.9	94.3	95.2	94.6	96.0	96.1	96.8	95.5
Paper, printing and publishing	87.4	88.7	89.2	86.2	88.9	92.5	95.0	96.9
Other manufacturing industries	99.5	100.1	100.9	101.2	97.4	100.0	100.6	101.6
All manufacturing industry	97.6	96.8	97.9	97.8	99.1	100.8	100.9	99.9
Mining and quarrying (not coal)	95.2	94.8	92.9	94.7	97.7	98.3	141.9	148.3
Construction	99.7	99.8	99.2	99.8	103.7	106.0	106.1	102.1
Gas, electricity and water	99.0	101.3	97.5	98.7	100.3	104.0	103.8	101.6
Transport and communications (excl. railways)	95.1	94.3	96.8	97.4	96.6	96.8	97.5	98.3
Certain miscellaneous services	101.6	91.7	104.7	103.0	107.0	105.5	109.7	107.4
Public administration	96.6	98.2	98.0	99.2	101.9	111.5	99.4	98.8
All industries covered	97.0	97.0	97.7	98.0	99.7	101.7	102.0	100.7

[1]Full-time manual men aged 21 and over.
Source: Scottish Economic Bulletin, no. 15 (1978).

The table shows general convergence in Scottish earnings towards
UK levels over the period 1971-7. However it can also be seen from the
table that the industry group called miscellaneous services seems to
have had an earnings level above the UK in 1971 and this trend con-

tinued over 1971–8. The industries under this category include distributive trades, insurance, banking and finance and other services. It is also interesting to note that the average earning in public administration and defence remains marginally below 100 except for 1974 and 1975. This could be indicative of some wage differential between national and local government employment.

It is useful at this stage to recapitulate the various caveats which we have examined so far. First, measuring value added in service industries poses more difficult conceptual problems than measuring value added in production industries. However, it is still possible to interpret the value added data which will help to link the results therefrom with employment and earning trends. Such analysis reveals that the evidence for Scotland does not support theoretical models such as an export base and there are possible reasons for this pattern. First, stimulus to manufacturing seems to be confined to a few industries and so it appears that the stimulus to local demand was more limited than if there was a more general stimulation or an expansion specifically among those industries with 'local linkages'. Second, and related to the first, is the role of immigrant firms rather than indigenous firms. Third, the time pattern of value added in 'public' and 'private' services showed some important features. In public services, the actual value added series remained below 'expected' for the most part except 1975–8. Important in explaining this pattern is the relatively faster growth in employment in local government over the latter period. But differences between Scotland and the UK in the proportion of total employment in public administration and defence constituted by employment in local government could be important, as salary levels, and therefore measured value added, have over most of the period been noticeably higher in central than in local government service, but the differentials have changed in a complex way. In 'private' services, where much of the induced growth may occur, the series of actual value added failed to confirm this. However, in explaining the upsurge in actual over 'expected', the catching up of earnings in Scotland towards the UK in these industries could be one of the factors along with possible stimulus from North Sea oil.

Conclusions

An analysis of Scottish and the UK growth rates led to several interesting conclusions. Firstly, for the entire study period of 1954–78, the Scottish GDP growth rate was only marginally below that of the UK, with the manufacturing growth rates being identical and the growth rate in public utilities being above that of the UK. To a certain extent the fact that the UK GDP series for the primary sector since

1975 is inclusive of value added in petroleum and gas makes any realistic comparisons of growth rates in this sector extremely difficult. This long time-period was conveniently divided into sub-periods, 1954–8, 1958–63, 1963–8, 1968–71, 1971–5, 1975–8.

At this sub-period level, it was found that for the first two sub-periods, the Scottish growth rates lagged behind those for the UK in most of the economic sectors, although there was a small gradual improvement in 1958–63 as compared to the earlier period. Over the sub-periods 1963–8 and 1968–71, Scottish growth rates exhibited remarkable revival albeit by the UK standards and this was most noticeable in manufacturing, but also in agriculture, forestry and fishing, and public utilities. However, despite this general revival, the overall growth rates in services lagged behind that of the UK and the overall GDP growth rate was just marginally ahead of that for the UK. Already in the 1968–71 sub-period, manufacturing and construction in Scotland showed signs of slack which were further accentuated in 1971–5. Thus, although for the entire sub-period of 1971–8, the Scottish GDP growth rate was a little ahead of the UK GDP, this was mainly due to some upsurge in service-sector growth rates, particularly in the period 1975–8. This pattern of growth in the services sector was therefore taken up for a further analysis in the growth standardisation analysis.

In the growth standardisation analysis, the relation between actual and 'expected' output was examined at sectoral and industry level. The general pattern of output change that emerges from this study is one of steady improvement since 1963. This spell of steady improvement was conveniently divided into 1961–6, 1966–70, 1970–5. It was found that the overall pattern in manufacturing appears to have been influenced heavily by the performance of the engineering and allied industries, particularly in the timing of the spurts of actual output above the 'expected' level, but the steady pull of actual output above the 'expected' level in food, drink and tobacco must also be important in explaining the growth of actual output above 'expected' in manufacturing since 1963. An important feature of the pattern in engineering and allied industries was the role played by electrical engineering. Diversity in the patterns within the engineering and allied industries may be taken as an indication that conventional regional policy may not be the only factor, most obviously in industries such as shipbuilding and vehicles.

The effects of regional policy can be analysed in terms of the roles of the indigenous and the immigrant sectors, since different policy instruments can be expected to have different effects on the two sectors. The data on movements of manufacturing industry into Scotland show that the annual number of firms moving into Scotland grew faster over the period 1958–66 but levelled off after 1966, a picture rather different from that of other development areas in the UK. The difficulties of disentangling the movements of industry data by manufacturing order prevents a definitive analysis of the role of mobile firms in specific industries but the overall pattern of actual output as against 'expected' output in manufacturing fits well with the data of the movement of manufacturing firms into Scotland and with the Scottish Office analysis which shows a relatively high contribution in the period 1961–6 by 'incomers' in total jobs created due to the openings of new plant. The conclusions therefore are that regional policy could possibly be one of the factors behind the pattern observed for manufacturing as a whole in the period up to about 1970. It also appears that movement of mobile firms into Scotland must be regarded as important in the growth of manufacturing output, especially perhaps in electrical engineering, but more rigorous analysis is needed before drawing any firm conclusions.

To summarise briefly the conclusions reached by applying standardisation technique to the other sectors of production, in the primary sector as a whole (and in agriculture, forestry and fishing) actual output was greater than 'expected' for most of our whole period of 1954–75. This may be partly due to differences between Scotland and the UK in the structure of production within agriculture, forestry and fishing. In mining and quarrying, Scottish actual value added was greater than the 'expected' from 1954 to 1957 and from 1971 to 1975, but otherwise the 'expected' value exceeded the actual. In public utilities, the pattern for the sector as a whole followed exactly that of construction, with gas, electricity and water in Scotland having a growth in value added much in line with the UK average. Value added in the construction industry grew faster in Scotland than in the UK for most years from 1965. Regional policy may be important in explaining the relatively good performance of the Scottish construction industry but further analysis is needed.

In Services, we focused our analysis to throw some light on the conventional wisdom that stimulation of the manufacturing sector will affect services through multiplier effects. In what was termed 'private' service industries (transport and communications; distributive trades; insurance, banking and finance; and 'other services'), there was close correspondence between actual and 'expected' over the whole period 1954–75, and there was no evidence of any spurt in private-sector service activity despite the improvement in the manufacturing sector in Scotland after 1963. The total value added in 'private services' remained below that 'expected' for the period 1963–75, but the actual value added was above the 'expected' for 1976–8.

The pattern of actual and of 'expected' value added in public services was examined fully both with reference to the value added data and employment data. In terms of growth standardisation analysis, the total of actual value added was below that of 'expected' for most part of 1963–75 but actual value added exceeded 'expected' since then. In public health and education, while actual was above that of 'expected' from 1954–63, for most part of the period since 1963 actual value added was below that of 'expected' up to 1975. In public administration and defence, we also examined the employment data which showed a greater relative importance of local government in Scotland as compared to the UK. The overall growth of local government employment appears to be much higher than that for the UK for the period 1960–75 but the acceleration was highest since 1971. If we look at the general data on the ratio of non-industrial to industrial employment and changes in it over the period 1961–78, in Scotland and the UK, it would appear that the base ratio for Scotland was higher than that for the UK but over the period, the percentage change in the UK ratio worked out much higher than that for Scotland. These data highlight several important features of employment growth in services in Scotland and the UK.

5

Government and the Scottish Economy, 1954–78

Introduction

In Chapter 3 we analysed output and input in Scotland and concluded that output per worker in the Scottish economy has improved both in absolute terms and relatively to the UK average over the study period. In Chapter 4, we examined the Scottish economic performance in terms of average growth rates by sector and industry. This analysis also supported the evidence of an improved economic performance in Scotland over the various sub-periods. Further analysis in terms of 'growth standardisation' technique enabled us to identify the industries and sectors in which Scottish growth pattern of actual output was noticeably different from what would be 'expected' if the Scottish output in a particular industry grew at the same rate as in the UK. So far we have not attempted to examine the possible role of external policy forces in explaining Scottish economic performance.

In this chapter we will examine the extent of central government activity in Scotland and analyse how far the pattern of Scottish economic performance can be attributed to central government activity. First, we examine the extent and pattern of central government expenditure in Scotland. We then discuss briefly the procedures followed and the conclusions reached by the earlier studies of the effects of regional policy on Scotland. We give the regression analysis of the main influences on Scottish manufacturing, examine the employment and output change in other sectors of economic activity, and finally draw our conclusions.

Central Government Expenditure in Scotland, 1961–78

The evidence of economic performance that was presented in Chapter 4 was of a selection of fairly conventional indicators. Table 5.1, which summarises the possible role of central government, is sufficiently unconventional to warrant a few words of explanation. First, the total of gross expenditure in this table measures the gross flow of expenditure incurred by the central government in Scotland before deducting the net revenue flows to central government.

Second, it does not include full estimates of the central government subsidies in housing and transport and communications, because of the difficulties of separating the local and central government elements in the totals for these items. What is more important to emphasise is the fact that the table does enable us to present the time pattern and structure of total central government expenditure in Scotland for the period 1961–78, the years for which these estimates could be constructed.

The first row of the table, which sets out for 1961–78 expenditure on regional policy, presents the measure usually chosen to indicate the total of central government regionally differentiated expenditure. Rows 2–4 indicate the extent of other kinds of central government expenditure in Scotland, grants to local authorities, capital expenditure by nationalised industries and wages and salaries bill in public administration and defence. Row 5 gives an estimate of central government expenditure on subsidies in agriculture, forestry and fishing; and trade, industry and employment. Row 6 gives total gross expenditure in Scotland. As row 7 shows, expenditure on 'special' regional policy is small in relation to the total of central government expenditure in Scotland. It does not of course follow that the total of 'special' regional policy expenditure was small in relation to the amount that systematically varied in Scotland's favour, though it is interesting to note that Wilson (1979) puts the extent of transfer to poorer regions in the UK at a little under 8 per cent of public expenditure.

The percentage of the total gross expenditure accounted for by the grants to local authorities varied from just under 30 per cent in 1961 to around 33 per cent in 1965 with some yearly variations around that until 1970 but rising steadily after that to reach just under 41 per cent in 1973, 43 per cent in 1977 and 45 per cent in 1978. The percentage share of total gross expenditure accounted for by the capital expenditure of nationalised industries also varied from just under 24 per cent in 1961 to around 21 per cent up to 1967, with a steady drop after 1967 ranging around 18 per cent up to 1972, but never recovering above that level except in 1975. The wages and salaries bill accounted for around 32 per cent of the total gross expenditure between 1961 and 1966, slightly under 30 per cent between 1967 and 1978 with the exception of 1978. The subsidies which could be measured separately accounted for a much smaller percentage of the total gross expenditure, varying from around 13 per cent in 1961 and 1962 but declining

Table 5.1 Central government expenditure in Scotland, 1961–78, £ million, current prices

	1961	1962	1963	1964	1965	1966	1967	1968	1969	1970	1971	1972	1973	1974	1975	1976	1977	1978
1 Annual exchequer cost of 'special' regional policy	14.4	15.4	9.6	9.5	27.3	29.4	46.7	49.9	95.9	96.1	89.2	85.7	102.5	136.5	206.2	223.4	162.7	153.4
2 Grants to local authorities[1]	113.8	120.8	133.5	145.4	158.2	177.0	195.9	218.5	245.7	289.5	338.7	402.5	519.5	706.8	852.5	1,077	1,198.8	1,316.3
	(117.8)	(125.2)	(139.1)	(151.0)	(164.1)	(185.0)	(200.0)	(230.0)	(244.6)	(288.2)	(337.1)	(400.2)	(503)	(679)				
3 Capital expenditure by nationalised industries[2]	93.0	87.8	93.2	98.8	104.9	113.4	132.7	130.6	125.9	144.0	162.4	182.8	188.1	288.7	457.8	456.5	429.5	380.2[3]
4 Wages and salaries public administration and defence[4]	120.0	130.0	138.0	149.0	159.0	170.0	184.0	195.0	211.0	237.0	273.0	322.0	363.0	454.0	632.0	764.0	793.0	919.0
5 Subsidies:[5] Agriculture, forestry and fishing	48.7	46.7	43.5	41.4	38.6	39.2	42.2	43.1	43.5	46.0	49.6	42.3	48.2	104.5	117.7	109.5	84.0	62.4
Trade, industry and employment	0.2	0.1	0.2	0.2	–	2.9	13.5	46.2	60.7	55.3	52.0	46.1	56.8	79.1	97.0	164.9	130.7	112.5
Total	48.9	46.8	43.7	41.6	38.6	42.1	55.7	89.3	104.2	101.3	101.6	88.4	105.0	183.6	214.7	274.4	214.7	174.9
6 Total gross expenditure	390.1	400.8	418.0	444.3	488.0	531.9	615.0	713.3	782.7	867.9	964.9	1,081.4	1,278.1	1,759.6	2,363.2	2,795.3	2,798.7	2,943.8
7 (1) as % of (6)	3.7	2.5	2.3	6.1	5.6	5.5	7.6	11.2	12.2	11.1	9.2	7.9	8.0	7.7	8.7	8.0	5.8	5.2
8 (2) as % of (6)	29.2	30.1	31.9	32.7	32.4	33.3	31.8	30.5	31.4	33.4	35.1	37.2	40.6	39.9	36.1	38.5	42.8	44.7
9 (3) as % of (6)	23.8	21.9	22.3	22.2	21.5	21.3	21.6	18.3	16.1	16.6	18.9	16.9	14.7	16.3	19.4	16.3	15.3	12.9
10 (4) as % of (6)	30.8	32.4	33.0	33.6	32.6	32.0	29.9	27.3	27.0	27.3	28.3	29.8	28.4	25.7	26.7	27.3	28.3	31.2
11 (5) as % of (6)	12.6	11.7	10.4	9.4	7.9	7.9	9.1	12.5	13.3	11.7	10.5	8.2	8.2	10.4	9.1	9.8	7.7	5.9

[1]Includes current and capital grants under rate support and general equalisation categories. The figures in the brackets are those calculated from the local financial returns directly. As the figures for the later years were not available from this source, the alternative source calculated from the figures published in Annual Abstract of Statistics is used.

[2]There are no estimates available in respect of the British Steel Corporation for the years 1969/70 to 1973/74 inclusive. The total for these years refers only to the other nationalised industries.

[3]The total is exclusive of the expenditure by Airways and Scottish Development Agency.

[4]Corresponds to the value added in public administration and defence.

[5]For the full breakdown of various subsidies, see Cox et al. (1978), Table 27. Most important items in central government subsidies are housing and transport and communications. However, it was rather difficult to estimate the precise breakdown between the local and central government subsidies from 1975 onwards due to non-availability of local financial returns.

Sources: Calculated from Scottish Abstract of Statistics, 1974, 1976, 1978, 1980; Annual Abstract of Statistics, nos. 106, 109, 110–12; Local Financial Returns, 1960–1 to 1975–6.

to under 10 per cent between 1964 and 1967, rising to around 12 per cent between 1968 and 1970, and declining steadily thereafter to 10 per cent or under.

Thus, we can conclude that 'special' regional policy really is only a very small part of total government expenditure in Scotland and although there is room for debate as to how much of that total is consciously regionally differentiated, the fact remains that it is misleading to focus on just a small part of government expenditure.

Earlier Studies of the Effects of Regional Policy on Scotland and the UK Regions

Since most of the earlier studies have been concerned principally with the effects of 'special' regional policy on manufacturing, it is convenient to start with a brief outline of how such policy might affect a regional economy. This is followed by a summary of results of earlier studies which include Moore and Rhodes (1973, 1974, 1976, 1980), Begg, Lythe and Macdonald (1975), Ashcroft and Taylor (1977, 1978). This brief analysis is followed by a summary and critique of the main findings of the more comprehensive literature surveys, namely, Ashcroft (1978), Schofield (1979) and Marquand (1980).

'Special' regional policy can be expected to work through its effects on indigenous enterprises (that is, those which are already there in the assisted region) and perhaps more importantly through its effects on immigrant enterprises (those which are new to the region). It is particularly relevant to start with investment since throughout much of the period of 'active' regional policy there was a consistent history of subsidisation of investment expenditure. Regional policy can bring to a region investment that would have taken place anyway but which is now induced by the availability of incentives to go to the favoured location. This can in many cases be associated with the immigration of a new enterprise. Regional policy can also induce new investment that would not have taken place anywhere in the absence of incentives but is now justifiable in the favoured region and not elsewhere. Such investment may either be in indigenous or immigrant enterprises.

It has commonly been argued that the principal way in which investment subsidies are likely to affect the indigenous enterprises is to raise their level of investment by the substitution of capital for labour as a result of a fall in the relative price of capital, but there are other effects, as shown, for example, by Blake (in Whiting, ed., 1976).

The full effect on the favoured region will not however be limited to either increasing the capital intensity among indigenous firms or causing in influx of migrants for whom the differential subsidy is a reward for relocation. For the former, there will be an 'income' as well as a substitution effect; the higher subsidy will not only change the price-relativity between capital and labour more than in unfavoured enterprise but will also, relative to other regions, lower the cost of factors in combination by a greater amount. As a result, firms already located in the favoured region will acquire a price advantage over firms outside such that, in the absence of spatial frictions, they are in a position to obtain a larger share than before of the output of their industry nationally. (p. 93)

The employment effects of investment subsidies are thus complicated because there are conflicting forces operating. The relative cheapening of investment will cause factor substitution in indigenous enterprises. At the same time, there will be a stimulus to indigenous enterprises as they are enabled to expand output. The movement into the region by immigrant firms will tend to increase employment in the region (and nationally, if it is completely new rather than displacement investment that is taking place). The relative strength of these is a matter of some debate (see for example, Blake and Thirlwall, in Whiting, ed., 1976). It is possible to generalise that for an assisted region, the employment creating effects of investment can be expected to be greater than employment displacing effects, the greater the labour intensity of the new investment attracted to the region and the fewer the possibilities of substituting capital for labour in the plants already in existence in the region.

The effects on output of investment subsidies also contain some elements of conflict. The lower the capital/output ratio in the particular industry involved, the higher will be the effects on output. At the same time, for the investment incentives to be effective, their impact on total costs of production must be noticeable and this implies a fairly high capital/labour ratio which may not be consistent with a low capital/output ratio. It can, however, be argued that in so far as investment subsidies attract new firms with high capital/labour ratios or reduce the demand for labour through factor substitution, output creating effects of investment subsidies are likely to be greater than their employment creating effects.

The practical implication of all this is that in seeking to examine the effects of 'special' regional assistance, it can be expected to create its impact initially on investment, and that the effects on employment and output will be complex, varying from one industry to another according to its factor intensity of production, its competitive structure and the extent to which the response is from indigenous and from immigrant firms.

The possible effects of a labour subsidy (such as Regional Employment Premium in Britain which was a per capita subsidy on the employment of labour during 1967–77) may be summarised briefly. Labour subsidy can have the same effect as a currency devaluation in so far as the subsidies are used to reduce the price of commodities produced in the development areas and are not used to pay higher wages or profits. A subsidy will thus stimulate the region's exports and thus regional income and employment. However, the effect of a labour subsidy will also be influenced by the extent to which the total cost of regional output consists of value added by firms located in other regions at an earlier stage of production. The lower the proportion of value added by the region exporting it, the smaller will be the effect of any given labour subsidy on final export prices.

The other related problems with labour subsidy arise due to the fact that, like a devaluation, the initial effects of the subsidy are to improve the competitiveness of the region but the long-term effects of this once and for all increase in exports are uncertain. Thus, although it appears that on purely theoretical considerations, labour subsidies are likely to have greater regional multiplier effects and possibly greater employment creating effects than is generally the case with investment subsidies, the reality is likely to be more complicated as is argued above.

The effects of regional policy on investment in manufacturing industry in Scotland over the period 1951–71 have been studied by Begg, Lythe and Macdonald (1975). They found that over the period 1960–71, the excess of actual over 'expected' investment amounted to a total of £220 million (averaging £18 million per annum) over and above what it might have been if Scotland's experience during 1951–9 had continued thereafter. A more detailed analysis by sub-periods, 1960–4, 1965–7 and 1968–70 showed that the annual average excess of actual over 'expected' was greater for 1968–70 (at £35 million) than for 1965–7 (£20 million) which in turn was greater than for 1960–4 (£12 million). These results need to be interpreted with caution because they assume that the improvement in actual investment over the time-trend is induced entirely by the regional policy, whereas in fact other forces such as changes in structure of economic activity in Scottish manufacturing could be relevant. Thus, the results of the examination of manufacturing investment must be placed in the context of what was happening to manufacturing output and employment.

Moore and Rhodes (1973, 1974) studied the effects of regional policy on employment in manufacturing in Scotland as well as in the UK development areas as a whole for the period 1951–71. For Scotland, Moore and Rhodes found that actual employment fell relative to 'expected' employment in what they regarded as a period of passive regional policy (1952–9) (in the development areas as a whole, actual and 'expected' employment moved closer together in this period). In the period they defined as 'active' regional policy from 1960 to 1971, Moore and Rhodes's analysis of employment changes showed that actual employment continued to fall though less fast than 'expected', in the indigenous sector. For immigrant enterprises, actual employment grew faster than 'expected' during the period of active regional policy, when both were rising. Moore and Rhodes put the direct effects of regional policy on employment in manufacturing in Scotland at 34–38,000 in the immigrant sector and 12–15,000 in the indigenous sector.

Moore and Rhodes (1973) estimated that for the development areas as a whole, the total number of jobs created directly due to regional policy was 220,000 manufacturing jobs over the period 1951–71. More recently, Tyler, Moore and Rhodes (1980) have re-examined the evidence for assisted regions of the UK, including Scotland. On their findings, regional policy during the 1970s continued to create jobs in the assisted areas, although at a slower rate than in the 1960s. They attributed the decline in employment growth to several factors: the reduction in the strength of regional policy – especially the gradual weakening of IDC controls and the abandonment for Scotland of Regional Employment Premium in 1977; the concept that any given instrument will produce effects that rise to a 'plateau' as it is fully taken up; possible statistical problems arising from the definition of the policy-off period; and the extent to which the problem may be one of urban decline. In their more detailed studies to examine the possibility that urban decline is responsible, they examined for Scotland the Clydeside conurbation which they reckon experienced relative decline from 1951 to 1961, and then a relative improvement, equivalent to 30,000 jobs in manufacturing by 1971. The group of smaller 'free-standing' towns they considered is predominantly Scottish – the group consists of Cardiff, Aberdeen, Dundee and Edinburgh – and for this group there was a relative improvement of 15,000 jobs in manufacturing in 1961–71.

Ashcroft and Taylor (1977, 1978) used an investment-demand model to explain the 'generation' of industrial movement which is then distributed to regions according to their relative attractiveness. Their latest estimates suggest that over 50 per cent of the moves to the development areas during 1961–71 were a direct consequence of regional policy. Scotland received some 15.3 per cent of the firms which moved within Great Britain in 1945–71, but the regional policy variables which Ashcroft and Taylor consider explain for Scotland under 60 per cent of the variation in the period from 1952 (as compared with 86 per cent for development areas as a whole). As far as policy instruments are concerned, Ashcroft and Taylor concluded that both location controls and capital subsidies had a substantial effect on the movement of industry to the development areas such as Scotland.

In summary, then, these studies are unanimous in identifying a continuous improvement in Scottish manufacturing from about 1960 or 1961 which can be attributed to regional policy: the nature of the posited policy effect and the measurement of employment gain varies from study to study, but the overall direction seems to be clear.

Ashcroft (1978), evaluating regional policy in the UK, comes to the overall conclusion that

> It must be concluded, therefore, that these estimates of the impact of regional policy on the number of moves to the Development Areas, while useful in assessing the number of decision units influenced by regional policy, must be seen to be of limited assistance to the identification of the number of *jobs* diverted to the Development Areas. Furthermore, since these estimates are concerned solely with the number of moves, we do not know the value of the investment directed to the Development Areas. Yet an understanding of the impact of regional policy on the value of investment in the Development Areas is of overriding importance if we are to have an appreciation of the possible success of the policy in raising the Development Areas' rate of growth and in consequence, the prospect of the eventual solution of the UK regional problem. (p. 35)

Schofield (1979) provides a comprehensive literature survey of macro-evaluations of regional policy in Great Britain. He argues that regional policies may be assessed from at least three perspectives: (i) their impact on the regional distribution of activity (their primary purpose), (ii) their aggregative efficiency effect on the economy (contribution to national output net of resource cost) and (iii) their financial impact on the Treasury (net Exchequer costs). So far as the impact of policy on the regional distribution of economic activity is concerned, Schofield classifies studies in three categories according to quantitative methods used, namely, simple statistical analysis, shift-share analysis and regression analysis. Schofield argues effectively that regression studies are preferable to shift-share studies in that, among other things, as compared to shift-share they enable a more precise estimate of counterfactual positions. Schofield's main conclusion from the survey of regression studies is that

> One line of inquiry would seem to be especially worth pursuing more fully, viz. the regression of actual employment change in depressed regions against expected employment change (defined as in shift-share analysis), a measure of change in national activity and separate policy variables. To date, only one study exists employing this approach (Moore and Rhodes, 1976) and then only in respect of indigenous employment in depressed regions. (p. 264)

Marquand (1980) sets out her objective to examine methods and problems of assessing the effectiveness of regional policy incentives, considering work which has already been done both within the Department of Industry and elsewhere. She summarises (para. 14) that the main regional incentives have attempted to stimulate growth and employment by aiding investment. Other measures such as Regional Employment Premium have attempted to operate directly upon the levels of employment. The methodology for a full evaluation of regional incentives not only requires that an increase in investment and employment be demonstrated above that which otherwise would have taken place but also that the link is demonstrated between any such increases and any observed increases in rates of growth, levels of incomes and decreases in unemployment.

She further argues that the methodology for a more modest partial assessment has yet to demonstrate an increase in investment and employment, disentangling the effects of the investment incentives from the effects of other factors; the latter may possibly include factors such as changes in the regional incidence of government transfer payments and public expenditure on goods and services, the consequences of changes in infrastructure, the effects of North Sea oil and gas, and the effects of other regional policies such as REP and IDC controls in the non-assisted areas. Indeed, her own conclusions on the examination of evidence from other studies are worth noting.

It remains necessary and possible to carry out further micro-work examining the relative merits of different regional policy instruments. But extensive macro-economic work to attempt to evaluate the general contribution of regional policy instruments to the achievement of self-sustaining growth does not appear a particularly fruitful route to follow. (para. 165)

It would thus appear that more recent literature surveys have somewhat different conclusions to offer on how worthwhile in general is the pursuit of macro approaches to the evaluation of regional policy. While both these studies emphasise the complex problems of estimation and methodology involved in partial macro evaluation, the routes suggested in particular by Schofield and Marquand are different. Again to a great extent the focus of these surveys is on the 'special' regional policy rather than the broader view of regional policy. It must be granted that even taking a broader framework of regional policy does not reduce the complex problem of measurement. However, if we were to focus more directly on an analysis of employment and output change in Scotland rather than indirect variables such as the number of moves, then the wider measure of the extent of central government activity becomes even more relevant. We believe that given the mass of data available on the Scottish economy, it should be possible to offer a more comprehensive partial evaluation than has been attempted for Scotland so far, and the conclusions offered pertaining to Scotland can hopefully be placed within the context of other development areas as well.

'Special' Regional Policy and Manufacturing in Scotland

If, as all the studies outlined in the previous section suggest, regional policy has indeed brought about an improvement in performance in the manufacturing sector in Scotland, it seemed to us that we should be able to see some effect of regional policy if we tried to model the behaviour over time of employment and output in manufacturing in total or in individual industries. We operated with as long data runs as possible to get a reasonably consistent series, so for employment we worked with data for 1954 to 1976 and for output for 1954 to 1978. For manufacturing employment, we were fortunate in being able to use the annual data collected by the Scottish Office under the Scottish Manufacturing Establishments Record SCOMER (*Scottish Economic Bulletin*, no. 17, 1979) which divide manufacturing units into incomers (that is, those units opening since 1945 having their origins outside Scotland or being sub-units of a unit which itself came into Scotland from outside) and non-incomers. The advantages of the data for analytical purposes are neatly expressed by the Scottish Office: 'Hitherto the use of employment data to analyse developments in the Scottish economy in the post-war period has been largely restricted to an analysis of net changes in Employment. These changes have been dominated by long-term declines in old established Scottish industries.' (*Scottish Economic Bulletin*, no. 17, 1977). For our purposes the chief interest was that we could expect to see regional policy working fairly directly on the 'incomer' groups and perhaps in a much more diffused manner on the rest.

We began by modelling all the policy variables which could be expected to have some influence on the employment and output change in Scottish manufacturing. Therefore, initially much of our effort was concentrated on analysing the possible effects of capital subsidies, labour subsidy, special development areas, Industrial Development Certificates and so forth. Of course there is a complex problem of specification of variables, multicolinearity and lags. To take each variable separately then, we tried capital subsidies in terms of real expenditure on capital subsidies, with varying lags, differential investment incentives available to firms expanding in development areas (Mellis and Richardson, 1976) and along with these we experimented with a number of dummy variables. These were for the Local

Employment Act, and the years in which labour subsidy was available. Alternatively, we experimented with the differential value of expenditure on labour subsidy in real terms. However, the evidence was conclusive that in terms of employment change in the indigenous sector and also more importantly for employment change in incomer units, the explanatory power of the 'special' regional policy variables was rather weak. This is to be expected if the broader dimension of regional policy was more important. In order to capture the possible effects of this broader dimension, we have included two kinds of variables and these are proxies for pressure of demand in terms of unfilled vacancies with appropriate lags and the Wharton index of capacity utilisation for Scotland.

Table 5.2 gives the best ordinary least square equations we could fit to explain employment changes in 'others' (or indigenous – EMPIND) and 'incomers' (EMPINC). EMPIND is interpreted as depending on VAC which is unfilled vacancies in Scotland (lagged one period) and is taken as proxy for pressure of demand, UKGRO which is the percentage growth rate in UK manufacturing, and LOCEMP which is a dummy variable (taken as 1 for the years 1961 to 1964, 0 otherwise). VAC and UKGRO are statistically significant at 1 per cent level and LOCEMP at 5 per cent level of probability respectively. For EMPINC, the statistically significant explanatory variables are again UKGRO and WHATI or alternatively, VAC and UKGRO. For both equations seeking to explain the employment change in 'incomers', the adjusted R^2 is lower than that for EMPIND. This is indicative of the presence of other factors (for example, multinationals) which are not captured in the specified variables.

To conclude, the results in Table 5.2 possibly raise a question mark on much of the conventional wisdom regarding the possible effects of 'special' regional policy. The dependent variables we have chosen are far superior to any of the variables used so far in earlier studies. Admittedly, our own variables WHAT and VAC capture not only the broader dimension of regional policy but also a particular phase of national macro-economic policy. But these results are more conclusive in suggesting that it is misleading to focus so much attention in terms of methodology and evaluation on narrowly defined 'special' regional policy. Schofield (1979) highlights this point when he recognises the need to analyse the relevant regional macro-aggregates directly and also the need to take the level of activity as one of the independent variables, given a considerable amount of central government's own infrastructural expenditure.

Table 5.3 gives the results of the regression analysis to explain output change in Scottish manufacturing. It can be seen from the table that in the equation explaining change in output in manufacturing two of the regional policy variables are statistically significant along with

Table 5.2 *The regression analysis of employment change in manufacturing in Scotland, 1955–75*

Dependent variable	Constant	VAC	LOCEMP	UKGRO	WHATI	Adjusted R^2	F-value	Standard error	DW
			Regression coefficients of independent variables						
EMPIND	−49,666.68 (−7.00)*	2,511.42 (5.89)*	784.92 (1.92)**	7,685.25 (1.72)**		0.67	15.45† (3,18)	7,567.12	2.11
EMPINC	−101,846.8 (−3.27)*			409.19 (1.80)**	1,122.19 (3.36)*	0.49	10.92† (2,19)	4,037.46	1.46
EMPINC	−9,066.23 (−2.81)*	770.53 (3.80)*		513.44 (2.48)**		0.53	13.05† (2,19)	4,310.27	1.83

Notes: Figures in the brackets are t-ratios which denote the following statistical significance:

  * = significant at 1 per cent level of probability
  ** = significant at 5 per cent level of probability
  *** = significant at 10 per cent level of probability

For F-values, † denotes the 1 per cent level of probability and § gives the 5 per cent level of probability.
Data used in this table are given in the Appendix (see Table A.3, p. 208).

List of variables used in Tables 5.2 and 5.3

CAPSUB = Expenditure in real terms on capital subsidies, unlagged.
EMPINC = The employment change in the incomers' firms in Scotland between t-1 and t (starting from 1955), in thousands.[1]
EMPIND = The employment change in the 'non incomers' manufacturing units in Scotland between t-1 and t (1955) in thousands.[1]
FOOD = The output change (in constant 1975 prices) in food, drink and tobacco (SIC order III) in Scotland, between t-1 and t, £ million.[2]
IDC3 = Official IDC refusals (in terms of expected employment involved) in the Midlands and south east regions as a percentage of refusals plus approvals in the development areas, 3 period lag.[7]
LABDIFF = The change in the expenditure on labour subsidy in £ million in real terms between t-1 and t.[8]
LOCEMP = Dummy 1 in cases 10 to 13, 0 otherwise.[8]
OUTENG = The output change in constant (1975) prices in engineering and allied industries (SIC order VII–XII) in Scotland between t-1 and t, £ million.[2]
SCOMFG = The output change in constant (1975 prices) manufacturing in Scotland between t-1 and t (starting from 1955), £ million.[2]
UKGRO = Percentage change in UK manufacturing output (1975 prices), one period lag.[9]
UKOUT = The change in UK manufacturing output, between t-2 and t-1, £ million, 1975 prices.[4]
VAC = Unfilled vacancies, Scotland, t-1.[5]
VACI = Unfilled vacancies, Scotland, t-2.[5]
WHAT = Wharton index of capacity utilisation, Scotland, unlagged.[3]
WHATI = Wharton index, Scotland, 1 period lag.[3]

Sources: 1 Calculated from *Scottish Economic Bulletin*, no. 17 (Spring, 1979). 2 See C. Lythe and M. Majmudar, *Scottish Gross Domestic Product 1961–1971: An Exercise in Regional Accounting and Analysis* (Dundee, 1978), p. 191. 3 Aggregate index of capacity utilisation, Scotland, for manufacturing, mining and quarrying, construction, gas, electricity and water. For methodology, see J. Taylor, D. Winter and D. Pearce, 'Capacity utilisation in the UK, 1948–1969', *Oxford Bulletin of Economic Statistics*, (1970), calculated and updated for Dundee data bank. 4 Calculated from C. Lythe and M. Majmudar (1978), op. cit. p. 193–4. 5 *Scottish Abstract of Statistics*; also *Scottish Digest of Statistics*. 6 Calculated from data on expenditure on regional policy in Scotland, *Scottish Economic Bulletin*, nos. 9 and 13. The UK price index for the government final consumption calculated from the *Blue Book* was applied to calculate the constant (1975) price figures of all components of central government expenditure. 7 See Ashcroft and Taylor (1977). 8 Dummy variable. 9 Calculated from C. Lythe and M. Majmudar (1978), op. cit. p. 193–4.

Table 5.3 *The regression analysis of output change in manufacturing in Scotland, 1955–78*

Dependent variable	Constant	Regression coefficients of independent variables					Adjusted R^2	F-value	Standard error	DW
		UKOUT	VACI	IDC3	WHATI	UKGRO				
SCOMFG	83.50 (1.67)**	0.04 (3.61)*	−5.6 (−2.11)**	2.09 (1.53)***			0.53	8.92 (3,18)	49.26	1.90
OUTENG	−275.24 (−0.88)			1.11 (1.08)	WHATI 2.94** (0.86)	UKGRO 0.26 (0.1)	0.03	1.28 (3,18)	35.76	2.69
FOOD	−114.50 (−1.15)				WHAT 1.36 (1.26)	UKGRO 0.07 (0.09)	0.10	1.62 (3,18)	11.63	1.49

Notes: Figures in brackets are t-ratios which denote the following statistical significance:
   * = significant at 1 per cent level of probability
   ** = significant at 5 per cent level of probability
   *** = significant at 10 per cent level of probability

For F-values, † denotes the 1 per cent level of probability and § gives 5 per cent level of probability.
Data used in this table are given in the Appendix (see Table A.3, p. 208).

Table 5.4 The regression analysis of the sectoral output and employment change in Scotland, 1962–78

Dependent variable	Constant	Regression coefficients of independent variables			Adjusted R^2	F-Value	Standard error	DW
ΔOUTAGR	-1.03 (0.15)	SCOMFG-1 0.19 (2.46)**			0.24	6.06 (1,15)§	24.30	2.6
ΔEMPAGR	-16.95 (-5.11)*	CENEXP 0.07 (3.97)*			0.48	15.78† (1,15)	2.71	1.8
ΔEMPMIN	-11.88 (-2.92)**	UNEMP 0.05 (2.46)**	EMPUTILI -7.71 (3.08)*	OUTAGGI -0.19 (1.80)**	0.24	6.04§ (1,15)	3.32	2.2
ΔSEROUT	33.56 (0.36)	EXPRDHO 0.68 (1.19)	DUM2 5.91 (1.46)***	ΔREGEMP -51.85 (2.09)***	0.44	5.25§ (3,13)	75.11	2.0
ΔEMPUTIL	-2.67 (-1.24)	ΔSEREMP 0.08 (2.41)**	SCOMFG 1.26 (5.05)*		0.29	3.17 (3,13)	6.15	1.8
ΔOUTAGG	51.25 (2.02)**	SCOMFG 0.89 (5.51)*			0.76	26.13† (2,14)	78.82	1.6

Notes: Figures in brackets are t-ratios which denote the following statistical significance:
  * = significant at 1 per cent level of probability
  ** = significant at 5 per cent level of probability
  *** = significant at 10 per cent level of probability
  For F-values, † denotes 1 per cent level of probability and § gives 5 per cent level of probability (see Table A.4, pp. 209–11).
  Data used in this analysis are given in the Appendix (see Table A.4, pp. 209–11).

List of variables used in Table 5.4 in Scotland, 1962-1978

AGRSUB	=	The central government expenditure on agricultural subsidies, Scotland, 1975 prices.
ΔAGRSUB	=	The change in central government expenditure on agricultural subsidies, 1975 prices.
CENEXP	=	The central government expenditure in Scotland, total £ million, constant (1975) prices.
ΔCENEXP	=	The change in total central government expenditure in Scotland, constant (1975) prices.
DUM-1	=	0 otherwise, 1 for last 3 cases.
DUM-2	=	0 otherwise, 1 for last 4 cases.
ΔEMPAGR	=	The change in employment in agriculture, forestry and fishing in Scotland, thousands.
ΔEXPMIN	=	The change in employment in mining and quarrying, in Scotland, thousands.
ΔEMPUTIL	=	The change in employment in public utilities, in Scotland, thousands.
EXPRD	=	The central government expenditure on roads, Scotland, 1975 prices.
ΔEXPRD	=	The change in central government expenditure on roads, Scotland, 1975 prices.
EXPRDHO	=	The central government expenditure on roads and housing, Scotland, 1975 prices.
ΔEXPRDHO	=	The change in central government expenditure on roads and housing, Scotland, 1975 prices.
EXPRDTR	=	The central government expenditure on roads and transport, Scotland, 1975 prices.
ΔEXPRDTR	=	The change in central government expenditure on roads and transport, 1975 prices.
EXPUTIL	=	The central government expenditure on public utilities, Scotland, constant (1975) prices.
ΔEXPUTIL	=	The change in central government expenditure on utilities, Scotland, constant (1975) prices.
NATIND	=	The capital expenditure by nationalised industries, Scotland, constant (1975) prices.
ΔNATIND	=	The change in capital expenditure by nationalised industries, Scotland, constant (1975) prices.

ΔOUTAGG = The change in GDP in Scotland, 1975 prices, £ million.

ΔOUTAGR = The change in output in agriculture, forestry and fishing, Scotland, £ million, constant (1975) prices.

ΔOUTMIN = The change in output in mining and quarrying, in Scotland, £ million, constant (1975) prices.

ΔOUTUTIL = The change in output in public utilities, in Scotland, £ million, constant (1975) prices.

REGEXP = 'Exchequer' cost of regional policy gross, Scotland, constant (1975) prices.

ΔREGEXP = The change in gross expenditure on regional policy, constant (1975) prices.

ΔSEREMP = The change in employment in services (SIC order XII–XVI), thousands.

ΔSEROUT = The change in output of 'private services' (SIC order XXII, XXIII, XXIV and XXVI).

UKMFG = Percentage growth rate of output in the UK manufacturing, one period lag.

UNEMP = The number of registered unemployed, Scotland.

ΔUNEMP = The change in the number of registered unemployed, Scotland.

ΔUNEMP-1 = The change in unemployment, one period lag, Scotland.

VAC = Unfilled vacancies, Scotland.

ΔVAC = The change in unfilled vacancies, Scotland.

EMPAGR-1
EMPMIN-1
EMPSER-1
EMPUTIL-1
OUTAGG-1 = The output and employment change in the relevant sector, one period lag, Scotland.
OUTAGR-1
OUTMIN-1
OUTUTIL-1
SCOMFG-1

UKOUT. However, the explanatory power of the equations explaining output change in engineering and allied industries is very weak indeed. It must also be pointed out that in an earlier paper (Majmudar and Lythe, 1981) we reported the results of regression analysis of output change in manufacturing in Scotland in 1970 prices. However, conversion to 1975 prices and inclusion of the 1975–8 period seems to have resulted in a considerable drop in the explanatory power of all the three equations reported in Table 5.3. On balance one would expect the latter to be more important.

In an earlier study (Lythe and Majmudar, 1978), we sought to show, by a comparison of 'actual' with 'expected' output in manufacturing and its individual industries, that regional policy over the period 1961–71 did indeed cause some rise in 'actual' output above 'expected' levels. We feel, however, that the conclusions of our present study must be decisive: broader regional policy contributed positively to change in employment in 'incomer' and 'indigenous' enterprises. But for the former this contribution was very small, and for both there were additional factors which must be taken into account. The effect of 'special' regional policy on output seems to have worked more importantly through location controls and pressure of demand (VAC).

Regional Policy and Other Sectors of the Scottish Economy

In considering the effects of regional policy on other sectors of the economy, it is appropriate to adopt a less restrictive view and indeed broaden the independent variables in terms of the various types of expenditure injections in the regional economy, including some variables representing intersectoral linkages along with pressure of demand and UK variables. We report in Table 5.4 the best equations for various sectors.

The following conclusions can be drawn from Table 5.4:

(1)   In explaining output change in agriculture, forestry and fishing, the percentage change in Scottish manufacturing output with one period lag is statistically significant.

(2)   The SCOMFG-1 is also statistically significant in explaining the employment change in agriculture, forestry and fishing. It is therefore interesting to observe the intersectoral link between these two variables working possibly through growth patterns in food, drink and tobacco.

(3)   In explaining employment change in mining total central government is statistically significant at 5 per cent level but fails to yield significant F-value. On the other hand, no satis-

factory explanation could be established for output change in mining and quarrying.

(4)   No satisfactory explanation was found for output change in utilities.

(5)   Employment change in utilities is interpreted to depend on ΔEXPRDHO which is change in expenditure on roads and housing, DUM-2 which is a dummy variable (with 1975 to 1978 = 1, 0 otherwise) and ΔREGEXP which is the change in gross expenditure on regional policy. The F-value for this equation is not statistically significant although the first two coefficients are statistically significant, at 5 per cent and 10 per cent level respectively.

(6)   The change in aggregate output in Scotland is interpreted to depend on the change in employment in services sector and SCOMFG which is the percentage change in output in Scottish manufacturing. The regression coefficients for these variables are statistically significant at 1 per cent level.

(7)   As compared to the results presented in Majmudar and Lythe (1981) the equation for services sector was not found to be statistically significant in terms of variables used in the earlier analysis or in terms of any other variables listed for Table 5.4. However, the change in output in 'private services' is seen to depend on variables UNEMP, EMPUTIL-1 and OUTAGG-1. No satisfactory explanation was found for output change in public services. It is important to note once again that there is little evidence to support the once popular view that improved growth in manufacturing evident for the period 1960 to early 1970s had a positive spin-off effect on the service sector. Indeed the spurt in the service-sector activity over and above what could be expected from the UK growth rates occurred in the much later period of 1975-8.

(8)   The results in Table 5.4 show a clear pattern in terms of the overall explanatory power of employment change vis à vis output change in various sectors. The equations explaining change in output in GDP in Scotland and output in utilities display good statistical fit, while those explaining employment change in agriculture, forestry and fishing, mining and quarrying and utilities show weak statistical fit. Again, there is no satisfactory explanation for employment change in services.

To summarise, it would appear that the results in Table 5.4 show that (i) output change rather than employment change has better explanatory power, (ii) intersectoral linkages are important in explaining output change in various sectors, (iii) in at least two of the equations (namely, mining and quarrying, and utilities) explaining employment change, expenditure variables are statistically significant. This is not the case for the corresponding equations for these sectors for output change.

Conclusions

This chapter examined fairly vigorously the contribution of external factors in the explanation of Scottish economic performance. We started off by looking at the extent of central government activity in Scotland over the period 1961–78. We saw that expenditure on 'special' regional policy accounted for a fairly small proportion of total government expenditure in Scotland. This is not to argue that all of central government expenditure presented in Table 5.1 varied systematically in regions. However it is important to point out that in addition to 'special' regional policy, there is an additional component which is quite consciously differentiated regionally and therefore it is misleading to focus on just a small part of government expenditure.

We then examined the evidence from earlier studies on the effects of regional policy on Scotland and the UK regions. Most of these studies are unanimous in identifying continuous improvement in Scottish manufacturing from about 1960 or 1961 which can be attributed to regional policy: the nature of the posited effect and the measurement of employment gain varied in the various studies but the overall direction seems clear. The three main literature surveys of Ashcroft (1978), Schofield (1979) and Marquand (1980) differ somewhat in their approaches and recommendations but these surveys are important in that they do highlight the complex problems involved in a partial evaluation and make some recommendations for further work. In the latter two, the routes suggested are different.

We argued that it is important to attempt a partial analysis using more direct dependent variables in terms of employment and output change and that such an analysis should not be restricted to manufacturing alone. We were fortunate in being able to use for manufacturing employment the data which could be disaggregated in terms of 'incomer' firms and 'indigenous' firms. For employment change in manufacturing our best results showed that the variables that could conventionally be regarded as indicating the effect of 'special' regional policy failed to yield statistically significant results. But variables such as unfilled vacancies (proxy for pressure of demand), percentage growth rate of manufacturing and Wharton index of capacity utilisation were found statistically significant. Again the explanatory power of the equation explaining employment change in 'others' (indigenous firms) was much better than that for incomers. The statistically significant variables in the equation explaining output change were not the same as for employment change. The analysis of employment and output change in other sectors also revealed a certain important pattern. We tried to model variables which would measure intersectoral linkages, pressure of demand, expenditure variables and the UK variables.

The overall pattern seems to be that the equations explaining change in aggregate GDP in Scotland and change in output in public utilities, did produce good statistical fit. In agriculture and mining the equations explaining employment change were more satisfactory than those for output change. For the services sector, and for output change in mining, we could not fit any statistically significant result at all. On the whole the best equations for other sectors have lower explanatory power than those for the manufacturing sector. Thus again the earlier conclusion of Chapter 4 that the improved performance of Scottish manufacturing failed to produce a significant spin-off effect in services and some other sectors is further supported by the analysis of this chapter. In the next chapter we will examine the question of the outlook on Scottish economy in terms of some of the more important recent developments in the 1970s.

6

The Outlook for the Scottish Economy

Introduction

In the last four chapters, we have examined in detail the performance of the Scottish economy since the mid 1950s and we have concluded that, whilst Scotland's economic fortunes have been dominated by the poor growth and productivity record of the UK, there is some evidence that from the mid 1960s Scotland has been doing a little better than the UK average. We have seen in Chapter 2 that Scottish income and output per head has risen up to near UK levels, and that expenditure per head in Scotland has matched that of the UK. Chapter 3 showed that labour productivity in Scotland has improved noticeably, and now approaches UK levels. Chapter 4 pinpointed the sources of growth, and identified the key role of certain industries, and in Chapter 5 we discussed how far the relatively good economic performance was attributable to the economic activities of government.

In this chapter, we intend first to deal with a number of special factors which we have not so far considered, and which can be expected to have had a noticeable effect on the Scottish economy. The first of these is the exploitation of North Sea oil and gas reserves, and the second is British membership of the European Communities. Both events only have economic significance from the early 1970s, and so cannot be expected to have featured importantly in the longer sweep analysis of Chapters 2-5. As we will show, the effects of oil development have been very great in restricted areas, but the overall impact on the Scottish economy has never been great and is now diminishing. In the case of the European Communities, whilst the assistance made available to Scotland has not been negligible, it has been relatively unimportant in comparison with the activities of the UK government. In both these cases, then, our conclusion is that the main significance is potential rather than actual.

The third special factor we will examine is the role of the multinational companies. It has been argued that the multinationals provide an initial source of growth but are a longer-term threat to the development of an economy because of the 'branch factory syndrome' – that when world economic climates deteriorate, it is the overseas branches that are closed first, and so instability is engendered in the host economy. We shall examine the plausibility of this case, again with an eye to the implications for the future economic progress of Scotland.

In the next section of this chapter, we will consider a topic we have not so far treated explicitly – the importance and nature of Scotland's trade. The discussion here is based solely on the evidence for the one year – 1973 – for which an input-output study of Scotland has been conducted. A similar exercise is now under way for 1979, but evidence from it is not yet available. What we will show in this section is how far it is really true that Scotland is dependent on the rest of the UK and so how far her economic destiny is not in her own hands.

After that, we will look at the actual and potential role of some of the more important governmental and quasi-governmental economic institutions in Scotland. We make no claim to deal here with a comprehensive list of agencies: we will discuss just some of those which have a potential to operate with some degree of autonomy from the UK, and the nature of the constraints which inhibit their freedom.

In the last two sections, we shall turn to a more direct treatment of the economic outlook for Scotland. We shall review the current state of the art in formal econometric modelling for Scotland, and discuss what is implied by the limited work so far undertaken in that direction. In the last section, we will attempt to put together all the material in the two penultimate sections of this chapter, together with the implications of the earlier chapters of this book, to offer our views on the economic outlook for Scotland over the next few years.

North Sea Oil and the Scottish Economy

In writings about the Scottish economy ten years ago, discussion of North Sea oil and gas was inevitably speculative, because it was very hard at that stage to make more than intelligent guesses about the employment and output that the exploration and extraction processes would generate. So much have we now become used to the oil-related activity, that it is difficult to remember that offshore oil-related employment in Scotland was only just over 5,000 in 1973, and the first production platform in the North Sea was installed in 1974. We will look shortly at the scale of the North Sea activities and of the shock they represented, to Scotland as a whole and to regions of Scotland, but as might be expected developments of such suddenness and such extensiveness have attracted considerable academic attention, and all we can hope to do here is offer a brief review of some of the numerous studies.

The economic effects of the discovery and exploitation of a major resource within a region can conveniently be distinguished into the relatively local effects – which are our concern here – and the national effects. The local effects are those of the moving in to the affected areas of specialised labour and equipment, and the creation of local employment opportunities, initially in supplying less specialised labour and equipment, eventually perhaps in acquiring the specialisations to displace the incoming resources. This moving in of labour and equipment requires the provision of suitable services – houses, schools, industrial sites – and of itself generates some employment – catering, distributive trades, etc. – through what is labelled the "multiplier" effect. The more underemployed resources there are in the area where the development takes place, the more scope there is for them to be drawn into employment through the multiplier effect: otherwise the tendency will be for servicing a new industry to be at the expense of older established industries (whose decline may be accelerated or even brought about by this process).

As far as the wider nation is concerned, it too may gain through multiplier effects, providing services that it is not possible or convenient to supply locally (and there is the corresponding possibility of displacement of resources from other activities), but the main effect from a major resource development like oil is to the balance of payments (by reducing imports of oil or by starting to export oil) and hence to the value of the currency in international exchange, and to the government's revenue, in so far as the resource exploitation gives rise to taxes on companies and perhaps to special taxes on the value of the output or to royalties for permits for companies to operate. Whilst it is possible for local areas to enjoy some of the fiscal benefits – through rate revenue or through special arrangements such as those negotiated with the oil companies by the Shetland local authorities – in practice the fiscal benefits are primarily to the national exchequer and the local benefits are mainly in the form of employment. One study (MacKay, 1977) did posit a scenario of the sharing of fiscal benefits between the UK government and some sort of self-governing body for Scotland, and demonstrated that the effects of tax revenues on Scotland would be sufficiently great to pose very interesting questions of resource allocation, but we will follow most commentators in being more realistic and in regarding the impact on Scotland as being primarily the 'local' effects we have discussed earlier.

We will start, then by looking at the total of oil-related employment in Scotland and at how it is distributed between regions of Scotland. The first part of Table 6.1 sets out the details for employment in companies wholly related to the North Sea oil industry – that is, excluding workers whose companies, whilst involved in North Sea activities, are also fairly heavily committed to other activities. The employment analysed in Table 6.1 can fairly be regarded as that most directly created by the North Sea developments. No regional analysis of its distribution within Scotland is available for 1973, but as the table shows the Scottish total was then quite low. Employment in wholly involved companies grew in Scotland more or less steadily through the period, but, as the quarterly data available for 1980 suggest, that growth is now pretty well at an end, and the total will at best be stable and will, as we shall see, probably decline somewhat.

The impact on the regions of Scotland has been very uneven. Much the biggest effect in absolute terms has been on the Grampian region: with about 9 per cent of total Scottish employment it had in the summer of 1980 about 69 per cent of the wholly involved employment, and the numbers in Grampian wholly involved in the North Sea have climbed fairly steadily. The next largest region in terms of absolute employment involvement is that of the Highland and Islands. At its peak, when there were over 7,000 people in the Highland region working on North Sea projects, the Highland region had nearly 25 per cent of the North Sea jobs, and only 3.5 per cent of the total Scottish employment: and the Islands' mid-1980 employment in the North Sea was 7.5 per cent of the Scottish total, but the Islands then had only about 1 per cent of total Scottish employment. The impact has, then, been very heavy on regions which are fairly small in terms of total employment; indeed, in some years employment in companies wholly involved in the North Sea has been of the order of 10 per cent of all employment in some regions, and of course within specific towns and villages the effect has been much greater. The table also brings out how the timing of the effects on regions has varied. In the Highland region North Sea oil employment peaked in 1977, so in that region the problems of adjustment to decline have already been encountered.

The second part of Table 6.1 presents some of the key to this diversity of experience, by showing how the nature of the activity in the North Sea has changed. Whilst exploration in northern waters is still going on, and new discoveries are being made, the emphasis has clearly switched from exploration, through appraisal of promising discoveries, to production, and the number of new wells being drilled reached its peak in 1977. As the growth in the number of new wells has started to diminish, so has the demand for new drilling equipment, and hence the areas in which drilling platform yards were set up, which were the first to experience the oil boom, have also been the first to see the end of that boom.

Table 6.2, in which we look at the industrial composition of employment both wholly and partly involved in the North Sea, shows

Table 6.1   *North Sea oil-related activity in Scotland*

A   *Employment in companies wholly related to the North Sea oil industry*

	Central and Lothian	Fife	Gram- pian	High- land	Strath- clyde	Tayside	Islands	Scotland
1973	–	–	–	–	–	–	–	5.29
1974	1.07	1.21	4.81	4.86	1.17	0.27	0.09	13.47
1975	0.42	1.62	8.97	4.45	3.30	1.10	0.21	20.05
1976	0.69	2.03	11.54	6.78	4.23	1.44	0.40	27.10
1977	0.62	0.81	15.68	7.09	1.92	1.76	0.77	28.63
1978	0.55	1.38	22.89	6.00	0.50	2.05	0.63	33.99
1979	0.62	2.26	28.06	4.81	0.77	2.32	2.92	41.76
1980 Q1	0.74	0.88	32.92	4.61	2.51	2.07	3.07	46.80
Q2	0.86	0.81	32.32	4.35	2.73	1.81	3.46	46.34
Q3	0.77	0.82	32.64	4.76	2.99	1.82	4.02	47.82

B   *Drilling activities in UK northern waters*

	Wells drilled			Oil production northern North Sea million tonnes
	Exploration	Appraisal	Production	
1967	7	–	–	–
1968	1	–	–	–
1969	8	–	–	–
1970	10	–	–	–
1971	17	4	–	–
1972	23	4	–	–
1973	34	13	–	–
1974	59	31	–	–
1975	75	35	8	1.1
1976	51	26	47	11.6
1977	58	27	89	37.3
1978	32	20	85	52.8
1979	13	6	53	76.1

Note: The areas defined for the statistics in this table vary slightly from one series to another.

Source: A *Scottish Economic Bulletin*, no. 22 (Spring 1981); B *Scottish Economic Bulletin*, no. 19 (Autumn 1979) and 22 (Spring 1981).

more clearly the change in the type of product demanded by the North Sea industry: in 1976 work on concrete and steel platforms and modules accounted for over 30 per cent of total oil-related employment in Scotland; by 1978 its share had fallen to under 13 per cent, and services constituted the dominant source of total oil-related employment. The Highland region had a disproportionately large

Table 6.2 The Industrial composition of North Sea oil employment in Scotland

SIC order	Industry	Unit	1974 Total	1976 Wholly involved	1976 Partly involved	1976 Total	1978 Wholly involved	1978 Partly involved	1978 Total
II	Mining and quarrying	'000	3.30	4.30	–	4.30 [6.10]	9.90	–	9.90
		%	11.1			15.2			21.3
IV and V	Manufacturing — Chemicals, coal and petroleum products	'000	0.15	–	0.20	0.20	–	0.30	0.35
		%	0.5			0.5			0.8
VI	Metal manufacture	'000	2.95	0.15	2.75	2.90 [2.60]	–	2.75	2.75
		%	10.0			6.5			5.9
VII (part) and XX	Concrete and steel platforms and modules	'000	6.50	12.55	–	12.55	5.90	–	5.90
		%	22.0			31.2			12.7
VII (part)	Rest of mechanical engineering	'000	5.70	1.30	3.40	4.75	3.60	2.40	5.95
		%	19.3			11.8			12.8
VIII and IX	Instrument and electrical engineering	'000	0.80	0.30	0.35	0.65 [0.70]	0.65	0.45	1.10
		%	2.7			1.7			2.4
X and XI	Shipbuilding and marine engineering	'000	2.20	0.15	1.95	2.10	–	–	1.10
		%	7.4			5.2			2.4
XII	Metal goods (not elsewhere specified)	'000	1.75	0.95	0.85	1.80	1.30	1.05	2.35
		%	5.9			4.5			5.1
XIII–XIX	Other manufacturing industries	'000	0.70	–	0.70	0.70	0.10	0.40	0.45
		%	2.4			1.7			0.9
III–XX	Total manufacturing	'000	20.85	15.45	10.20	25.65 [25.70]	11.90	8.15	20.00
		%	70.4			63.9			43.1
XXII	Transport and Communication	'000	2.20	3.25	0.30	3.55	4.65	0.55	5.20
		%	7.4			8.8			11.2
XXIII	Distributive Trades	'000	1.15	1.20	0.40	1.60	1.85	0.75	2.60
		%	3.9			4.0			5.6
XXIV and XXV	Professional, Scientific Services; Insurance, Banking, Finance	'000	1.30	1.05	0.45	1.50 [1.55]	3.70	0.90	4.55
		%	4.4			3.9			9.8
XXVI	Miscellaneous Services	'000	0.85	1.45	–	1.45 [1.75]	3.90	0.25	4.10
		%	2.9			4.4			8.8
XXII to XXVI	Total Services	'000	5.50	6.90	1.15	8.10 [8.45]	14.15	2.40	16.55
		%	18.6			21.0			35.6
	Total All Industries	'000	29.60	26.65	11.35	38.00 [40.2]	35.90	10.55	46.45
		%	100			100			100

SCOTTISH ECONOMIC BULLETIN

Note: The totals for 'wholly involved' in this Table differ from those in Table 6.1 because of differences in definitions and some revisions of data.
Source: 1978 figures from Scottish Economic Bulletin No. 18.
1976 figures from Scottish Economic Bulletin No. 11 1976. Figures in brackets by deduction from Scottish Economic Bulletin No. 18. Percentages for 1976 calculated from Scottish Economic Bulletin No. 18 figures.
1974 figures by deduction from Scottish Economic Bulletin No. 11.

share of the platform and module construction yards, and the Grampian region and the Islands a disproportionately large share of the service activities. The typical pattern of oil development, and its implications for the type of employment required, are carefully documented by Lewis and McNicoll (1978), and the Scottish experience has so far proved very close to their description. The difficulties for some areas of decline are very well brought out in the report by MacDowall and Begg (1981).

Another way of seeking to analyse the local employment effects of North Sea oil-related activity is to ask how far this employment has been of incomers to the area and how far the jobs have gone to those already located there. To pose the question is immediately to raise problems of definition of what we mean by incomers and these problems can never be satisfactorily resolved. Despite these limitations, the Scottish Office has published in *Scottish Economic Bulletin*, no. 21 (Summer 1980) an analysis conducted in September 1979 of the place of origin of those working offshore on oil and gas production platforms and mobile rigs in Scottish waters.

Of those whose place of residence was known, 26 per cent lived in Grampian region, 14 per cent in Strathclyde, just under 60 per cent in total in Scotland, 33 per cent in England, and 6 per cent were from outside the UK. Of those reported as residing in Grampian, about 6 per cent appear to have a permanent place of residence elsewhere, and about 40 per cent had moved their permanent address to Grampian on or after taking up their oil-related jobs – most of these had come either from other parts of Scotland (31 per cent of them) or from the rest of the UK (44 per cent of them). So in numerical terms, though not necessarily in each skill category, most of the offshore jobs in Scottish waters are filled by Scots residents, though the English contingent is substantial. Similar figures are not available for on-shore employment, but one would expect it to be rather more closely related to the local labour force.

So far, we have outlined some of the key evidence about the local impact on employment. What of the local impact on output? The last column in Table 6.1 offers an estimate of the physical flow of oil production from what are at least arguably Scottish waters. In dealing in Chapter 2 with Scottish output, we followed what is the convention in the official analysis of UK income. This convention is to attribute to each of the regions of the UK activity which take place on its land and inland waters and to add a region labelled 'the Continental Shelf' and attribute to it all off-shore activity. So the value of the output from the North Sea (oil and gas) is assigned to the Continental Shelf and is not allocated between Scotland and, for example, regions of eastern England on the basis of some legal definition of what constitutes Scottish and what English waters. As long as there is no direct mechanism whereby Scotland receives as, for example, regional assistance, a proportion of 'her' oil production, the social accounting conviction represents quite well the true state of affairs: while Scotland has gained directly and indirectly through the employment opportunities created by the North Sea activities, she has not experienced any additional *direct* gain through the value of the output extracted.

We turn now to a brief consideration of the likely longer-term effects of oil activity on Scotland. Despite its date, much the most rigorous discussion here remains the report prepared for the Scottish Office in 1973–7 by Gaskin and MacKay (1978). The statistics have of course been updated, by the Scottish Office in *Scottish Economic Bulletin*, by various academic studies especially in the University of Aberdeen, and by the estimates of commercial bodies such as Wood MacKenzie & Co., but the changes to the fundamental arguments of the Gaskin and MacKay report have been slight.

Probably the most important long-term consideration for Scotland is the use made by the UK government of the tax and balance-of-payments windfalls represented by the existence of the oil. So far, these windfalls have not been used in any very obviously long-term advantageous way: the balance-of-payments benefits have shown most clearly in a rather high international valuation of the £ sterling and this seems to have led to problems of price competitiveness for British manufacturers; the tax benefits have accrued in an economic environment where it has proved difficult to use them to promote industrial expansion and the oil companies have claimed that the tax take in one form or another is so great that some of the smaller fields are not commercially viable. Our scepticism about the current use of the uncovenanted benefits should not, however, blind us to the opportunities they would present in a more favourable set of circumstances, and the fact remains that potentially much the most important long-term benefit to Scotland would come from a substantial improvement to the economic situation of the UK.

More readily quantifiable is the likely pattern of the future local impact on Scotland. Forecasts here depend critically on assumptions made about the nature of future discoveries of reserves – their location and their commercial viability. Geology can give us some hints about the location and possible extent of hitherto undiscovered reserves. Estimates based on geology diverge: most such estimates suggest that about half the total recoverable resources in the UK Continental Shelf have already been discovered – this is, for example, the view of the Department of Energy as quoted by Gaskin and MacKay (p. 65) – but some, such as Odell and Rosing (1974) think that these figures represent serious under-estimates of the potential. Commercial viability depends partly on the size of the field, partly on the price of the product and partly on the tax regime. The sheer difficulty of getting oil ashore from locations far below the waters of the North Sea is such that there is no chance of the average cost of production and delivery of North Sea oil being anywhere near as low as that of oil from some of the Arabian Gulf countries, despite the much greater transport distances involved. World prices of oil could therefore conceivably become so low as to make all the North Sea deposits commercially unviable.

It was argued early in the 1970s that cost of production considerations were not very important in the pricing of oil, because the cartel operated by the Organization of Petroleum Exporting Countries (OPEC) was faced with an inexorably growing demand for energy and so could expect a steadily rising real price for its oil. Between 1960 and 1973 the share of oil in world primary energy consumption rose from 36 per cent to 46 per cent, and total world primary energy consumption rose at over 6 per cent *per annum*. Between 1973 and 1979, however, primary energy consumption rose by only just over 2 per cent *per annum*, and oil's share of that total fell fractionally to 45 per cent (Pearce, 1980). How far this fall in the expansion of energy consumption, and of oil consumption in particular, is a result of the world-wide depression and how far it is a response to perceived price rises is a matter for considerable speculation, and that speculation makes forecasting future prices particularly difficult.

Reviewing the range of forecasts made, Pearce (1980) concluded: 'The few comparatively "hard" judgements that emerge are therefore that the future demand for OPEC exports is likely to exceed OPEC's willingness to supply oil. The basis for real price rises therefore exists' (p. 22). If so, there is no question but that the existing commercially viable North Sea oil fields will continue to be viable, and perhaps some that are now marginal will cross the threshold to becoming commercially worthwhile.

The other element in the calculation is the tax regime. The British government has experimented with a great variety of types of tax – indeed the sheer variety and variability has been a subject of complaints by the oil companies – broadly with the object of creaming off some of the profits on the more profitable fields whilst leaving the marginal fields relatively untaxed. Given sufficient ingenuity, and accurate information from the companies, there is no reason in principle why the tax system should affect oil output at all in the short term, although of course it is much more likely to have some long term effects through the removal of profits which they might otherwise have ploughed back into further development in the North Sea.

As our discussion has tried to indicate, there are many imponderables in trying to forecast the future levels of employment in the North Sea sector of Scotland. Gaskin and MacKay (1978) formed what is still the most plausible judgement.

It is our view that the peak level of exploration activity in Scottish waters has passed, and that although the fifth and subsequent licencing rounds may temporarily increase interest, from now on there is likely to be a slow decline in the number of exploration rigs operating. The crucial factors are the number, size and commercial viability of any oil and gas discoveries: we expect these to be less attractive and successful than hitherto, although for many areas not yet licensed it is obviously impossible to make any confident statements. Our estimates of oil and gas reserves and production are higher than official estimates and suggest considerable opportunities for downstream gas processing in Scotland (pp. 71–2).

The employment prospects therefore depend on the maintenance of the service activities – which as we have shown are already very important in total Scottish oil-related employment – and on whether any of these 'downstream' developments in gas processing and perhaps in petrochemicals get under way. In the absence of 'downstream' developments, employment in oil-related activities in Scotland can be expected to settle to a level of some 30,000 workers, of whom perhaps two-thirds will be in the Grampian region, and to stay at around that level till well into the 1990s.

The European Economic Community and Regional Policy

The overall subject of the EEC and regional policy can be approached in various ways. Firstly, it can be approached in terms of the development of EEC regional policy. Secondly, it can be examined in terms of the possible impact of joining the EEC on the evolution of the UK regional policy. Thirdly, there is the wider issue of the possible effects of economic integration on the extent of regional problems in the UK – especially the possible short-run and long-term consequences for a peripheral region such as Scotland.

Since its foundation the European Economic Community has had commitment to develop policies to reduce regional imbalances within the community. Community regional policy is still in an evolving stage but its focus is on reducing existing regional imbalances and on preventing new regional disparities. Of course the problem regions within the community do take a wide variety of forms. Community action in the field of co-ordination of regional policy dates back to June 1971. (Commission of the European Communities, Communication of the Commission on Regional Aid Systems, 23 June 1971). Earlier effort was directed towards bringing together community regional policies and individual regional policies of member states. 'The initial concern was to distinguish between central and peripheral areas of the community and to limit the discretion of member states with regard to regional incentives in the central areas.' (EEC Regional Policy and the Scottish Economy, *Scottish Economic Bulletin*, no. 18 (Summer 1979), p. 7). As the same article points out the next stage of co-ordination policy was set out in the communication on general regional aid systems in February 1975 which described the principles which were to operate for a three-year period. Five different categories of regions were distinguished in terms of the overall severity of their regional need. Various elements of the co-ordination policy identified in 1971 were also expanded.

The co-ordination principles developed in 1975 were partly re-defined in December 1978 and the methods for their implementation amended and supplemented as from 1 January 1979. The data in the *SEB* article show that Northern Ireland is in the group whose regional problems are regarded most severe, along with Ireland, 'Mezzogiorno', W. Berlin and the French Overseas Departments. Nearly the whole of Scotland falls into the second group, where maximum of net grant equivalent of initial investment cost is 30 per cent as compared to 75 per cent in the first category of regions on Ceiling 1. On the alternative scheme, Ceiling 2, grants in Scotland can be up to 40% if the cost per job is less than 5,500 e.u.a. The total value of regional assistance pro-vided to an individual project including Selective Financial Assistance and Regional Development Grants provided under the Industry Act, 1972, must not exceed one or other of these ceilings.

In terms of the specific financial arrangements the European Regional Development Fund (ERDF) was established on 18 March 1975. In establishing the Fund, it was accepted that financial induce-ment was an important element of regional policies which already operated in member states. The *SEB* article gives details of the operation of ERDF. But using the data on allocation to Scotland a brief comparison can be made with allocation under ERDF and expenditure on regional policy in Scotland. Table 6.3 gives these data. It can be seen that Scotland received a fair proportion of total grant commitments for the UK as a whole and Scotland's share in the total varied from around 27 per cent in 1975 to around 25 per cent in 1978. A comparison of allocation under ERDF to that under regional policy shows that the expenditure under ERDF is fairly small in relation to the total expenditure on regional policy in Scotland. Thus for an assisted region such as Scotland, the UK regional policy is by far the more important.

To summarise, the EEC regional policy itself is in an evolutionary stage and as the new directives emerge, these would inevitably lead to some changes in the UK regional policy and allocations under the Industry Act of 1972. Of course the UK regional policy itself is in a fairly passive phase since 1975 and thus the problems of co-ordination

Table 6.3   *Expenditure on regional policy and European Regional Development Fund: grant commitment*

	1973	1974	1975	1976	1977	1978
European Regional Development Fund[1]						
Scotland (£m)	–	–	9.8	14.6	13.9	24.8
Scotland as % of UK	–	–	27.4%	24.7%	25.2%	24.8%
Expenditure on 'special' regional policy in Scotland	102.5	136.5	206.2	223.4	162.7	153.4
Grants from European Regional Development Fund as % of gross expenditure on regional policy in Scotland	–	–	4.7%	6.5%	8.5%	16.2%

[1]ERDF was set up in 1975.
Source: Compiled from Table 5.1 and *Scottish Economic Bulletin*, no. 18 (Summer 1979).

have not been particularly acute. Nevin (in El-Agraa, 1980) points out that on the positive side, membership of the EEC should in principle increase the effectiveness of British regional policy in three separate respects.

First and most obviously, the existence of ERDF ensures the availability of resources over and above those extracted from the pockets of inevitably reluctant national taxpayers. Second, the steady development of the Community regional policy mechanism will involve the British government in an experience with which it has been unhappily unfamiliar for many decades – the necessity of formulating coherent statements of intent and forward plans concerning its regional policy and of explaining and defending those statements to the representatives of other member governments in the Regional Development Committee. Third, the insistence by the Community on the avoidance of operating subsidies, open or concealed, and on the essential aim of reducing or eliminating productive inefficiencies may well help to bring a long overdue element of economic reality into British regional policy.

As regards to the third aspect of the possible impact of integration on the peripheral region such as Scotland, the overall prediction is not difficult to obtain. As Nevin (1980) puts it,

The effect of any movement towards a customs union and *a fortiori* a common market is to reduce the extent to which its member countries can conduct their affairs as sovereign independent states and to increase the extent to which they acquire the characteristics of a single unitary economy. On strictly *a priori* grounds therefore the likely consequences for the 'problem' regions of the participating country are obvious enough (p. 236).

It would appear that increased specialisation, fiercer competition and the realisation of economies of scale is likely to accentuate rather than reduce the disequilibrating factors operating in peripheral regions. In addition, in so far as the overall impact of integration on the UK growth rate or its overall competitive position is disequilibrating, this in itself acts as a further negative feedback on a peripheral regional economy. Not only is 'active' regional policy easier to pursue in the context of growing economy but, as we pointed out in Chapter 5, in explaining the employment change in 'incomers' and 'non-incomers' and the output change, the UK growth rate in manufacturing was a significant variable. To conclude with Nevin (1980):

> On the evidence of first six or seven years of membership of the Community, the British regional problem must necessarily appear more rather than less serious and difficult than before. At the root of that conclusion lies the fundamental cause of so much of Britain's difficulties at the end of the 1970s – the failure of its productivity to keep pace with that of its neighbours and competitors (p. 255).

The Impact of Multinational Companies

There is growing literature on the general subject of external control in Scotland and in particular the possible role of multinationals in regional development. Firn (1975) showed that while over 70 per cent of manufacturing plants in Scotland were domestically owned in 1973 such plants provided only 41 per cent of employment leaving the remaining 59 per cent as the branch factory sector. He also pointed out that external control was greatest in the fastest growing industrial sectors and was concentrated in the largest enterprises. External control in this context refers to non-Scottish control and most branch plants are controlled by companies located elsewhere. We examined earlier the data on employment change which was disaggregated in terms of 'incomers' and 'indigenous' or others. These data included both the branch plants from other regions of the UK as well as those where the ultimate control lies in companies outside UK. While the general pattern of behaviour of multinationals can be expected to fit in within the overall pattern of 'branch plant syndrome' there are some additional implications of inward foreign investment in Scotland and we may review some of the literature in this area and the main conclusions of various studies. As Hood and Young (1976) point out, North American plants occupy a highly significant position in the Scottish economy. They pointed out that the number of such plants almost doubled in the ten years up to 1973 and by 1973 accounted for about 15 per cent of manufacturing employment. Forsyth's (1972) study gives the relevant data in terms of investment, output and employment and some of his findings may briefly be summarised. Table 6.4 gives employment in Scotland and the share of US-owned firms for selected years.

Table 6.4 *Employment in Scotland and the share of US-owned firms: selected years, 1950–69*

Year	Scotland (total)	US-owned as percentage of total
1950	734,500	2.8
1954	750,600	4.0
1964	720,700	7.2
1966	740,400	8.2
1969	745,500	12.3

Source: Forsyth (1972), p. 56.

It is significant to note that the relative importance of employment in the US-owned firms in total employment in Scotland started to rise in the 1960s. Forsyth's data also shows that out of the total new jobs in Scotland in manufacturing over the period 1961–9, 11.4 per cent were contributed by US new jobs and that this percentage varied for different manufacturing industries. In particular in chemical and allied; mechanical engineering; electrical engineering; textiles; and paper, printing and publishing, US new jobs as percentage of all new jobs in manufacturing were 21.3, 25.3, 12.0, 40.4, 51.9 and 48.3 per cent respectively.

Hood and Young (1976) point out that a principal consequence of the time span of this investment is its concentration in the highly scientific and technologically based industries. Thus North American plants accounted for nearly one-third of employment in the mechanical and electrical engineering sectors and 60 per cent of employment in instrument engineering. As a result, the areas of major growth potential are placed under a very significant degree of American control.

The potential further gains from inward direct foreign investment in Scotland which are generally highlighted in the literature are listed below:

(1)   The capital contributions of incoming firms may help in filling the resource gap and have a favourable effect on the balance of payments.
(2)   The provision of foreign management may fill the management and skill gap and may contribute towards the training of local managers and workers.
(3)   Transfer of technology may provide increased R and D inputs.
(4)   Indirect benefits of inward foreign investment could be significant if through purchase of intermediate inputs the level of activity in the indigenous sector is raised. If such input-ouput linkages are established over a longer time-period, then it could be an important contribution to self-sustained growth of the region.

Thus while the importance of US investment in terms of employment gains cannot be denied there are wider issues involved. The central issue is what would have happened in the absence of US foreign investment. It is fairly easy to admit that unemployment rates would have been different in the period up to 1973 in the absence of US investment. It is also possible to accept the reasoning (Hood and Young, 1976) that even if the resources used by US firms had been employed elsewhere the control of such resources may still be outside Scotland.

Forsyth concludes that

the diffusion of technological and managerial know-how is as has been pointed out, widely regarded as one of the most important benefits of inward foreign investment. In the Scottish case, however, the impact on technology and management methods seems to have been minimal, and it is probable that this is the direct result of the generally backward nature of the region's economy . . . an examination of US-owned firms in Scotland suggests strongly that they do not provide an adequate basis for subregional growth points. This is because of their low degree of integration with indigenous industry; manifested in poorly developed inter industry and inter firm linkages and information flows and the general inability of indigenous firms to internalise the external economies generated by the American firms (p. 257).

Forsyth also points out the potential for inflationary consequences of the regional policies due to the fact that leakages into other regions in these circumstances of limited internal absorptive capacity could be very large indeed. These leakages may be more important in the context of branch plants from the UK but even more so for the foreign firms.

Hood and Young (1976) examined the evidence on R and D and marketing activities of the US firms in Scotland. They conclude that

> the data presented do seem to lend some support for such fears (fears of increasing external control and potential effects of the loss of autonomy) since a majority of US firms in Scotland either undertake no R & D in Scotland or the functions delegated are not particularly meaningful. Moreover parent company controls over Marketing and R & D activities seem in general fairly tight (p. 292).

McDermott (1979) examined the evidence drawn from 51 establishments, of which 23 were under non-Scottish control. Of the total 24 firms who fell into the component category 16 were in capital equipment and 11 in instruments and computer peripheral equipment. The external-indigenous dichotomy treats all English subsidiaries as elements of multinational organisations and may obscure potential within group differences. The following hypotheses were tested using these data:

(1) The presence of multinational firms should stimulate the generation of indigenous enterprise.
(2) The presence of the multinational sector will be reflected in the development of related indigenous enterprise.
(3a) Multinational subsidiaries should be no more complex than local firms with similar proportions of technical and management staff.
(3b) Multinational subsidiaries and indigenous firms will have similarly structured environments.
(4) There will be strong linkages between multinational subsidiaries and local industrial infrastructure.
(5) There will be local firms which have reduced their dependence upon the local multinational sector and have developed external market contacts.

The first hypothesis could not be rejected completely but few Scottish firms could be traced which owed their existence to spin-off from multinational electronics firms. The second hypothesis was not rejected and the indigenous firms covered in the survey grew at the same rate as multinationals. Externally controlled firms were not found to be impeding the growth of existing indigenous enterprises. The differences between the two groups were sufficiently marked with respect to employment structure and task structure. Purchasing linkages between multinationals and Scottish suppliers were not strong. While the multinationals were an important element in the environment of indigenous firms the converse was apparently not true. McDermott emphasises that the overall question of net gain or loss attendant upon a policy of encouraging multinational investment in problem regions could not be resolved in his study. He concludes that

> in more direct policy terms it can be concluded that the requirement for a significant indigenous electronics industry has changed little since the 1950s; the development of organisations suitably structured to deal with the commercial and market environments which have to be confronted if technological ability is to be exploited successfully. Only through an adequate organisational response will the indigenous sector be able to capitalise in the long-term on the opportunities proferred for development by the presence of multinational enterprise (p. 305).

Hood, Reeves and Young (1981) analyse the European dimension of foreign direct investment in Scotland with particular reference to the method of entry used by these companies. It is important to note that, as Hood and Young point out, in 1978 manufacturing firms from continental Europe employed 14,000 people and accounted for about 14 per cent of employment in the foreign sector as compared to only 6,000 people (about 6.5 per cent) employed in the European-based foreign sector in 1973.

To summarise, briefly, their sample data showed that the acquired firms in Scotland have been fairly small. A comparison of product and market rates revealed an interesting pattern which differs from that for the UK as a whole where takeovers have been most evident in high-technology, capital-intensive sectors. In Scotland nearly half the takeovers were in food, drink and tobacco which is not a dynamic sector in terms of research intensity, etc. Hood, Reeves and Young conclude that 'all points considered, it must be concluded that "the jury is still out" when it comes to assessing the desirability of foreign takeovers for the Scottish Economy' (p. 183).

The emerging pattern of multinationals in Scotland can be summarised. It would appear that in terms of employment the gains from inward foreign investment have been perhaps greatest over the longer time-period since 1954. However, the events in most recent years highlight the uncertainties and problems that arise in a changing international and national environment and thus exacerbate the unemployment problem which tends to be somewhat more acute in the depressed regions in any case. We also noted that most studies highlighted that in terms of linkages with indigenous enterprises, research and development, contribution to the technological and skills development in the remaining sector, the potential gains appear to be more limited.

Our own analysis of Chapters 4 and 5 shows that the stimulus to manufacturing output evidenced for much of the 1961–75 period was not particularly reflected in higher than expected growth in the services sector. The regression analysis of Chapter 5 failed to yield significant coefficients for explaining employment change in services in terms of variables measuring the pressure of demand, manufacturing growth rate and other variables which were proxies for inter-industry linkages. The analysis of Chapter 3 showed that among the manufacturing industries: food, drink and tobacco; electrical engineering; timber and furniture; and 'other manufacturing' were the industry groups exhibiting relative fast growth in output per worker. The overall growth in productivity in manufacturing was relatively faster in 1963–71 and in 1975–8.

Forsyth (1972) and a recent study of labour performance of US-owned plants in Scotland (Scottish Development Agency, September 1979) analyse data on overall labour performance in the US-owned plants. The Scottish Development Agency examined the labour performance in US-owned plants in terms of absenteeism, labour turnover, labour stability and productivity. From the data examined, 72 per cent of firms recorded absenteeism below 8 per cent. The weighted average for 57,000 workers surveyed was 7.2 per cent. Turnover of labour was well in line with firms' expectations. 5.6 per cent of plants reported under 10 per cent. In terms of productivity, labour productivity was considered to be good or very good, and the Scottish workforce fared well in international comparisons. The quality of output was also found to be very good. More rigorous analysis of labour performance in the foreign owned sector is needed to identify the various explanatory factors.

In overall terms, it is difficult to disagree with McDermott's (1979) proposition that 'unless it can be demonstrated that long-term damage to the Scottish economy has resulted from this, it would be difficult to argue for any change to the policies which have encouraged such investment' (p. 303). However, what is arguable is not so much the reversal from the policies which encourage inward foreign investment, but the most desirable approach for inducing such investment that incorporates some safeguards on the wider welfare considerations.

Scottish Trade: the Input–Output Evidence

One of the characteristics of an economic region, as we saw in Chapter 1, is its dependence on trade outside its borders. In a country which is economically advanced, one would expect that the more narrowly an area is defined, the more dependent it would be on trade with other areas: so, for example, it is likely that Dundee is more dependent on trade outside its borders than is Scotland as a whole, and that a suburb of Dundee will be more dependent on trade outside its boundaries than is Dundee itself. To some extent, then, the amount of trade in an economy – its openness – is a function simply of some indicator of economic size. There is, however, obviously more to it than that, as even a small economy can choose to pursue the target of self-sufficiency if it so wishes. Further, dependence on trade does not of itself mean that a small economy lacks autonomy: it will surrender autonomy if it becomes very specialised in one product or in a small group of products where it does not have enough monopoly to influence world prices, and it will surrender autonomy if it chooses to concentrate its trade into the markets of a single country or a group of countries much larger than itself.

It had long been suspected from casual observation that Scotland fitted the picture of an economically dependent region in her trading relationships with the rest of the UK, but decisive evidence on the matter was hard to find before the completion of a special input-output study for 1973. The international trading patterns of a country with its own currency and its own tax regimes are normally fairly well known, because the movement of goods and of currency across its borders is monitored as part of the customs and foreign exchange mechanisms. For these reasons, something is known year-to-year about Scotland's overseas trade in so far as that trade takes the form of movements into and out of Scottish seaports and airports. But there is no mechanism that automatically records the flow of goods between Scotland and other parts of the UK, and so some goods exported from Scotland, for example, to the Continent, transported by road to the channel ports, would not appear in the record as Scotland's foreign trade, and similarly goods imported to England and Wales whose ultimate destination is Scotland would not be registered as Scottish imports. So port returns are of limited value even for measuring overseas trade. It should be noted, however, that HM Customs and Excise do now attempt to identify the inland origins and destinations of UK non-fuel international freight: the first such comprehensive survey was carried out for 1978, and its results for Scotland are described in *Scottish Economic Bulletin*, no. 22 (Spring 1981). Much more acute is the problem that they give no record at all of exports from Scotland to the rest of the UK or of imports to Scotland from elsewhere in the UK. No other regularly collected statistical series helps here either. To identify Scottish trade flows, a special study was needed.

That special study was undertaken for the year 1973, as part of the

Scottish input–output tables. We have referred briefly in Chapter 2 to the social accounting implications of these tables: while in terms of social accounting they are of little interest, on the whole creating more problems of reconciliation with other evidence than the light they cast, the tables are invaluable to a study of Scotland's trade and the similar study currently being undertaken for 1979 should be at least as useful in giving some basis for time-period studies. As things stand, the 1973 evidence has always to be interpreted with the proviso that we have no means of knowing how representative that year is, or what is the likely implication of the sampling errors inherent in the exercise.

The 1973 tables are compiled from information supplied to the sponsoring bodies – IBM United Kingdom Scientific Centre, the Scottish Council Research Institute, and the Fraser of Allander Institute for Research into the Scottish Economy. The data was collected from government and other public agencies (with 100 per cent coverage) and from a sample survey of Scottish establishments (coverage there was in some cases fairly low in terms of number of establishments, though not in terms of employment). The respondents were required to complete a questionnaire designed to identify the amount and the origin of all their inputs and the amount and the destination of all their outputs. Once the establishments were assigned to industries, their input and output flows could be aggregated by industry, to enable the construction of tables which identify for each industry what kind of inputs it bought from Scotland, industry by industry, and what it bought from the rest of the UK and from the rest of the world, and similarly what outputs it sold to each industry in Scotland and what it sold to the rest of the UK and to the rest of the world. It is, then, a fairly straightforward matter to use the input–output table to construct a picture of Scotland's trade, with the rest of the UK and with the rest of the world. The evidence is presented initially in the input–output table reports, from which Table 6.5 is constructed, and discussed in Draper and McNicoll (1979).

Table 6.5 shows clearly the importance of trade to the Scottish economy. For primary goods – agriculture forestry and fishing, and mining and quarrying – imports, mainly from the rest of the world, were over half as much as total Scottish output, and nearly 20 per cent of Scottish output was exported, predominantly to the rest of the UK. In the metal goods group – the metal and engineering industries – exports were crucial for Scotland, nearly three-quarters of Scottish output being exported, mainly to the rest of the UK. At the same time, imports from the rest of the UK were equivalent to about 57 per cent of home production. Other manufactured goods show the same kind of pattern: well over half the Scottish output was exported, and nearly the same quantity imported, in both cases the major market being the rest of the UK. (The importance of the rest of the UK as an export

market here is perhaps a little surprising: by far the biggest trade item in the input–output table is for exports of whisky and other drinks to the rest of the world, at £234.6 million.) Trade in the public utilities sector was insignificant – the only trade being the sale of electricity to the rest of the UK – and as might be expected it was not very important in services either. As the last line in the table shows, however, in aggregate 23 per cent of Scottish output was exported, and nearly 15 per cent of Scottish output was sold to the rest of the UK. Imports accounted for nearly 25 per cent of total domestic output, and the rest of the UK was even more important in that total, providing Scotland with the equivalent of 17½ per cent of her domestic output. Overall, Scotland was running at a slight trade surplus in her dealings with the rest of the world, but at a distinct deficit in her dealings with the rest of the UK.

To make the table comprehensible, the evidence in it is presented in a very aggregated form. Draper and McNicoll (1979) deal with the evidence at industry level, and using the criterion of proportion of exports to total domestic industry output identify the export dependence of Scottish industries. As they show, on this criterion vehicles and aerospace; electrical engineering; textiles and clothing; miscellaneous manufacture; shipbuilding; and drink and tobacco stand out as exporting over two-thirds of their output. As they conclude

> The export column . . . demonstrates clearly the export dependence of key Scottish industries and the classically open nature of her economy. Such dependence emphasizes the heavy reliance of the Scottish economy on external markets. These figures . . . raise serious questions as to the stability of these industries in changing world conditions, and in particular emphasize the need to examine critically changes in trading relationships with England (and the EEC) which might arise through constitutional changes. Several of the above industries, notably textiles, shipbuilding and vehicles are already suffering from intense foreign competition in relatively static markets (p. 30).

Further, as Draper and McNicoll suggest but do not clearly identify, not only is Scotland in the sense they suggest a very open economy, but she is also an economy very closely linked in trade with a larger near neighbour, and thus the general considerations we raised in Chapter 1 about the limited scope for economic decision-making clearly apply. Even if Scotland were institutionally able to pursue her own monetary and fiscal policy, she could not without serious problems break the trading links between her and England, and thus the Scottish economy would have to be managed in such a way that Scottish exporters could sell their goods to England in much the same volumes and at much the same (Scottish) prices as before, and that Scottish importers could buy materials from England on much the same terms as before: and that in turn entails that to keep their currencies related the two countries would have to adopt similar budgetary and monetary stances. To lose Scottish markets would be uncomfortable but not crucial for England. To lose English markets would, as Table 6.5 clearly suggests, be very damaging indeed to Scotland's manufacturers. Further, if England is in an economic depression, then the major market for Scotland's goods is depressed, and so the usual multiplier effect will spread the depression to Scotland, and again because England is proportionately so much bigger the reverse argument does not apply so forcefully. Again the conclusion has to be to question the scope for independent action to affect the Scottish economy.

There is one more consideration we think it appropriate to raise here. Draper and McNicoll (1979) draw attention to the implication that the open nature of the Scottish economy may have served to dissipate the intentions of regional policy. The usual justification for concentrating regional policy so heavily on manufacturing industry is that in that way the multiplier effects – the first expenditure is reflected in second-round expenditure, which in turn is reflected in the third round, and so on – are as high as possible. The smaller the size of the multiplier, the greater are the leakages of demand from the economy, and one such kind of leakage is imports. If, as Table 6.5 and the tables Draper and McNicoll construct suggest, something of the order of 50 per cent of total demand in some manufacturing industries is met by imports, the leakages are then very high. On that criterion regional policy directed towards the services would be much more effective, because the leakages into imports there are so much smaller. We have seen in Chapter 5 that the spin-off to services from regional policy directed towards manufacturing has been very slight: it would be interesting if a government were brave enough to offer regional incentives to service industries to see if the spin-off into manufacturing was significant.

The Role of Governmental Institutions

In this section, we consider the possible roles of Scottish governmental and quasi-governmental institutions in influencing the economic performance of Scotland. In Chapter 1, we outlined the administrative framework, but said very little about the economic agencies and what powers they have. We turn to this question now.

Scottish Office

As we have already indicated, Scotland has its own administrative structure in the form of the secretary of state for Scotland and the civil servants under his control. The secretary of state is not responsible for all the civil-service employees in Scotland: Pottinger (1979) points out that of the approximately 64,000 civil servants employed in Scotland, the Scottish Office employed 9,300. The vast majority, then, are in branches of UK departments, such as the Departments of Health and Social Security and of Employment, which happen to be located in Scotland. At first sight, this might suggest that the powers of the secretary of state even in Scotland do not extend very widely, but such an impression is deceptive: as Pottinger (1979) put it, the civil servants outwith the formal control of the secretary of state 'are for the most part concerned with the execution rather than the shaping of policy. They take their instructions from headquarters in Whitehall, but their senior officers also maintain close contact with the Scottish Office, particularly in the many matters which involve local authorities' (p. 21).

Within the Scottish Office, there is one department, the Scottish Economic Planning Department (SEPD), which is the main economic service. The list of its responsibilities is extensive:

Coordination of North Sea oil policy; oil research and intelligence; applications to European regional development fund; liaison with ports, aircraft, steel and shipbuilding industries; relationships with the Scottish Development Agency. Liaison with the Manpower Services Commission; careers service, policy and administration. Economic and statistical advice. Selective financial assistance to industry – policy and casework; promotion of industrial expansion and inward investment; export promotion; information to small firms.

Electricity: relations with the two Scottish electricity boards. Energy policy.

New Towns: relations with the Development Corporations.

Highland development and tourism: policy relations with Highlands and Islands Development Board and Scottish Tourist Board.

Coordination of Scottish Office interests in the Scottish construction industry (Drucker and Drucker, 1979, p. 173).

Some of the other departments of the Scottish Office also have some economic responsibilities – for example, the Department of Agriculture and Fisheries for Scotland look after the various agriculture and fishing subsidy schemes, and there are economic aspects of the Scottish Development Department's work on physical planning, but the main economic responsibilities rest with the SEPD.

The SEPD as such is a relatively recent creation – it was formed in 1973 – but Scottish Office responsibility for many of its functions goes much further back. When the Scottish Office structure was reorganised in 1939, to form the four main departments it was recognised that in addition to the functions specific to those departments (Agriculture, Education, Health and Home) there was a more general role for the secretary of state in promoting Scotland's interests. These more general functions were described in the Gilmore Report of 1936 as 'penumbral', perhaps, as Milne (1957) suggests 'because they are carried out in that twilight world where more than one Government department operates and the responsibilities of each are difficult to distinguish' (p. 173). It is in this penumbral area that the most important aspect of the economic activities of the secretary of state lie, as Scotland's interests have in practice been identified with the promotion of industrial growth.

Specific action within the Scottish Office to promote industrial growth dates to the Second World War, when an industry division was created within the Scottish Home Department, and was given the responsibility for preparing an annual white paper on the prospects for the Scottish economy. Looking at the administrative structure in 1961, the Toothill Report by the Scottish Council (Development and Industry) listed the prevailing allocation between departments of economic responsibilities and concluded

> This distribution of responsibilities does not seem to us to be well calculated to promote the co-ordination of activities related to economic development. We do not think that these activities could satisfactorily be brought under any one of the existing departments. It seems to us that the importance of these subjects warrants the creation of a new department which would be responsible for those functions of the Secretary of State most closely related to economic affairs (p. 176).

Although there was some reorganisation of the economic functions in 1962 this was in practice to divide them between two bodies, the Scottish Home and Health Department and the Scottish Development Department, with industrial development being assigned to the Scottish Development Department along with various physical planning functions. Co-ordination between departments within the Scottish Office was supposed to be achieved by the Scottish Development Group. Thinking in the mid 1960s favoured the formulation of economic strategic plans, and two such plans were prepared for Scotland.

The first, in 1963, was a White Paper *Central Scotland: a Programme for Development and Growth*, which argued for the promotion of growth areas. The second arose out of the Department of Economic Affairs' National Plan of 1965: in 1966 there was published *The Scottish Economy 1965-1970: A Plan for Expansion*, which traced out the implications for Scotland of the growth targets for Britain in the National Plan, and looked at the consequences for the regions of Scotland. In attempting to put together, on the same footing, information about the economic sub-regions of Scotland, the 1966 plan pioneered the more recent actions of the Scottish Office to co-ordinate the economic aspirations of local authorities, but the broad-sweep economic planning approach embodied in the style of the report has passed out in fashion in favour of concentration on industrial strategy for individual industries.

When the SEPD did come into existence as a department in its own right, it inherited many of its functions from activities already conducted in the Scottish Office, particularly in the Scottish Development Department. One of what is in practice the most important functions of the SEPD – its responsibilities for selective assistance under the framework of the Industry Act of 1972 – had not been exercised anywhere in the Scottish Office. The administration of the various schemes of regional assistance, whose effects we have discussed in Chapter 5, was undertaken for the whole of Britain by the Departments of Trade and Industry and their predecessors. It was only in 1975 that this responsibility was transferred to the secretary of state for Scotland.

The list of functions of the SEPD appears impressive, even if we discount those involving coordinations with other bodies (and as we shall see later, when we look at the Scottish Development Agency and the Highlands and Islands Development Board, even coordination can involve considerable practical responsibilities). What, however, do they amount to in practice? The views of the person who in the important period of 1976–9 was Secretary of State for Scotland are clear and interesting.

Describing the changes in the secretary of state's functions in and after 1975, Bruce Millan observes that before 1975

> the Secretary of State's actual powers in the fields of industry and the economy were extremely limited. As the 1969 memorandum stated, 'the arrangements (were) without prejudices to the primary responsibility of the other Ministers concerned'.
>
> The situation in respect of industry was radically changed when, in 1975, the function of providing selective assistance for industry under the Industry Act 1972 was transferred from the Department of Industry to the Secretary of State. His industrial role was enhanced by the establishment of the Scottish Development Agency at the end of 1975 and another significant accretion of powers came in 1977 when the Secretary of State became jointly responsible, with the Employment Secretary and the Welsh Secretary, for the Manpower Services Commission.

I do not think the full significance of these changes has yet been properly appreciated in Scotland. In Whitehall there is no shortage of 'consultation' or 'liaison', but whether at Civil Service or Ministerial level, power depends essentially on responsibility. A Minister's power is immeasurably increased when he has actual responsibility for a function rather than just an interest in it. Of course, it would be foolish to claim that the Secretary of State has, on general issues of industrial policy, a role as important as that of the Secretary of State for Industry and a lot will depend on his relationship with the Industry Secretary and his political clout, or lack of it, in Cabinet. However, he *is* an industrial minister and will be actively involved in the determination of industrial policy in a way which would not be possible if he was a Ministerial 'outsider' (Millan, 1981, pp. 98–9).

Millan goes on to review examples of the specific industrial intervention that is the responsibility of the secretary of state.

The role of the Scottish Office in the Chrysler rescue in 1975 – with several thousand jobs at stake at Linwood – was crucial. I doubt if even the most energetic Department of Industry intervention would have kept the Marathon yard at Clydebank open when it went repeatedly to the brink of closure but, as Secretary of State, I was able to mount successive rescue operations (p. 99).

The points Millan is making are twofold. First, the secretary of state for Scotland does, through the SEPD, have a very active role in industrial policy in Scotland. Second, and, as we shall see, even more important, as a member of Cabinet he can try to affect UK industrial policy, drawing on his Scottish experience. If, as we shall suggest, the freedom of action of Scottish institutions is closely constrained by UK policy, then any tempering of the UK policy to suit Scottish interests is of major significance.

In industrial policy it is, then, clear that the SEPD executes important functions. On matters of more general economic policy, the functions of the secretary of state and of his civil servants are much more restricted. The apparatus of advice and consultation is there: a group of professors of economics at Scottish universities operates as a panel of economic consultants and meets with the secretary of state; and the Scottish Economic Council – selected to represent industry, trade unions, the banks, nationalised industries and other groups – also meets regularly with the secretary of state and advises him. His civil servants in the SEPD, particularly in its economics and statistics unit, provide him with an excellent information service and prepare useful analyses (some of which, in *Scottish Economic Bulletin*, have been used by us in the preparation of this book). But at the end of the day he can do very little to influence UK macro-economic policy. As Millan puts it:

> While, therefore, the Secretary of State (like Ministers in other Departments), can be briefed on major economic issues as they arise and can use his experience of the discussions in the Scottish Economic Council and elsewhere in forming his views, in practice major economic decisions are dominated by Treasury Ministers . . . This does not mean that there is no real Cabinet discussion, nor that no one puts forward different, or contrary views. Nor does it mean that policy is not modified in ways which the Treasury do not like. It does remain true however, that a Chancellor of the Exchequer who has the Prime Minister's support is likely to get his way in most things. In view of his crucial role in the Government he could hardly operate without full Prime Ministerial support. The combination of Chancellor and Prime Minister is, therefore, a formidable one (p. 107).

The implications, therefore, are that in matters of macro-economic policy the secretary of state for Scotland stands in the same position as any other 'spending' minister. He can put his case to show why the Scottish Office should be treated in some exceptional way, but he has very little influence over the overall budgetary stance of the UK or over how much is to be made available to the 'spending' ministers. This is despite the fact that he has at his disposal many sources from which he can draw evidence of how the Scottish economy is faring and of what the needs of that economy are. Except through the industrial strategy, he can do very little to change things.

The Scottish Development Agency
The Scottish Development Agency (SDA) was established in 1975, as one of three agencies with the remit of development of peripheral areas of the UK (the other agencies were for Wales and for Northern Ireland). The objectives of the SDA were explained in the SDA evidence to the Wilson Committee as being 'the furthering of economic development, the provision, maintenance or safeguarding of employment, the promotion of industrial efficiency and international competitiveness, and the furthering of environmental improvement.' (Wilson Committee, Vol. 6, 1978, p. 153.) As we shall see, concepts of precisely how these objectives are to be achieved and of their relative importance have changed even during the relatively short period that the SDA has been in existence.

It was envisaged right from the start that the SDA should co-operate with other agencies. This co-operation has taken the form of

UK agencies minimising their activities in Scotland – for example, the National Enterprise Board (NEB) whose area of influence stated in the 1975 Industry Act clearly covers all of the UK, has been required in its guidelines of 1976 to

> develop effective arrangements for consultation and collaboration with the Scottish . . . Development Agenc(y). These arrangements shall be such as to ensure that the NEB consult the Agenc(y) before taking action on proposals affecting companies with significant interests in Scotland . . . The Agenc(y) will take the initiative in dealing with companies which are wholly or predominantly of concern to (it) but will consult the NEB if necessary (Wilson Committee, Vol. 4, 1978, p. 17).

Within Scotland, the SDA's sphere of influence has been defined to avoid undesirable overlaps with the Highlands and Islands Development Board (HIDB) and to ensure positive co-operation with the economic development section of the Scottish Office. The co-operation with the Scottish Office is built in primarily by the arrangement whereby the SDA is not responsible for administering the various grants available, under the 1972 Industry Act, for companies investing in certain selected industries or in Development or Special Development Areas. Discussion in the Wilson Committee of the SDA evidence considered at several stages the relationship between the SDA and the Scottish Office's Scottish Economic Planning Department. 'The great majority of the cases we [the SDA] handle involve also Industry Act money and selective financial assitance, and therefore will, to a greater or lesser extent, be discussed with the Scottish Economic Planning Department' (Wilson Committee, Vol. 6, 1978, p. 191), and later,

> it is more sensible for us . . . to be the basic investor and for them (the Industry Act agents) to be, if you like, the giver. They are in many cases giving grants, interest-relief grants; and in some cases giving limited-term loans, often at reduced rates of interest. Their money is, in practical terms, softer than ours and their criteria are slightly different, in that they are very much tied to the number of jobs and we, despite the references to employment in our statute, do not interpret jobs as the only, or even the immediately dominant, consideration that we must have regard to. We are interested, of course, in employment, which is part of what it is about; but in employment in the longer term and on a more solid basis. Industry Act money is shorter term, shorter perspective money as a rule (op. cit. p. 196).

Perhaps equally important, the SDA requires the explicit approval of
the secretary of state for Scotland for expenditure on any one project
which exceeds specified limits.

The resources made available to the SDA are quite considerable. It
had at March 1980 717 members of staff, mainly based in Glasgow. It
has an upper limit to the total committed budget of £700 million. In
1978/79 it spent £67.2 million (£12.9 per head of the Scottish
population). As clearly documented by Yuill and Allen (1981), that
makes the SDA one of the largest regional development agencies in
Europe: although dwarfed by the main Italian agencies, the SDA is
very big by the standards of the rest of Western Europe, both in
staffing and in resources. How it has deployed its staff, and how it has
spent its resources, have changed over time, partly because of its
growth process and partly in response to changing political concepts
of how best to promote development. Initially, the SDA's role was
very much to respond to proposals brought to it, but latterly it has
exercised more initiative, to the extent of formulating three-year
rolling plans on matters such as the number of jobs to be created, the
area of factory space to be constructed or acquired, and the number of
new projects to be attracted. In the provision of factory space, the
SDA operated initially extensively through local authorities, but it has
increasingly proceeded under its own auspices – so that in 1979/80 it
spent £30 million on factory provision itself, and lent only £0.3 million
to local authorities for that purpose.

In terms of annual expenditure, much the most important activities
of the SDA are the provision of factories and industrial estates, and
work on urban and land renewal for industrial development. These
two activities in recent years accounted for nearly 90 per cent of the
total annual expenditure. But the SDA's own concept of its important
functions lays much more stress on the financial assistance and more
general information and guidance it can provide to existing and
potential business. The financial assistance can come in the form of
loans, on their own or, more frequently, accompanied by the purchase
of equity shareholding. Explaining to the Wilson Committee its policy
about equity shareholding, the SDA made it clear that in its view
'there is an equity gap, with uneven edges, which becomes sharper
with small size, unconvincing management, apparent risk, and short
history' (Wilson Committee, Vol. 6, 1978, p. 162). The problem, then,
is rarely just financial; even for small firms, there are also other
elements involved. The SDA is charged in its lending and equity
investment to observe something close to commercial criteria: thus, in
lending it is required to charge a rate of interest at least equal to that
paid by firms 'of good standing', and in its financial dealings it is
supposed to aim at an 'adequate' return on capital employed 'whilst
being prepared, having regard to its wider purposes of development

and the creation of employment, to wait longer for a return than a private investor would' (op. cit. p. 154). The interpretation that the SDA has put on this is perhaps best illustrated by the comment made by the SDA Chairman to the Wilson Committee when pressed on the extent of SDA support to 'lame ducks' 'if . . . a project came to us and the only, but quite considerable, defect lay in the field of management we would feel that nevertheless we would have to try to do something about it, by persuasion or leverage or whatever other means we could find, to bring about a filling of the management gap' (op. cit. p. 194).

The general information and guidance is very much in this area of improvement of management. This was undertaken initially through the Small Business Division, and thus restricted to smaller enterprises, but now the SDA provides its management advice through the Industry Services Division, available to concerns of all sizes. Of the further services the SDA has provided for some time perhaps the most important are its work, through the Small Business Division, in promoting sub-contracting and its attempts to attract industrial investment to Scotland from the rest of the UK and from overseas (now through Locate in Scotland, a joint SDA–Scottish Office activity). The SDA's functions were redefined most recently in January 1980, when the main change, in line with central government policy towards industry, was to stress the desirability of the 'privatisation' of the Agency's activities wherever possible; by the SDA's selling its assets to the private sector as soon as commercially possible; and by its being charged particularly to try to encourage private investment.

Because the SDA has been in existence for only a fairly short period; because even in that time it has experienced some fairly sharp changes in objective; and because for much of that time it has been working against an environment that was becoming increasingly hostile to business investment (particularly in manufacturing), its success cannot yet be assessed. It has certainly built or redeveloped a lot of factories – it is the largest industrial landlord in Scotland – and its financial support has preserved some jobs in the short period. The real test, however, is how successful the SDA is in providing long-term development, and we cannot offer any judgement about that until there is some substantial upturn in the economic fortunes of Scotland. It would be quite unreasonable to expect the SDA itself to generate such an upturn: the SDA will have cause to congratulate itself if the upturn is more marked in Scotland than one might reasonably expect and, especially, if the higher level of industrial activity is sustained more firmly than would otherwise be the case.

The Highlands and Islands Development Board
By dealing separately with the problems of the Highlands and Islands

this book might appear to lay itself open to the change of lack of proportion: whilst the Highlands and Islands represent a large part of the area of Scotland, they have been of little economic importance except, as we have seen earlier in this chapter, in absorbing the North Sea oil boom. In quantitative terms, this accusation is undoubtedly true, but the economic problems of the remote rural areas of Scotland (illustrated most clearly by the Highlands and Islands, but relevant also for the Borders and Dumfries and Galloway regions) are analytically interesting and, more relevantly for this book, have proved empirically intractable.

In Table 6.6, we illustrate the diversity of employment structure within Scotland. Without wishing in any way to suggest that either the pattern for Scotland as a whole or that for any particular region is ideal, we nevertheless suggest that it is apparent that the structural differences are sufficiently great to cause some questions to be germane. Most obviously, there is the issue of the importance of manufacturing. We have already alluded to the argument of Bacon and Eltis (1976) that 'deindustrialisation' which can be translated more or less into 'location of low proportion of total employment in manufacturing' is a danger sign for a developed economy. On that criterion the Highland region and the three Island regions (Orkney, Shetland and the Western Isles) all stand out clearly as having under 20 per cent of their total employment in manufacturing, although on that criterion the other two areas of low population, the Borders and Dumfries and Galloway, look quite well placed.

If we take a large proportion of employment in the primary sector as an indication of lack of development, the Borders, Dumfries and Galloway, Fife and Orkney are conspicuous, with 10 per cent or more of their employment in the primary sector. In the public utilities sector, there is little that can be said when it is appreciated that the effects of oil-related developments are part of the explanation for the extraordinarily high figures for Shetland and to some extent for the figures recorded for the Grampian, Highland, Orkney and Western Island areas. The high figures for service employment in the Lothian region is attributable to the presence there of the administrative capital of Scotland. To North Sea oil can be attributed at least part of the high service sector employment in the Highlands and the Western Isles.

If, then, we put together the conclusions we can draw from Table 6.6, it is apparent that of the rural areas the Borders appears to have a reasonably balanced employment structure except, perhaps, for a little too much concentration on agriculture (and, within manufacturing, on woollens but the table is not refined enough to show the more detailed structure); much the same is true of Dumfries and Galloway, though the dependence on agriculture is more marked there; in the

Table 6.6 *The regional structure of Scottish employment in 1977*

	Primary		Manufacturing		Public utilities		Services		Total number
	'000	% of total	'000	% of total	'000	% of total	'000	% of total	'000
Borders	4.2	10.9	14.2	37.0	3.1	8.1	16.9	44.0	38.4
Central	3.5	3.3	37.5	35.4	10.4	9.8	54.6	51.5	106.0
Dumfries and Galloway	6.3	12.3	12.4	24.3	5.3	10.4	27.1	53.0	51.1
Fife	12.6	10.0	42.3	33.7	10.5	8.4	60.3	48.0	125.7
Grampian	14.7	8.2	38.3	21.5	19.0	10.6	106.5	59.7	178.5
Highland	4.2	5.8	11.6	15.9	11.3	15.5	46.0	62.9	73.1
Lothian	12.7	3.9	67.9	21.0	26.9	8.3	215.3	66.7	322.8
Strathclyde	17.5	1.8	342.4	34.5	87.2	8.8	545.6	55.0	992.7
Tayside	7.2	4.5	45.5	28.4	13.9	8.7	93.7	58.5	160.3
Orkney	0.8	13.6	0.5	8.5	0.8	13.6	3.8	64.4	5.9
Shetland	0.4	4.7	1.1	12.8	2.3	26.7	4.8	55.8	8.6
Western Isles	0.3	4.2	1.1	15.3	1.1	15.3	4.7	65.3	7.2
Scotland	8.5	4.1	6.5	29.7	19.2	9.3	117.9	56.9	2,071.0

Source: *Scottish Abstract of Statistics*, no. 10 (1981).

Highlands there is very little manufacturing and perhaps too much service employment, and the three Island areas all show a very low employment in manufacturing with, in the case of Orkney, a very high share of agriculture and, for both Orkney and the Western Isles, a perhaps dangerous dependence on service employment.

What this discussion of employment structures has shown most clearly is, however, the coexistence within Scotland of areas of quite diverse employment structure. When one group of areas is heavily urbanised and based on manufacturing, and another group of areas is rural and based on agriculture and services, we approach the situation described in economic theory as that of a 'dual' economy. Theoretical analysis of dual economies suggests that there may be great dangers to the continued viability of the rural economy, as it loses population impatient of the poor facilities and limited employment opportunities offered and attracted to the 'bright lights' of an urbanised way of life. Whether influenced by economic theorists or whether simply responding to what they perceive to be the case, politicians have devoted much time and effort to trying to ameliorate the economic problems of the Highlands and Islands, and the Highlands and Islands Development Board is but one, albeit the most obvious, manifestation of such concern.

Specific responsibilities for the Highlands had long been part of the remit for Scottish Office, in the form of assistance to crofters and of arrangements to ensure the continuance of ferry and other shipping services, and a Highlands Advisory Panel was created within the Scottish Office to coordinate the exercise of these responsibilities and more generally to keep the development of the Highlands under review. This mechanism was felt to be unsatisfactory, however, because it lacked clear executive machinery with powers to initiate and sustain economic development, and eventually the Highlands and Islands Development Board (HIDB) was set up in 1965. It was not intended as a substitute for existing agencies – for example, the Crofters Commission still looks after crofting arrangements, and the existing functions of Scottish Office departments remained in the Scottish Office and were not transferred to the new Board. Instead, the HIDB was given what was in effect a new job – to promote development generally but especially in industry, by the giving of grants and loans or by acquiring equity in new or existing companies. In the words of the Highlands and Islands Development (Scotland) Act 1965 which created the HIDB, its object was to assist 'the people of the Highlands and Islands to improve their economic and social conditions'. The HIDB then has a broad remit and because there is no parallel body elsewhere in the UK (and because the amount of finance it needs in UK terms is very small) it has been allowed unusually wide scope to pioneer some interesting experiments.

To understand what the HIDB has done, we need first to identify what characterises the problems it has been attempting to overcome.

Sparseness of population and the very small size of the majority of settlements (there are only four towns with populations of 8,000 or more) creates quite distinct problems for economic activity of any kind – external economies and economies of scale and of proximity to markets and suppliers of specific skills are all lacking. Within the Highlands and Islands it is common for the distance between 'adjacent' communities with populations of only a few hundreds to be twenty or more miles, and many communities of the Highlands and Islands are separated from the mass markets of the Scottish Central belt (itself a suboptimal market when measured against the scale necessary for some modern technologies) by 200 miles or more (Alexander, 1981, pp. 74–5).

Add to these concepts of distance an understanding that, despite considerable development efforts in recent years, the road system in the Highlands is poor, and the money cost and, perhaps even more important, time cost, inhibitions on industrial development become clear.

In some respects, the HIDB's activities look much like those of any development agency. Thus, the annual reports list, among other tables, the nature and amount of financial assistance made available and the corresponding employment created; so, for example, in 1971–9, at 1979 prices, the total of grants made by the Board was £35.4 million, and loans and share purchases represented another £52.2 million. This was reckoned as responsible for creating 14,070 jobs, and for retaining another 4,090 jobs, at a 'grant equivalence' cost of £2,800 per job. Of the total expenditure, the biggest share (nearly half) was on tourism, despite the relatively high cost of assistance there (£5,300 per job). The lowest cost per job was for manufacturing – at £1,400 per job – and manufacturing accounted for around a fifth of total assistance. In other respects, however, the HIDB has been a very unorthodox body.

The background to this unorthodoxy is well explained by the HIDB's former Chairman.

The approach of the HIDB to its development task takes four forms: the *responsive* role, the *fostering* role, the *research* role and the *lobbying* role. In its responsive role the Board reacts to the initiative of commercial enterprises by helping to provide capital and in a variety of other ways . . . In adopting the fostering role, the Board will for example, bring together an appropriate mix of people, a product or products, money and probably several other factors, which can combine to form the basis of a business venture. Experience demonstrates that the central resource in development is not money, not land, not ideas, not plans, but *people* with the relevant attributes and skills . . . Research activity plays a very important role in the work of the HIDB, exploring the possibilities and practicalities of development in the region (ibid.).

By the lobbying role, Alexander means the efforts of the HIDB to set up community initiatives.

> In the relatively egalitarian social structure of a crofting community, or indeed of most of the rural communities of the Highlands and Islands, individual initiative pushed beyond a certain level may meet community resistance rather than attract community support. Very often communal action is judged to be more appropriate, both socially and culturally, perhaps because it is seen as less socially divisive. A strong sense of community is generated through work and mutual help arrangements associated with work (op. cit. p. 77).

In practical form, the fostering and lobbying functions have produced results most strikingly in the form of community co-operatives. These are, as might be expected, very small in scale, but interesting in concept. By October 1980 nine such co-operatives were in existence, and a further five at the planning stage. The production aims of co-operatives are diverse – embracing traditional activities like servicing tourist trade and extensions on those activities like fish processing, mechanical peat-cutting, and craft production. Their financial arrangement is that members have to subscribe a minimum shareholding – between £20 and £50 – and each cooperative has a share subscription target. The HIDB support the co-operatives with a £ for £ grant matching local funds, by providing specific assistance with equipment and with training for the co-operative staff, and, more crucially, by fostering the initial establishment of the co-operatives. Official initiatives of this nature are to some extent based on Irish experience, but are without parallel in the economic development framework of the UK.

The specific problems the HIDB was set up to try to solve were those of the economic decline of the Highlands and Islands – low income (by Scottish standards) and population emigration. These problems were in economies which had been more or less bypassed by industrial development, remaining agricultural in employment structure. The successes of the HIDB is hard indeed to measure, because the time when the HIDB reasonably could be expected to start to produce some results was also the time when oil-related employment really started to become significant in much of its area. The evidence in the

HIDB reports suggest that at least some of the recent relative prosperity in the areas of its influence is due to the HIDB itself – both in the relatively small schemes we have looked at in detail and in its more ambitious large-scale developments such as those at Fort William – but the real test will come as the Highlands and some of the Islands have to adapt to the decline in oil-related jobs. Accommodating its policies in such a way as to replace the oil employment will test to the full the considerable ingenuity so far displayed by the Board.

Constraints

At various points in our discussion of these governmental and quasi-governmental institutions, we have alluded to the limitations on their freedom of action because of the extent to which they are constrained directly or indirectly to operate in consistence with UK government policy. In this section we propose to outline the nature of those constraints.

In Chapter 1, when we sketched the rationale of region policy, we stressed that regional policy can appear to be in accord with the aims and interests of government macro-economic policy if the role of regional policy is conceived as that of relieving congestion and bringing into use resources that would otherwise be idle: thus regional policy can appear to be a way of increasing output without any inflation cost. The changing official attitude is well summarised by Wilson (1979).

> When a country is faced with great economic difficulties, should it persist with policies selectively designed to foster industrial development in the less prosperous regions? On two important occasions in Great Britain, 1947 and 1977, the response of the government of the day was in the negative . . . Thus, on these two occasions, it was apparently decided that the special needs of the less prosperous areas would have to give way to the more general needs of the economy as a whole. That attitude implies, as does the phrasing of our opening question, that regional policies can impose a burden on the rest of the community. It is a burden that may be accepted at times of national prosperity, but is liable to be laid down while the times are bad. A very different official attitude was adopted in the 1960's . . . During this period, regional policies were commended not only for the help they were expected to bring to the regions concerned but also for the benefits to be conferred on the nation as a whole . . . In particular it was held that the national labour force might thus be raised by something like one per cent and this would add to the level of national output (p. 81).

There is no very plausible economic reasoning that could reconcile these changing government attitudes. If we explain the retrenchments in 1947 and 1977 as being occasioned by inflationary or balance of payments pressures, that argument should have applied even more strongly in the 1960s when national employment levels were so high and when the economy was jolted through stop-go policies. If Keynesian-style demand-management arguments are used to justify regional policy in the 1960s, those same arguments should apply even more forcibly where national unemployment levels rise, as in the 1970s. Part of the explanation lies in changing perspectives of the macro-economic target – a theme outside the scope of this book – but part is inherent in changing attitudes towards regions. These changes in attitude are a more critical appraisal of the costs of regional policy as conventionally defined and a switch from treating regions to treating industries as the frame of reference.

We have discussed in Chapter 5 the problems of measuring the costs and benefits of regional policy. One important aspect of those problems is the difficulties of measuring the displacement effects of any 'successful' scheme. Suppose a factory sets up in Scotland, and would otherwise have set up, in say, Bedford. We can perhaps identify fairly accurately the effects of its setting up in Scotland – the people it employs, the extra jobs it creates through the multiplier effect, and so on – though we might have some difficulties in making sure that we have allowed properly for the effects if our new factory draws some of its workforce from factories already in the area. What, however, of the effect on Bedford?

One line of analysis – that, for example, used by Moore and Rhodes in their early work (see Bibliography for examples) – would be to say that we can ignore the effects on Bedford if there is more or less full employment there, because if our factory had set up in Bedford it could do so only by drawing labour from existing factories, and thus to the increase in employment and output from our factory there would be a pretty closely corresponding decrease in employment and output somewhere else in Bedford. So if the factory had been located at Bedford, employment and output gain there (and to the UK) would have been negligible. So the effect on Bedford can safely be ignored.

There are in practice very few circumstances which are sufficiently close to this abstract case for the displacement effects to be properly negligible, and the growing realisation that this is so is no doubt part of the background to the changing perspectives. The changes in focus of policy from geographical areas to industries is however also relevant.

The thinking behind industrial policy is at times somewhat confused. A nice illustration is provided by Cameron (1979).

In terms of efficiency the Department of Industry seeks to aid companies that can become viable and maintain profitability with specific and controlled aid and thereafter do not require continuing subsidies apart from those such as Regional Development grants available to all eligible enterprises. However, and here the dilemma is portrayed by two possibly opposed objectives,

'In considering an assessment of viability along with an assessment of the social costs and benefits involved, the Government have always been more prepared to give proposals for assistance the benefit of the doubt as to the prospects of viability when the social cost of withholding assistance would be particularly high and in particular in areas of high unemployment where the creation of new employment is specially difficult.'

Contrast this statement with another in the same document:

'The government are conscious of the desire for job security, and of the natural resentment of redundancy which require that all reasonable measures should be taken to provide the former or cushion the impact of the latter. At the same time if we are to break through the balance of payments constraints and thus achieve more room for manoeuvre in the management of the economy more and not less emphasis will be required on competitiveness in home and export markets.' (p. 301).

Cameron's quotations from official sources are both from p. 38 of the Department of Industry's 1976 *Annual Report of the 1972 Industry Act*, and illustrate the dilemmas between the aims of regional and industrial policy and indeed the inherent problems of seeking to provide aid in such a way as to ensure that it is diverted to concerns which are about to become profitable but are at the moment sufficiently far off being profitable to need help. Industry policy, by being microeconomic in thrust, is perhaps better at being selective than the older forms of regional policy, but as soon as the concept changes from automatic assistance to concerns that satisfy some predetermined criteria, whether or not they really need help and whether or not they have any likely future, to a more discretionary approval, these problems of defining *ad hoc* what are the relevant criteria have to be faced.

So far, we have used the vicissitudes of regional policy in the UK as illustrative of the changing nature of the politically perceived constraints against which the institutions we have discussed earlier in this section have operated. We now broaden the perspective a little to identify some of the macroeconomic constraints we mentioned in describing Millan's views.

Any government's economic policy is a matter of striking a delicately poised balance between conflicting considerations. Too slow a rate of growth can lead to frustration of expectations in the economy and inflationary pressures. Too rapid a rate of growth can lead to balance of payments or exchange rate problems. The list of contrasts could be extensive, and the solution which satisfies one set of constraints – for example, the 'right' rate of growth – may well be inconsistent with a solution that satisfies another set – for example, the 'right' rate of interest. Similar complexities characterise the relationships between regions and the countries of which they are part. Even if we have a clear concept of what is the desirable relationship between the regions and the country, it may be impossible to move towards that relationship for some reason of national policy. For example, we might wish to suggest that regional disparities within the UK should be reduced, by raising the levels of income, employment, etc. in the less prosperous regions. Some measures whereby we could bring about this result might do so only at the cost of lowering income in the more prosperous regions, and this might be regarded as undesirable. Some measures to promote development in less prosperous regions, whilst not lowering income in any region in the short term, might damage long-term growth prospects, by forcing firms to operate in a location where extra costs are so high as to inhibit their growth. Conflicts of aim and of interest can arise within a region: for example, the promotion of new towns as a measure to relieve congestion particularly in Glasgow has been one of the causes of the inner city urban decay within Glasgow which the SDA is now trying to correct.

It is, then, hardly surprising that the institutions we have discussed in this section have operated against a background of rapid changes in policy and of differing degree of constraint on their freedom of manoeuvre. When management of the economy is so uncertain a matter the uncertainty is bound to make for panic reactions as things appear suddenly to get out of control, and the swings of perception of what is thought of as the paramount macro-economic consideration lead in due course to swings in concept of what regional development agencies should be doing. Because it is relatively small, the HIDB has been largely insulated from these changes in policy, but the Scottish Office, as an area of government, and the SDA, as a big spender, have been particularly subject to changes in role. When the intention is to promote development, some degree of stability in the range of incentives on offer is, it is generally thought, to be desired so that businessmen who are being invited to undertake investment commitments can do so with reasonable confidence about what is on offer. That the institutions we have discussed have achieved any success in promoting development in these circumstances is either a comment on the naïveté of businessmen or a tribute to the effectiveness of the agencies. Without any very decisive empirical evidence, we think it is at least partly the later.

Forecasting the Future

In this section, we will examine what work has been done in formal forecasting that can be used, in the next section, to help us formulate our views of the outlook for Scotland.

It is conventional, and useful, to divide economic forecasting models into categories according to the period they cover. Short-term forecasts, which are usually constructed on quarterly data, tend to look no further than one or at the most two years ahead. Medium-term forecasts, which might well be based on annual data, usually offer prognostications for three to five years ahead. Long-term forecasts, nearly always using annual data, are designed to give indication of the future say ten or twenty years ahead, sometimes even further away than that. The degree of sophistication of the models, and their accuracy, tends to be in inverse proportion to the length of period for which the forecast is constructed, for the obvious reason that the further into the future one looks the least certain one is about institutional and policy parameters – as our discussion in the last section tried to illustrate. We intend in the rest of this discussion to ignore the long-term forecasts – such models are useful when directed to specific problems, such as identifying the likely future demand for and supply of oil in the world, or the probable consequences of an afforestation programme, but they are not of much relevance to the more complex issues we have in mind in asking about the economic outlook of a country or a region.

Ignoring for the moment whether it is a short or a medium term forecast we want, what is the best way to try to go about obtaining a forecast for the Scottish economy? Statistical models for an economy – which are usually labelled 'econometric' models – can be constructed in various ways. For a national economy, the normal procedure is to forecast output on a kind of source of expenditures method, by constructing separately forecasts for consumption expenditure C, private sector investment (including stocks) I, government current and capital expenditure G, exports X, and imports M, and constructing national income Y by the equation

$$Y = C + I + G + X - M$$

For each of the items on the right hand side, C, I, G, etc., there may be one equation or there may be many equations. The equations for at least some of the items on the right hand side will not be identities (as the equation above is an identity) but will contain explanatory variables – for example, C might well be modelled as dependent on Y and on the income-tax rate and perhaps on previous levels of C or of Y and perhaps on the rate of inflation. As each new item is introduced, like the income-tax rate or the rate of inflation in the example above, it must either be placed on the left hand side of another explanatory equation or identity or treated as exogenous – something whose level is determined outside the model, and whose value is either held constant throughout the model or is changed on the judgement of the modeller. Items which are treated as exogenous variables really are in one or other of three categories: they can be items which the modeller believes really are constant over the period he is interested in; they can be items which the modeller regards as government or other agency policy variables, changes in which are a matter for the discretion of that agent; or they can be items which the modeller believes do change but not in a manner that he can discuss within the confines of his model.

The last type of exogenous variable is very important when the modeller is concerned not with a nation but with what is in economic terms a region. In Chapter 1 and earlier in this chapter we have alluded to the openness which characterises a region. In terms of econometric modelling, the implications of openness are that the model for the region will contain a lot of references to national variables, which will be exogenous to the model. When a region sells the output of some industry mainly to the rest of the nation of which it is part, it is natural to seek to model regional demand for that product as at least in part dependent on whatever determines national demand for that product, and that will entail using in the model either some exogenous variable for national consumer demand or, as a proxy for that, national output of the commodity. The first characteristic, then, that we can expect to find of a regional econometric model is extensive use of national items as exogenous variables in the model.

The second characteristic follows from this first consideration. If a forecast is to be made for the region, then a forecast for the nation has to be available first, so that the modeller knows what to assume about the exogenous variables. Whilst it is possible to construct a forecast for a nation by making and adding together forecasts for all its regions (and there has been a successful attempt in France to carry out this exercise), it is normal to start with a national model, because much more work has been done on national models and within understood limits they can be treated as reasonably reliable.

Third, we can expect that data limitations will affect the form and presentation of the regional model. Particularly, the absence in most cases of any regional information about trade flows means that since X and M cannot be measured, let alone modelled, the basic formulation for a national model as described above cannot be followed. Instead, the models start from a sum of outputs or of income rather than a sum of expenditures formulation, and so usually build up national income industry by industry, identifying what determines output in each industry. A further kind of data problem which can affect the presentation of the model might well be the absence of quarterly data. If quarterly data are not available for key variables in the model, then there is limited prospect for constructing any short-term forecast, and medium-term modelling is all that is feasible.

Regional econometric modelling is a relatively new art in the UK, but sufficient work has been done for states and for other areas of the USA that UK researchers have been given a head start, and there is no problem in finding a national model to use – the only difficulty is in deciding which of the different competing models is most appropriate, in terms of its technical definitions and of the general attitude towards the economy adopted in guesses about its exogenous variables.

The structure of a typical regional model is best illustrated in a simplified diagram. Figure 6.1 portrays the structure of the Dundee model, which we will discuss later in this section, but could stand for many reasonably fully fledged regional models. The rectangles in the diagram represent 'blocks' of equations. Each of these blocks may contain several equations – for example, the output block will contain one equation for each of the industries into which it is convenient or practicable to divide output. The lines with arrows are meant to illustrate the connections within the system. For instance, employment in each industry will typically be modelled as dependent on the output of that industry, and employment will be relevant in explaining income through wages and salaries, and unemployment through some sort of labour-force model. In some cases connections flow both ways – for example, income feeds into output through income-related demand factors and output feeds into income through income from self-employment.

The more complex the flows within the system, the more realistic and interesting the model becomes, because it is illustrating the circularity of processes: if income rises, investment will rise, and that will increase output, which increases employment, which increases income again, and at the same time income rises further through its two-way connections with output. The block in the model which is relatively isolated from the rest – in that it is not affected by any change other than those to income – is the tax block, and that is probably realistic for a region since there is no direct connection between taxes taken from the region and government expenditure in the region and so there is no linkage between taxes and investment or output or employment other than through income.

Regional models corresponding more or less to the structure in Figure 6.1 have been constructed within the UK for Wales (Wanhill, 1978), Northern Ireland (Jefferson, 1978) and Scotland (Bell, 1978, Dewhurst and Lythe, 1982). Although in all cases work on the models

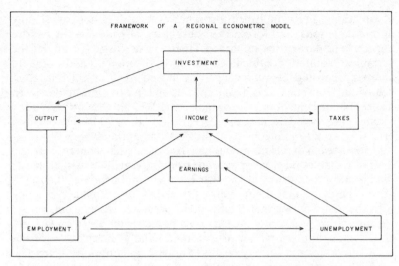

Figure 6.1   *Framework of a regional econometric model*

is continuing – Wanhill's work for Wales is now being followed up at the University College of North Wales; Jefferson is going on with his work for Northern Ireland; and the two Scottish models are being developed at the Fraser of Allander Institute and at Dundee respectively – none of them has yet got to the stage where their authors are prepared to produce formal forecasts from the models for critical inspection. This is mainly because all the work has been relatively recent, and a lot of effort is needed to get the model in good shape by fitting successive versions of it to past data and doing some 'within sample period forecasting' (that is, fitting the model to information for some years and using it to 'forecast' other years for which the factual outcome is already known) to identify the likely forecasting errors. Most of the models we have mentioned are somewhere in this latter stage. But to use the regional model to produce a forecast there is also the problem of where to look for a suitable 'national' model to plug the regional one into. In modelling Scotland, we need to find a suitable UK model.

As we have already said, there is no shortage of UK econometric models, but the choice of a suitable model is rather complex. First, there is the question of identifying for each national model whether it offers forecasts of the variables needed. Since national models are expenditure-based, and regional models are output-based, the problem of finding the right variables is far from negligible. For example, in terms of equation structure the Treasury model of the UK economy is much the most sophisticated, containing many hundreds of equations. In its published form, however, it does not contain any output equations, and forecasts of output by individual industries are not made as part of the published Treasury forecasts. If some of the variables required are included in one UK model, and some in another, it would be very dangerous indeed to draw their forecast behaviour from the two different models and use that mechanically to determine the behaviour of exogenous variables in the Scottish model, because the two UK models used as sources might well be (and probably would be) inconsistent in their assumptions.

Second, even if a UK model can be found that contains all the desired variables on what appears to be an internally consistent basis, the question then arises of whether the assumptions about their exogenous variables that the framers of the UK forecast made are in line with the assumptions that the Scottish forecaster wants to make. As we have already suggested, using an econometric model to make forecasts is not simply a matter of turning a handle and waiting for the results to pour out. For any results to appear, assumptions have to be made about key exogenous variables, and what assumptions are made depend ultimately on the economic intuition of the forecaster. This can be illustrated again by the UK Treasury model. The equations for that model are published, and it has been made easy for independent groups who wish to do so to run the Treasury model on their own assumptions about exogenous variables.

One group which regularly does this with the Treasury model is the St James's Group, which is a group of industrial, commercial and financial companies, and which runs the Treasury model with help from *The Economist* magazine. The forecasts made by the St James's Group are published in *The Economist*. In presenting its most recent forecasts, the Group's secretariat, after outlining its main prognostications, points out 'whether that gloomy picture is being painted inside the treasury itself is uncertain. The St James's Group forecasts depend heavily on the various assumptions made about world trade, oil prices, government spending and tax plans: on all, there is ample room for disagreement.' (*The Economist*, 24–30 October 1981, p. 40.)

One way of avoiding these difficulties is for the same team to prepare the regional and the national forecasts. The only attempt so far to do this for the UK is that of the Cambridge Economic Policy Group, which in the July 1980 issue of the *Cambridge Economic Policy Review* presented forecasts of unemployment for the regions of the UK, including Scotland, for 1983. According to that forecast, unemployment in Scotland in 1983 will be 12.7 per cent, only a little above the UK forecast level of 12.0 per cent. As we show in the Appendix, the data on which the Cambridge forecasts are based are unfortunately a bit too rough and ready to be acceptable. In the interests of uniformity of methodology for all the regions of the UK,

the Cambridge group made rather too heavy use of crude apportionment of UK totals for items for which published official statistics are
lacking. If the data are a little dubious, then any model based on them
must be suspect. Although the Cambridge group were unquestionably
going about regional forecasting in an eminently sound way, they did
not devote to the task the very considerable resources necessary to do
it properly, and thus the results are rather disappointing.

The second way of proceeding is to try to make intelligent *ad hoc*
decisions on how to incorporate the general tenor of UK forecasts.
This can be very difficult when, as has happened not infrequently,
there are sharp disagreements between the forecasts, but there have
been many studies of the track records of the different models so the
judgement which is most likely to be sound on some variable can
usually be reasonably well informed. The problem of consistency if
material is drawn from different model forecasts may not be too acute
if the researcher is aware of the dangers. Experience in the USA
suggests that, however suspect it might appear to be, there is a way
forward here.

Even within the regional models as they stand, there are clues that
we can use to help us formulate some ideas about the outlook. We can
read the equations as telling us something about the responsiveness of
one variable to changes in another. For example, if as in the Dundee
model, the output in Scotland of bricks, pottery, glass and cement is
represented as dependent on output in construction in Scotland, both
in the current year and one year ago, we can use the parameters in the
equation to identify the short-term and long-term change in output in
bricks, pottery, glass and cement if an extra £1 were to be spent on
construction. In that way we can use individual equations in the model
to make a guess at the order of magnitude of the extra demand for the
brick, pottery, glass and cement industry in Scotland if government
dispersal of civil service jobs requires the construction of a large office
building in Glasgow. But such informal uses of a formal model cannot
trace round the eventual effects – the model has to be run on the
computer and as soon as the interactions get at all complicated and
even with a great deal of effort in inspecting the equations, it may be
difficult to guess even whether the eventual effect will be greater or less
than the initial effect. For forecasting the major macroeconomic
variables, like income, informal methods are likely to be so
unreliable as to be useless, and there is no option to running the
model formally.

To revert to the question we posed at the beginning of this section –
how much can formal modelling tell us about the future of the
Scottish economy? – the answer at the moment must be 'not much'. In
two or so years' time there is the reasonable hope that either the Fraser
of Allander model or the Dundee model or both will be being used to

generate formal forecasts. It will, however, take a few years' experience after that before we will be able to judge how reliable the models are.

The Outlook

We round off this chapter and the book by trying to draw together the threads in a discussion of what the analysis we have undertaken so far has to tell us about the future prospects for the Scottish economy.

As we hope is obvious from the numerous occasions on which we have demonstrated the extent of Scotland's reliance on the rest of the UK as a market and source of materials as well as institutionally, the prime influence on Scotland's economic outlook must be the outlook for the UK at large. It is never easy to write with confidence about the outlook for the UK and it is particularly difficult to do so now when all the indicators suggest that in the near future the economic prospects are very bleak, but when there is a profound division among politicians but also among economists as to whether the UK is or is not on what will eventually prove to be the road to sustained economic growth.

The most recent St James's Group forecast, covering the period to the end of 1983, expects that output will rise very fractionally (0.6 per cent) in 1982 and a little faster (1.3 per cent) in 1983, that inflation will fall gradually but still be over 11 per cent in 1983, that unemployment will rise a little in 1982 over its level at the end of 1981, and fall only fractionally in 1983, and that the balance of payments will move into a (small) deficit in 1982 and 1983. Whilst some of the commentators more enamoured of government policy might think the 1983 picture is a bit gloomy, there seems a fair degree of unanimity about 1982, unless labour productivity grows abnormally quickly.

All past experience suggests that, whatever happens in the UK, things will be a little worse in Scotland. We saw in Chapter 2 that income per head in Scotland has crept up towards but shows no sign of consistently exceeding UK income per head. Chapter 2 showed, too, that government expenditure was disproportionately important in Scotland, so that Scotland is particularly vulnerable if the government does manage to cut the public sector. In Chapter 3 we noted the rise in Scottish labour productivity in recent years, but the movements have not been so dramatic as to give hope for a sharp swing in Scotland's favour of competitive advantage, particularly as earnings levels seem to have risen more or less in step with productivity. Chapter 4 demonstrated that the relative improvements in Scotland, in terms of excess of output over what could be 'expected' on extrapolation of past trends, was really concentrated in a few industries, and we saw in

Chapter 5 that these industries are those which are generally thought to have been those most favourably affected by conventionally defined regional policy. Chapter 5 also analysed less conventional concepts of regional policy and showed that whilst government policy is important in explaining output and employment in some industries, in others its influence is insignificant compared with that of the general prosperity of the UK. The earlier parts of this chapter have shown that the Scots cannot look to North Sea oil or to the EEC as a source for much further growth, and that indeed there is some contraction to be absorbed as the North Sea oil-related activity settles down to its long-term steady level.

In the next two or three years, then, we cannot be optimistic about the outlook for the Scottish economy, in absolute terms or by the standards of the UK. Our pessimism here is much in line with the views of the prospects of the Scottish economy in 1982 expressed by the Fraser of Allander Institute in their most recent *Quarterly Economic Commentary*.

It has been claimed by the government that the Scottish economy has weathered the recession better than the rest of the UK and that Scottish industry is poised to benefit from the economic discipline imposed by the recession. Certainly it is possible to point at a number of notable recent successes such as the Weir Group, Motorola, John Brown and Govan Shipbuilders. However, these have been balanced by a number of major closures and contractions. While some individual firms seem to have a brighter outlook the general economic climate does not appear conducive to a sustained, economy-wide improvement in industrial output. Interest rates are high, inflation is likely to increase, real consumer spending to decrease, public contracts scarce, and our trading partners are also in recession. Consequently, even the most efficient producers will find it difficult to sell their products domestically or internationally if the level of demand remains low. With regard to unemployment, the recessionary influence has yet to run its course . . . The conclusion of this analysis is therefore extremely pessimistic. Regardless of the success or failure of current policy on the level of industrial output, unemployment will remain high for a considerable period . . . Yet even if the government follows the advice of a broad spectrum of economic and political opinion, including this Institute, and reflates the economy, it is unlikely that unemployment will fall in the next year. High unemployment is therefore going to be with us for a considerable period of time whichever policies are pursued and regardless of their success. (*Quarterly Economic Commentary*, vol. 7, no. 2, October 1981, pp. 25, 26.)

Looking to the more distant future is even more difficult. As we have tried to argue several times in this book – in Chapter 1 and earlier in this chapter – we do not believe that it will make much difference to the economic prospects for Scotland whatever is the fate of the recurrent proposals about some measure of political devolution. Unless Scottish industry agrees to accept a really radical restructuring, devolution would have very little economic effect for a substantial number of years – the fifty years we have cited for Eire might be near the mark. So constitutional developments would have little economic relevance. Political developments, more narrowly defined, will work through the UK economy but is a rather magnified way in Scotland, because of the importance of the government sector, but what these developments might be is anybody's guess.

On economic developments, however, we can be a little clearer, and we can claim that there are grounds for some confidence about Scotland's future. Eventually, we believe there must be some return for the UK to a period of modest but reasonably steady growth such as that experienced in the 1950s and 1960s. Once that happens, Scotland should be well placed. As we have seen, at the beginning of the period covered by this book she inherited a heavy industry appropriate to the late nineteenth but not to the mid-twentieth century. Perhaps the major achievement of regional policy in Scotland in the 1960s – and the trend has continued since thanks to the industrial strategy and to the multi-nationals – is a steady but fundamental change in the structure of the economy, out of the old and into more modern industries.

Provided that the current view that future developments lie in fields like micro-electronics and bio-engineering is accurate, Scotland now has an industrial structure very well suited to the demands of the future. If the 1990s are going to be a decade in which those who are in work are farmers, scientists designing new microchip circuits and new genetic engineering programmes, and people working in personal service industries and in administration, Scotland should by then be if not the most prosperous region of the UK, at least the region with the most fully employed workforce.

Appendix

Introduction

In this Appendix, we discuss in some detail the sources and methods we have used in constructing the basic data about the Scottish economy on which we draw, throughout the book but especially in Chapters 2–5. We deal first with the employment figures, then with social accounting estimates; we include a chronology of regional policy and, finally, the evidence used in Chapter 5.

Employment in Scotland, 1961–78

In this section we discuss the employment data used in our analysis of the Scottish and UK employment structures and in calculating value added per worker for Scotland and the UK. The total labour force is made up of employees in employment and of the self-employed (including employers): we consider these two components separately. We deal later with the particular issues in estimating the manufacturing labour force.

Employees in employment
Department of Employment data on employees were collected on the basis of a national card-count system for all years of the study period up to 1970. From 1971, the data were compiled from the Census of Employment. This means that there are problems of discontinuity between the old and new series (see *SAS*, 1974, p. 74 and Department of Employment *Gazette*, March 1975, for a discussion of these discontinuity problems). The Department of Employment *Gazette*, however, gives UK data on employees in employment as a new continuous series for the years 1959–78, compiled by linking the two series. Corresponding details for regions (including Scotland) are available only for 1965–78. Thus, for the years 1961–4, we had to calculate a series of employees in employment in Scotland. We did this by scaling the card-count data of employees in employment, order by order, using scale factors for each order from the new published data for Scotland for 1965. The procedure used here, of applying scale factors to relate the card-count data to those from the Census of Employment, is similar to that used by the Department of Employment in calculating its new series, but since the new Scottish data were not available for MLH's we had to make our calculations at order level.

Self-employed and employers
There is one continuous run of information for the UK, covering the years 1961–74 by order (Department of Employment *Gazette*, December 1976). For 1971–5, details of self-employment (including employers) are available by order for Great Britain (Department of Employment *Gazette*, June 1977). Since the 1961–74 series is also available for Great Britain (Department of Employment *Gazette*, December 1976), it is possible by subtraction to estimate

the industrial analysis for Northern Ireland and thus adjust the Great Britain figures to produce more or less consistent figures for 1961–75 for the UK.

There is, however, no means whereby the series can properly be extended to 1978. In the official statistics, even the total number of self-employed and employers in the UK has not been estimated since June 1975. The only device that could be used to generate the UK working force data was, therefore, to assume that the industrial analysis and total number of self-employed and employers in 1976–8 was the same as that in 1975.

For Scotland, the problems are more acute, as the only official series is of the total number in self-employment (including employers) and these cover only 1966–75. However, the Censuses of Population of 1961, 1966 and 1971 provide evidence of the industrial distribution of employers and the self-employed, and so we used those three observations, by assuming linear trends, to produce estimates of the industrial distribution of self-employment in Scotland in 1961–5. We were, however, hesitant to extrapolate our trend beyond 1971, and so we applied the 1971 Census of Population distribution to the total number of self-employed and employers for each year after 1971. As for the UK, we did not even have a reliable total for 1976–8, and so simply repeated the 1975 figures.

Manufacturing industries
For the estimates of employees in employment in manufacturing industries, the procedure described earlier was applied to each manufacturing order so as to arrive at a continuous series of employees in employment in Scottish manufacturing. For 1963, 1968 and 1970 onwards the Census of Production was, however, an alternative source of information, and the Census of Production employment estimates are based on concepts and definitions which differ from those in the Census of Employment. The Census of Production estimates of employees in employment exclude workers who do not work on the factory site, but include working proprietors. The Department of Employment figures exclude working proprietors and directors not under contract of service, but include outworkers. As a result of these differences, the Census of Production figures of employees are lower than our corresponding estimated figures for Scotland for 1963, and lower also than the new continuous estimates for 1968, 1970 and 1971. In aggregate, our estimates are about 8 per cent higher than the corresponding Census of Production figures for 1963, 1968 and 1970. For 1971, the difference is just under 4 per cent.

Since we used Census of Production evidence in preparing our estimates of manufacturing output, we would ideally have liked to use Census of Production data as the basis for our estimates of the number of employees in manufacturing, but that would have led us into three difficulties. First, we would have had to compile estimates for years in which there was no Census of Production. Second, we would have had problems of comparability between the figures for manufacturing and those for other industries. Third, we would then have had some difficulty in measuring what deductions to make for working proprietors, so as to avoid double-counting when we added our allowance for self-employment. For these reasons, we have used in our calculation for manufacturing estimates of employees in employment based on Department of Employment returns.

The total number of self-employed and employers in manufacturing is small. To estimate the industrial distribution we first calculated the percentage each industry contributed to the total for the sector in 1961 and 1971, according to the Census of Population, and then estimated the number for each industry using 1961 ratios for the year 1963 and 1971 for the years from 1968 onwards.

Social Accounts

We start this section with a summary review of the published social accounts for Scotland, where we will consider in turn the estimates of Campbell (1955) (for 1924-49), McCrone (1965) (for 1951-60), Woodward (1970) (for 1961), Begg, Lythe and Sorley (1975a) (for 1961-73), Scottish Office (*Scottish Economic Bulletin*, nos. 4-11) (for 1961-74), Central Statistical Office (CSO) (1978, 1980) (for 1966-79), the Scottish Input-Output Project (SIOP) (1978) (for 1973), the Cambridge Economic Policy Group (1980) (for 1966 and 1970-78) and Lythe and Majmudar (1981) (for 1961-71). We will then specify the background to the figures used in our text.

Summary review
Campbell (1955): Campbell's analysis of Scottish incomes, for the years 1924-49, sought to measure the aggregate of income received by or attributable to individuals ordinarily resident in Scotland. Campbell calculated wages, salaries and agricultural income from published Scottish data. The values of the other components of Scottish income were obtained by applying proxy ratios to UK totals to give the Scottish figures. Two categories gave Campbell important conceptual and measurement problems. In the case of income from property, Campbell used the analysis of estates given in Inland Revenue reports to establish the extent of ownership, by individuals ordinarily resident in Scotland, of the companies operating in the UK, and allocated the appropriate share of UK trading profits of companies to Scotland. To measure Scotland's net income from abroad, Campbell attributed to Scotland a share of the UK total, thus ignoring flows within the UK.

McCrone (1965): McCrone's estimates for 1951-60 measured Scottish territorial GDP by the sum of products method. He measured the contribution of an industry to Scottish GDP directly from production data wherever possible, and in this way was able to make his estimates of value added in agriculture; mining and quarrying; manufacturing; gas, electricity and water; and construction. For most other industries he used relevant Inland Revenue Schedule E and Schedule D data. In a few industries, McCrone used employment as the indicator to apportion to Scotland a share of UK value added. His estimates for public health and local authority education services were made by direct use of Scottish data. By measuring value added directly from production data in the Census of Production industries, McCrone was able to overcome the conceptual and measurement problems involved in estimating profits. However, McCrone's estimates for years in which there was no Census were a lot less firmly based, as he himself recognised.

Woodward (1970): Woodward compiled estimates of residents' GDP for all the regions of the UK for the year 1961. Because he attempted to use a uniform method for all regions his choice of data sources was dictated by those for the least well documented regions. His method was sum of incomes. For wages and salaries, the Inland Revenue Survey of Personal Income (which for 1959/60 and 1964/65 had a 5 per cent sample) provided the necessary data, to which Woodward made adjustments for those items which are not included in PAYE statistics. For estimating income from self-employment, Woodward again drew on Inland Revenue Survey data, with appropriate adjustments to national accounting conventions. For gross distributed profits in manufacturing, Woodward used data from the Census of Production of 1958, and this of course led him to an estimate of territorial, not residents', profit income. Calculating the regional distribution of profits of non-manufacturing companies presented even more intractable problems, and Woodward had to use indicators such as employment and turnover of retail establishments. For gross trading surpluses of public enterprises and rent Woodward used regional data where possible, again producing what is fundamentally a territorial estimate. In Woodward's calculations, gross profits and surpluses of public enterprises and rent were all estimated at industry level and then aggregated. His industrial breakdown of income from employment was calculated from earnings and employment data, but lack of information made it necessary for him to treat the wage-bill of some industries as the residual between the total wage-bill and the sum for the industries for which he could make a separate estimate.

Begg, Lythe and Sorley (1975a): The estimates of Gross Domestic Expenditure (GDE) for 1961-71 and 1972-3 made by Begg, Lythe and Sorley (1975b), Lythe, Begg and Majmudar (1977), and Cox, Devlen and Lythe (1979) try to measure territorial expenditure incurred in Scotland. The calculation was made in term of the normal components of expenditure: consumers' expenditure, public authorities' current expenditure, gross domestic fixed capital formation and stock formation. The major data source used for consumers' expenditure was the *Family Expenditure Survey*. There are both statistical and conceptual difficulties associated with this source. Statistical problems arise because the Survey is based on sampling, and the sample size for Scotland is dangerously small. This has led to some problems, for example in measuring certain items of consumers' expenditure in Scotland in 1972. The conceptual difficulties spring from the fact that the survey gives a measure of expenditure by families domiciled in Scotland, not of expenditure in Scotland. The figures for public authorities' current expenditure were derived from Treasury totals where possible but contain a fairly significant amount of apportionment of UK totals. The estimates for gross domestic fixed capital formation in manufacturing are derived from Census of Production returns: other investment is calculated by a variety of means, but a large part is directly measurable. The estimates for stock formation are analytically the least satisfactory part of the accounts: they rest largely on estimation by proxy ratios.

Scottish Office (Scottish Economic Bulletin, nos. 4-11): The Scottish Office estimates are of residents' GDP, by the sum of incomes method. They itemise income from employment, income from self-employment, gross trading profits and surpluses, rent and the adjustment for stock appreciation. The basic source of data for the estimate of wages and salaries up to 1971 was the Inland Revenue Quinquennial Survey of Personal Incomes for 1959-60, 1964-5 and 1969-70, linked by the annual trend observed in the Inland Revenue assessments of gross income charged under PAYE in Scotland. Self-employment income except that of farmers was derived from Inland Revenue assessments under Schedule D with an addition for wives' Schedule D earnings based on the Inland Revenue Quinquennial Survey. The estimates of rent were built up from direct Scottish data. The estimates of trading surpluses of the Electricity, Gas and Coal Boards were made direct from their returns; the estimates of surpluses in most of the remaining public corporations, and of gross trading profits, were made by using employment as the indicator. The main problems of the Scottish Office estimates result from their reliance on Inland Revenue data, which leads to two difficulties. First, the estimates of income from employment may be distorted because of the small sample size of the surveys. Secondly, there is the problem of the difference between place of assessment for tax returns and places of residence: such differences may give rise to few discrepancies in total, but are important in some industries. The Scottish Office has compiled an industrial analysis of GDP for the years 1962-72, based on their factor income estimates, but the total GDP figures on which the industrial analysis was based have now been superceded by Central Statistical Office estimates, and there has been no official attempt to recalculate the Scottish Office industrial analysis to bring it into consistency with the new totals.

Central Statistical Office (1978 and 1980): Central Statistical Office (CSO) has published regional GDP accounts for the UK for the years 1966-79. The basic method is the sum of income approach, and the totals are intended to be of residents' income: 'We have tried to measure the total income from employment accruing to the residents of each region, rather than the accruing to those working in each region'. (Kent-Smith and Hartley, 1976, p. 78.)

CSO has compiled an industrial analysis of regional GDP for the years 1971-9. In the CSO estimates of income from employment, the Inland Revenue Surveys of Personal Incomes (most recently 1977/78) provided the initial benchmark, which was modified by use of the 1 per cent sample of graduated contributions carried out by the Department of Health and Social Security (DHSS). This use of residence-based data from the DHSS helped to produce a series which more faithfully reflects place of residence than the Inland Revenue statistics. Profits were estimated by the use of proxies. Employment was used as the main indicator for manufacturing profits for the years before 1971, but for the years 1971 onwards these profits were estimated from Census of Production data by region and industry. For other industries, employment was used as the indicator to distribute UK profits.

Scottish Input-Output Project (1978): This study is quite different from any that we have considered earlier in this Appendix, in that it has been compiled from survey data assembled for the purpose. Its main object is to present an inter-industry analysis, but a by-product of the analysis is that it produced estimates of GDP (by the sum of incomes and value added methods) and of GDE. The Scottish Input-Output Project (SIOP) has produced an input-output table for Scotland for 1973. The whole calculation is, of course, territorial in basis. The principal data source for the SIOP was an extensive industrial survey. The survey of manufacturing was the most substantial part of the project and returns covered nearly 40 per cent of manufacturing employment. For other industries, the sample coverage varies, but it was generally inadequate in the service sector. As the authors emphasise, 'In some of the manufacturing sectors, we felt that our estimation of other value added was too high, primarily due to the under-reporting of the purchase of services in the survey questionnaire. In these cases, we transferred some of the other value added to the services to bring the proportion of total services purchases to gross output closer into line with the UK' (SIOP, 1978, Chap. 5). In addition to the differences in data base between SIOP and the other regional GDP estimates, there are important differences in the industrial sectoring of activities (Bulmer-Thomas, 1978). On the whole it is difficult to evaluate the contribution of SIOP to the Scottish social accounting framework. The SIOP framework was designed to produce a detailed analysis of inter-industry flows, and the totals which can be used to calculate an industrial breakdown of value added are essentially a by-product of the project. It is therefore hardly surprising that those totals are in a form which does not admit of easy comparison with the conventional social accounting estimates.

Cambridge Economic Policy Group (1980): The Cambridge Economic Policy Group (CEPG) has published social accounts for all regions of the UK. These accounts cover the period 1966 and 1970–8, and embrace most of the components of the sum of income method (with a limited industrial breakdown), the components of the sum of expenditure method, sum of outputs (with a limited industrial breakdown) and personal incomes. This exercise is valuable mainly in that, like Woodward's, it produces a set of information on the same basis for all regions and thus is a useful starting-point for inter-regional comparisons but, again like Woodward's, the attempt to achieve consistency across regions is at the cost of ignoring some Scottish data. The main interest of the CEPG estimates for Scotland is not in the most recent information, which is drawn or adapted mainly from CSO statistics, but in the details for 1966 which are calculated following Woodward's procedure.

Lythe and Majmudar (1981): We have ourselves constructed estimates of Scottish territorial GDP by the sum of output method for each year 1961–71, and disaggregated manufacturing GDP into that by the component orders for the Census of Production years 1963, 1968, 1970 and 1971. Our procedure as far as possible has been to measure value added directly in terms of output (less appropriate inputs): only where we could find no suitable details (as in manufacturing in years where there was no Census of Production) or where there is no tangible output to measure (as in service industries) did we use income-based information (like Inland Revenue tax statistics). We believe that by measuring output wherever possible we have avoided some of the problems of income statistics – particularly that of making sure that the statistics are of territorial rather than residents' income – and in practice our own figures are the only available set for 1961 and 1970 apart from the now superceded Scottish Office estimates. Thus, the methods we have used in compiling the tables for this book are very similar to those in Lythe and Majmudar.

Sum of incomes

The data we used in Table 2.2 came from various sources. The figures for 1954-9 are drawn from McCrone (1965), Chap. 3, Table I and VI (pp. 42, 46). The remaining data came from official estimates, as published by the Scottish Office in the *Scottish Abstract of Statistics* and *Scottish Economic Bulletin*. The most recent source used was *Scottish Economic Bulletin*, no. 22 (Spring 1981), p. 67, which printed details for 1971-9. The figures for the earlier years came from earlier issues.

It should be noted that there are these two discontinuities in the series; that as we move from McCrone's estimates to the Scottish Office series, and a discontinuity in the Scottish Office series as we move from estimates made within the Scottish Office to those made by the Central Statistical Office. The latter discontinuity is described in *Scottish Economic Bulletin*, no. 10 (Summer 1976) p. 46. To overcome the former discontinuity we adjusted McCrone's estimates for 1960 in the light of revisions to the UK figures in the *Blue Book*: this had the effect of moving our new 'McCrone' figures closer to the 1961 official figures, and thus smoothing out the quite sharp discontinuity that otherwise existed.

Sum of outputs

Again, the sources used for Table 2.3 are diverse. McCrone (1965) is the source for all the figures quoted for 1954-7. (See McCrone, Chap. 2, Table I, p. 31). For 1958-60, we have used McCrone's estimates for agriculture, forestry and fishing; mining and quarrying; manufacturing; construction; gas, electricity and water; and ownership of dwellings, but have altered his figures for the service sector and so his totals for all industries. The alterations we have made here are simply to incorporate the effects of revisions in the UK official statistics in the national income *Blue Book*: since McCrone's procedure for services is to calculate Scotland/UK ratios from Inland Revenue statistics and apply those ratios to the figures for the UK reported in *Blue Book*, it follows that when the *Blue Book* figures change, so do those for Scotland. We have therefore altered McCrone's figures in accordance with his own procedures.

For 1961-70, the estimates we quote in Table 2.3 are drawn from Lythe and Majmudar (1981). As we have explained earlier in this Appendix, the Scottish Office estimates for this period are now superceded, for at least part of the series, and so we have no alternative data with which we could properly compare our own estimates.

For 1971-9, we have used officially published figures. Since we had to determine early in the writing of this book what figures we were going to use, to enable the calculations for Chapters 4 and 5 to go ahead, we were not able to incorporate the most recent updatings. The most recent figures used are based on the data presented in *Scottish Economic Bulletin*, no. 22 (Spring 1981), p. 67, which covers all of 1971-9. We have divided some of the totals in the tables as presented there into parts - distinguishing public health and education services and 'other services' from the conglomeration of professional and scientific services and miscellaneous services by using Inland Revenue data to calculate income from employment and self employment in public health and education services, as described in Lythe and Majmudar

(1981), and attributing the rest of the miscellaneous group total to other services. When we lacked the relevant Inland Revenue data we used employment shares as a proxy.

The series for output at constant prices in Tables 2.5 and 2.6 was entirely our own calculation. The sources and methods are exactly as described in Lythe and Majmudar (1981), although of course the data run is longer than is that published and the calculations for this paper were rebased to 1975 prices.

Sum of expenditures
The estimates used in Tables 2.4 and 2.7 are almost entirely our own. We have described our original sources and methods in Begg, Lythe and Sorley (1975a), and this description has been updated by various working papers – Begg, Lythe and Sorley (1975b), Lythe, Begg and Majmudar (1977), and Cox, Devlen and Lythe (1979). A paper outlining the background to the most recent revisions, used in this book, is currently under preparation (Forbes and Lythe, 1982).

The only other attempt to measure several parts of the sum of expenditures totals for Scotland for other than occasional years is that of Central Statistical Office (published in the November issue of *Economic Trends* of each year: the most recent available to us was for 1980). The Central Statistical Office series covers the years 1972 to 1979. These estimates are of consumers' expenditure, parts of gross domestic fixed capital formation, and taxes and subsidies. The sources and methods are described in Central Statistical Office's *Regional Accounts* (1978). Consumers' expenditure in Scotland has been analysed by Henderson (1980) and the alterations in techniques described in Forbes and Lythe (1982) are mainly an attempt to incorporate some of the improvements suggested by Henderson. In the estimates quoted in this paper and discussed in Forbes and Lythe (1982), we have taken account of the Central Statistical Office estimates as far as possible, but as they are presented at a much less fine level of disaggregation than our own, detailed comparison is difficult.

A Chronology of British Regional Policy, 1928–77

The evolution of British regional policy can best be traced in terms of the chronology of British regional policy over the period 1928 onwards. Given that the focus of regional policy, the instruments and the geographic areas receiving assistance have changed throughout the period, it is most appropriate to outline the main legislative acts with reference to instruments and geographical areas. Such a chronology is already presented in Armstrong and Taylor (1978) and we reproduce their chronology with their kind permission.

Major policy measures are in italics

Date	Policy measure	Main provisions
1928	Industrial Transference Scheme and Juvenile Transfer Scheme	Minor grant and loan assistance for unemployed migrants. Retraining centres established.

Date	*Policy measure*	*Main provisions*
1934	*Special Areas (Development and Improvement) Act*	Four Special Areas designated in South Wales, Scotland, the North-East and West Cumberland, with two Special Area Commissioners appointed to administer the limited loan and aid powers. Establishment of first Trading Estates. Loan powers strengthened by the Special Areas Reconstruction (Agreement) Act of 1936.
1937	Special Areas (Amendment) Act	Extension of loan powers in Special Areas. Tax, rent and rates subsidies for firms in Special Areas. Extension of Trading Estates. Initial sum of £2 million provided.
1940	General Transfer Scheme	Wartime, much-strengthened migration assistance for displaced workers. Replaced Industrial Transference Scheme.
1940	*Royal Commission on the Distribution of the Industrial Population* (Barlow Report)	Strong, influential report. Has had a major effect on postwar regional policy. Urban congestion and regional problems seen as interrelated. Redistribution of population and industry recommended.
1944	White Paper on Employment Policy	Commitment to full employment.
1945	*Distribution of Industry Act*	Assisted areas enlarged and designated as Development Areas. Basic responsibility for regional policy given to the Board of Trade, which acquired (from the Special Area Commissioners) powers of factory building and leasing, finance for Trading Estates, land reclamation, and grants and loans for firms on the advice of the Development Areas Treasury Advisory Committee (DATAC). The system of building licences was retained as a disincentive to expansion in the prosperous regions. The Distribution of Industry Act marks the beginning of the first 'active' phase of British regional policy.

Date	Policy measure	Main provisions
1946	Resettlement Scheme	Gradual replacement of wartime General Transfer Scheme. Unemployed migrants from *all* regions eligible. Wide range of migration costs met. Incorporated a facility to assist temporary migrants (the Voluntary Temporary Transfer Scheme), as well as provision to assist key workers required by their firms to move to assisted areas. Extended in 1946 to workers sent by new firms in assisted areas for retraining in other regions (subsequently known as the Nucleus Labour Force Scheme).
1947	*Town and Country Planning Act*	Extension of wartime building controls into the full Industrial Development Certificate (IDC) system. All new manufacturing establishments or extensions of over 5000 sq. ft. required an IDC. This exemption limit has been altered frequently since 1947.
1950	Distribution of Industry Act	A further, but small, extension of Board of Trade loan and grant powers for firms moving to Development Areas. Regional policy throughout the 1950s was only weakly applied.
1951	Key Workers Scheme	Assistance to migrating key workers of firms moving to Development Areas separated out from the Resettlement Scheme, becoming a scheme in its own right. As with the industrial location policies, the resettlement policies were also less actively pursued in the 1950s. Assistance to temporary migrants discontinued from 1950–7.
1958	Distribution of Industry (Industry Finance) Act	Extension of loan and grant assistance to a number of development 'places' (high unemployment locations outside the Development Areas). Marks a gradual renewal of the vigour of regional policy, with a tightening up of IDC restrictions and increased policy expenditure.

Date	*Policy measure*	*Main provisions*
1960	*Local Employment Act*	Repeal of Distribution of Industry Acts. Broad Development Areas replaced by fragmented patchwork of Development Districts delimited on the basis of unemployment rates exceeding 4½ per cent. Retention and strengthening of earlier Board of Trade powers. Introduction of new building grants. Reform of Industrial (formerly Trading) Estate policy. IDC policy retained.
1962	Resettlement Transfer Scheme	Resettlement Scheme replaced by a strengthened Resettlement Transfer Scheme, along with the retained Key Workers Scheme and Nucleus Labour Force Scheme. Marks a more active resettlement policy.
1963	*Local Employment Act*	Introduction of standard investment and building grants.
1963	*Budget*	'Free' depreciation introduced for firms in assisted areas. This allows firms to write off investment in plant and machinery against Corporation Tax at any rate they wish. Allows Corporation Tax to be avoided in the initial years of new projects. Marks the beginning of the second major 'active' phase of regional policy.
1963	White Papers on Central Scotland and North East England (Hailsham Report)	Critical of Local Employment Acts and their emphasis on localised unemployment. Growth pole strategies emphasised, together with the need for public infrastructure investment in depressed areas.
1964	Regional Planning	Regional Economic Planning Councils and Boards set up by the Department of Economic Affairs.
1964	*Industrial Training Act*	Industrial Training Boards (ITBs) established for (an eventual) twenty-four industries, with a levy on firms. The programme of Government Training Centres slowly expanded.

Date	Policy measure	Main provisions
		Training schemes, as with resettlement schemes, are controlled by the Department of Employment.
1965	Control of Office and Industrial Development Act	Controls on office development in London and Birmingham. Office Development Permits. Rapidly extended to other areas in prosperous regions.
1965	*Highlands and Islands Development (Scotland) Act*	Highlands and Islands Development Board established with extensive powers of grants, loans, equity participation and new factory building for a wide range of economic activities within the area of the Board.
1966	*Industrial Development Act*	The 165 Development Districts replaced by 5 broad Development Areas covering almost half of the land area of Britain. Replacement of 'free' depreciation by a system of 40 per cent investment grants in Development Areas (20 per cent elsewhere). Retention of remainder of policies – IDC's building grants (25–35 per cent), etc. Land reclamation grants of 85 per cent (50 per cent elsewhere).
1967	*Finance Act*	A labour subsidy, the Regional Employment Premium (REP), introduced. Administered through the Selective Employment Tax (SET) system, with manufacturing firms in Development Areas reclaiming not only their SET, but also a Selective Employment Premium (37½p per man per week), and a Regional Employment Premium (£1.50 per man per week – lower rates for women and juveniles). SET and SEP subsequently withdrawn after 1970, but REP continued in existence until 1977.
1967	*Special Development Areas*	Special Development Areas established in Scotland, the North East, West Cumberland and Wales, with additional incentives of rent-free premises, 35 per cent building grants

Date	Policy measure	Main provisions
		and some operating cost grants, compared with their Development Area counterparts.
1969	Commission on the Intermediate Areas (Hunt Report)	Examination of the problem of Intermediate (or 'Grey') Areas. The recommended strong incentives for these areas were not fully accepted.
1969	Strategic Plans	Series of *ad hoc* regional strategy teams set up – beginning with South East region. Preparation of regional economic and land-use plans as framework for structure plans of local government and as a framework for central government policymaking.
1970	*Local Employment Act*	Seven Intermediate Areas established. Government-built factories, building grants and derelict land clearance grants. Financed by withdrawal of SEP from Development Areas.
1970	*October Mini-Budget*	Investment grants replaced by 'accelerated' depreciation in the Development Areas. Other existing powers retained and strengthened.
1972	*Industry Act*	A major strengthening of regional policy, involving: (i) extension of 'accelerated' depreciation to whole country; (ii) return to investment grants (Regional Development Grants) for plant and machinery, and for building; (iii) proposed phasing out of REP by 1974; (iv) IDCs ended in Development Areas and Special Development Areas; (v) increase of other forms of existing assistance; (vi) selective assistance (Section 7) for industry; grants and low-interest loans for services; (vii) post of Minister of Industrial Development.
1972	*Training Opportunities Scheme (TOPS)*	Major extension of government training centre programme. Financial allowances for trainees.

Date	Policy measure	Main provisions
1972	Employment Transfer Scheme	Strengthening of Resettlement Scheme and re-named Employment Transfer Scheme. Key Worker and Nucleus Labour Force Schemes retained.
1973	*European Economic Community*	Britain entered the EEC and became eligible for loans, grants and other assistance from Community financial instruments – the European Coal and Steel Community (ECSC), European Investment Bank (EIB), European Social Fund (ESF), European Agricultural Guidance and Guarantee Fund (EAGGF). Britain also required to adhere to Competition Policy of EEC. This sets limits on investment subsidies on 'central' regions of the EEC (including Intermediate Areas), and disapproves of continuing subsidies such as REP. Regional subsidies must also be 'transparent' (i.e., easily assessed).
1973	*Employment and Training Act*	Manpower Services Commission set up to oversee the Employment Services Agency (which controls the extended and reformed Jobcentre and local employment office functions of the Department of Employment), and the Training Services Agency (which operates the expanded TOPS retraining programme and the Industrial Training Boards). Rapid expansion of government training schemes.
1973	Royal Commission on the Constitution (Kilbrandon)	Qualified support for elected Scottish and Welsh assemblies and English Regional Advisory Councils. Devolution of limited economic powers proposed.
1973	Hardman Report	Proposals to disperse 31,000 London-based civil service jobs.
1974	Reform of Local Government	New system of County and District Councils established.
1974	Regional Employment Premium	REP rate doubled.

1974	White Paper on Devolution	Scottish and Welsh elected assemblies proposed.
1975	*Industry Act*	National Enterprise Board (NEB) established with an initial £1,000 million available for wide-ranging intervention. Planning Agreements with firms proposed. Designed to assist depressed areas in particular. Some relaxation of rules of selective assistance of 1972 Industry Act.
1975	*European Regional Development Fund*	An EEC Fund established to offer investment grants, and interest rebates on European Investment Bank loans in depressed regions. A Regional Policy Committee also established to co-ordinate member state and EEC regional policies and to stimulate regional research and planning.
1975/76	*Development Agencies*	Scottish and Welsh Development Agencies established. Scottish Development Agency in particular has substantial powers to invest in industry, create new companies, provide finance and advice for industry, to build and manage Industrial Estates, to lease or sell advance and custom-built factories, to reclaim derelict land and rehabilitate the environment.
1976	'Fire-fighting' Employment Policies	Series of *ad hoc* policies designed to alleviate temporary unemployment problems. Includes: Job Creation Programme; Training Award Scheme; Youth Employment Subsidy; Temporary Employment Subsidy; Community, Industry and Work Experience Scheme, etc. Employment Subsidy for small manufacturing firms.
1976	Service and office location subsidies	Strengthening of grants and rent relief for service and office firms locating in assisted areas. Preferential loans.
1977	*Regional Employment Premium*	REP abolished in Britain. Selective Employment Premium continues in Ulster.

| 1977 | *Development Board for Rural Wales* | Development Board for Rural Wales established with powers to build houses for incoming key workers, control over advance factories, and financial assistance for infrastructure and social projects within the Board's area. |
| 1977 | *EEC Regional Policy* | Proposals for a major extension of scope and powers of the European Regional Development Fund. |

Sources: Randall, P., 'The history of British regional policy', in G. Hallet, P. Randall and E. G. West, *Regional Policy for Ever?* (London: Institute of Economic Affairs, 1973); Department of Industry, *Incentives for Industry* (London: HMSO, n.d.); McCrone (1968); *British Economic Survey*; Department of Employment, London; 'Proposals for a community regional policy', *Official Journal of European Communities*, OJ C86 (16 October) and OJ C106 (6 December) (Brussels: Commission of the European Communities, 1973); 'Regulations establishing a Community regional policy', *OJEC*, OJ L73 (21 March) and OJ L128 (19 May) (Brussels: CEC, 1975); 'First report of the Regional Development Fund', *Bulletin of the European Communities* Supplement (Brussels: CEC, July 1976); *Guidelines for a Community Regional Policy*, COM(77) 195 final (Brussels: CEC, 1977); *Second Report of the Regional Development Fund*, COM(77) 260 final (Brussels: CEC, 1977).

Background Data on Government and the Scottish Economy

We set out in this section the background tables of data used in the analysis of Chapter 5. Table A.1 and A.2 give central government expenditure details in Scotland in current and constant prices for 1961–78. Table A.3 gives the data used in the regression analysis of Table 5.4 and Table A.4 gives the data used in the regression analysis of Table 5.5.

Table A.1   Identifiable public expenditure in Scotland, gross domestic fixed capital formation: 1961–78
Current prices, £ million

	1961	1962	1963	1964	1965	1966	1967	1968	1969
Agriculture, forestry and fishing	63.0	60.1	60.7	58.3	56.7	59.8	66.6	71.9	73.9
Coal	9.8	9.5	8.3	8.6	9.4	9.7	9.1	9.5	7.1
Gas, electricity and water	48.2	55.4	62.0	67.7	69.4	69.2	79.8	80.4	80.4
Housing	56.5	52.1	74.4	87.8	93.4	106.8	121.3	146.4	148.5
Roads[1]	7.5	8.1	18.5	21.0	23.7	28.9	34.9	41.2	45.4
Transport and communications[2]	15.3	15.7	11.5	21.4	26.1	32.9	36.1	42.9	50.2

	1970	1971	1972	1973	1974	1975	1976	1977	1978
Agriculture, forestry and fishing	73.9	87.3	87.0	88.3	125.4	141.3	148.5	144.8	154.3
Coal	4.7	3.9	4.4	3.8	6.2	10.8	13.2	12.9	16.2
Gas, electricity and water	90.4	97.4	102.6	102.5	157.3	246	216.7	173.3	151.4
Housing	138.2	113.7	118.9	156.3	241.5	291.2	285.7	269.2	261.5
Roads[1]	47.7	53.1	54.0	65.6	85.2	101.9	102.2	112.8	116.3
Transport and communications[2]	58.6	69.1	69.3	80.4	95.1	109.7	129.7	121.8	139.9

[1] Includes GDFCF in Scotland in motorways and trunk roads, etc., and local roads and transport.
[2] Includes GDFCF in transport and communications by nationalised industries as well as capital expenditure on ports and shipping and civil aviation.

Sources: Compiled from *Scottish Abstract of Statistics*, no. 9 (1980) p. 146; no. 7 (1977) pp. 189–202; *SAS*, no. 6 (1976), pp. 185–93; *Scottish Digest of Statistics* (October 1968, October 1970).

Table A.2 Central government expenditure in Scotland, 1961–78, at constant (1975) prices, £ million

	1961	1962	1963	1964	1965	1966	1967	1968	1969
Annual exchequer cost of 'special' regional policy	51.0	52.4	31.6	29.8	80.3	81.4	123.8	199.7	225.4
Grants to local authorities	402.8	410.7	439.2	456.6	465.1	490.3	519.1	546.2	577.4
	(417.0)	(425.7)	(457.6)	(474.1)	(482.4)	(512.4)	(530.0)	(575.0)	(574.8)
Capital expenditure by nationalised industries	329.2	298.5	306.6	310.2	308.4	314.1	351.7	326.5	295.9
Wages and salaries, public administration and defence	424.8	442	454.0	467.9	467.5	470.9	487.6	487.5	495.8
Subsidies:									
Agriculture, forestry and fishing	172.4	158.8	143.1	130.0	113.5	108.6	111.8	107.7	102.2
Trade, industry and employment	0.7	0.3	0.7	0.6	–	8.0	35.8	115.5	142.6
Total	173.1	159.1	143.8	130.6	113.5	116.6	147.6	223.2	244.9
Total gross expenditure	1,381.0	1,362.7	1,375.2	1,395.1	1,434.7	1,473.4	1,629.8	1,783.2	1,839.4

Table A.2 Central government expenditure in Scotland, 1961–78, at constant (1975) prices, £ million (cont'd.)

	1970	1971	1972	1973	1974	1975	1976	1977	1978
Annual exchequer cost of 'special' regional policy	203.7	171.3	150	164	178.8	206.2	196.6	130.2	110.4
Grants to local authorities	613.7	650.3	704.4	831.2	925.9	852.5	947.8	959.0	947.7
	(611.0)	(647.2)	(700.3)	(804.8)	(889.5)				
Capital expenditure by nationalised industries	305.3	311.8	319.9	301	378.2	457.8	401.7	343.6	273.7
Wages and salaries, public administration and defence	502.4	524.1	563.5	580.8	594.7	632.0	672.3	634.4	661.7
Subsidies:									
Agriculture, forestry and fishing	97.5	95.2	74.0	77.1	136.9	117.7	96.4	67.2	44.9
Trade, industry and employment	117.2	99.8	80.7	90.9	103.6	97.0	145.1	104.6	81.0
Total	214.8	195.1	154.7	168.0	240.5	214.7	241.5	171.8	125.9
Total gross expenditure	1,839.9	1,852.6	1,892.5	2,044.9	2,318.2	2,363.2	2,459.9	2,239.0	2,119.5

Table A.3 *Data used in employment and output change in manufacturing in Scotland, 1954–76*

	EMPINC	EMPIND	SCOMFG £m.	FOOD £m.	ENG. £m.	WHAT Index	WHATI Index	UKOUT £m.	VAC Thou.	VACI Thou.	LABDIFF £m.	IDC3 %	LOCEMP (dummy)	UKGROI	CAPSUB Ton
1955 over 1954	4,967	9,006	−39	—	—	95.4	96.8	1,072.7	17.8	19.2	0	15.7	0	6.52	0
1956 over 1955	4,781	7,290	34	—	—	96.3	95.4	−48.8	20.2	17.8	0	7.7	0	−0.28	0
1957 over 1956	2,409	−994	24	—	—	96.3	96.3	387.5	20.0	20.2	0	6.4	0	2.22	0
1958 over 1957	4,060	−8,127	54	—	—	96.3	96.3	−117.2	17.2	20.0	0	6.3	0	−0.66	0
1959 over 1958	1,863	−17,738	32	12	−10	91.8	96.3	943.8	11.6	17.2	0	1.8	0	5.32	0
1960 over 1959	2,343	−21,909	109	22	6	91.7	91.8	1,508.6	10.1	11.6	0	2.1	1	8.07	0
1961 over 1960	6,292	12,606	15	8	21	95.2	91.7	−24.8	13.5	10.1	0	13.8	1	−0.12	50.98
1962 over 1961	−4,205	−1,884	−2	8	44	93.2	95.2	−23.8	15.7	13.5	0	13.7	1	−0.12	52.36
1963 over 1962	6,005	−17,261	32	20	−5	91.3	93.2	660.9	11.2	15.7	0	16.7	1	3.03	31.58
1964 over 1963	3,876	−25,777	183	15	77	89.7	91.3	1,938.8	10.4	11.2	0	19.1	0	9.31	29.83
1965 over 1964	8,844	3,838	91	21	36	93.9	89.7	656.6	15.7	10.4	0	24.2	0	2.89	67.03
1966 over 1965	8,370	11,459	40	19	29	97.1	93.9	314.0	20.0	15.7	0	21.6	0	1.34	79.97
1967 over 1966	13,744	−794	1	16	13	97.3	97.1	−1,001.2	21.3	20.0	0	26.1	0	4.22	98.05
1968 over 1967	1,574	−16,451	100	20	11	93.7	97.3	2,632.2	15.7	21.3	88	23.7	0	11.58	102.75
1969 over 1968	6,212	−2,641	135	8	68	93.0	93.7	−67.9	18.2	15.7	24	29.9	0	−0.27	103.87
1970 over 1969	13,013	−1,931	89	38	71	96.6	93.0	5.4	19.3	18.2	−23	22.6	0	0.001	106.21
1971 over 1970	7,814	−8,175	−24	19	−61	96.3	96.6	923.8	16.1	19.3	−20	22.1	0	3.65	96.38
1972 over 1971	−4,658	−31,245	42	14	−38	91.4	96.3	784.4	9.4	16.1	−12	16.0	0	2.99	89.25
1973 over 1972	−3,865	−20,243	188	23	60	90.3	91.4	2,256.1	9.5	9.4	−5	17.1	0	8.36	105.60
1974 over 1973	9,789	1,701	−23	24	13	94.7	90.3	−594.5	22.9	9.5	8	9.5	0	−2.03	108.60
1975 over 1974	10,717	7,059	−116	−19	60	93.3	94.7	−1,776.0	19.3	22.9	5	10.2	0	−6.20	131.90
1976 over 1975	−7,042	−24,745	7	5	−30	86.5	93.3	400.0	11.3	19.3	−3	9.4	0	1.27	125.31

Table A.4 Data used in sectoral output and employment change in Scotland 1962–78

	EXP RD	ΔEXP RD	VAC	ΔVAC	UNEMP	ΔUN EMP	ΔUN EMP -1	ΔUK MFG	ΔOUT AGR-1	ΔEMP AGR -1	ΔOUT MIN -1	ΔEMP MIN -1	ΔOUT UTIL -1	ΔEMP UTIL -1	ΔEMP SER -1	ΔOUT AGG -1	ΔSER OUT
1962 over 1961	26.5	1	15.8	-4.6	64.6	13.5	-10.2	-3.5	1	-2.5	-5	0	74	-11.9	-8.3	529	18
1963 over 1962	27.5	33.4	11.2	-0.7	78	20.2	13.5	3.4	2	-4.2	-3	-7	11	-1.4	33.5	141	-59
1964 over 1963	60.9	5	10.5	4.6	98.2	-20.1	20.2	3.3	4	-4	-2	-9.1	17	5	4.4	58	61
1965 over 1964	65.9	3.8	15.1	4.9	78.1	-14.7	-20.1	9.3	13	-7.1	-5	-5	68	-7.9	9.2	275	10
1966 over 1965	69.7	27	20	0.7	63.4	-3.5	-14.7	2.9	11	-15.3	-5	-3	20	5	-2	141	101
1967 over 1966	96.7	-4.2	21.3	-5.4	59.9	20.9	-3.5	1.3	9	-6.7	-11	-5	65	7.7	3.4	225	33
1968 over 1967	92.5	10.5	15.9	2.3	80.8	-0.1	20.9	0.1	13	-7.8	0	-2.9	41	-1.5	-2	167	61
1969 over 1968	103	3.7	18.2	1.1	80.7	-1.4	-0.1	8.9	10	-2.6	-19	-8	93	0.6	1.8	260	138
1970 over 1969	106.7	-5.6	19.2	-3.2	79.3	11.6	-1.4	1.7	9	-4.6	-12	-3	34	-4.6	59.8	238	14
1971 over 1970	101.1	11.5	16.1	6.7	90.9	34	11.6	0.4	19	-3.3	-5	-3	-88	-10.4	51.5	108	143
1972 over 1971	112.6	-18.5	9.4	0.1	124.8	12.7	34	-0.7	1	-5.2	11	0	-28	-13.2	166	133	266
1973 over 1972	94.5	10.5	9.5	13.4	137.5	-38.6	12.7	3.0	13	-1.5	-19	-2	64	-4.2	359	459	122
1974 over 1973	105	6.6	22.9	-3.6	98.9	-10.5	-38.6	8.3	12	-1.5	17	-2	80	16.2	146	440	-194
1975 over 1974	111.6	-9.6	19.3	-8.0	88.4	25	-10.5	-2.0	45	-2.5	-15	-1	-85	4.2	-165	-245	51
1976 over 1975	102	-12.1	16.9	-2.4	113.4	25	25	-6.2	-30	-1.7	-11	2	33	0.8	115	15	104
1977 over 1976	89.9	-0.3	14.3	-2.6	152.9	39.5	25	1.3	-61	0	-5	-1	-14	1	196	123	50
1978 over 1977	90.2	-5	16.3	2	182.8	29.9	39.5	1.8	71	0	-8	1	45	-8	29	127	177

Table A.4 Data used in sectoral output and employment change in Scotland, 1962–78 (cont'd.)

	ΔOUT AGR	ΔEMP AOTR	ΔOUT MIN	ΔEMP MIN	ΔOUT UTIL	ΔEMP UTIL	ΔSER EMP	ΔOUT AGG	CEN EXP	ΔCEN EXP
1962 over 1961	2	-4.2	-3	-7	11	-1.4	33.5	141	1,381	-18.3
1963 over 1962	4	-4.0	-2	-9.1	17	5	4.4	58	1,362.7	12.5
1964 over 1963	13	-7.1	-5	5	68	-7.9	9.2	275	1,375.2	19.9
1965 over 1964	11	-15.3	-5	-3	20	5	-0.2	141	1,395.1	39.6
1966 over 1965	9	-6.7	-11	-5	65	7.7	3.4	225	1,434.7	38.7
1967 over 1966	13	-7.8	0	-2.9	41	-1.5	-2	167	1,473.4	156
1968 over 1967	10	-2.6	-19	-8	93	0.6	1.8	260	1,629.8	153.4
1969 over 1968	9	-4.6	-12	-3	34	-4.6	59.8	238	1,783.2	56.2
1970 over 1969	19	-3.3	-5	-3	-88	-10.4	51.5	108	1,839.4	0.6
1971 over 1970	1	-5.2	11	0	-28	-13.2	166	133	1,840	12.6
1972 over 1971	13	-1.5	-19	-2	64	-4.2	359	459	1,852.6	39.9
1973 over 1972	12	-1.5	17	-2	80	16.2	146	440	1,892.5	152.5
1974 over 1973	45	-2.5	-15	-1	-85	4.2	-165	-245	2,045.0	273.2
1975 over 1974	-30	-1.7	-11	2	33	0.8	115	15	2,318.2	45
1976 over 1975	-61	0	-5	1	-14	1	196	123	2,363.2	96.7
1977 over 1976	71	0	-8	1	45	-8	29	127	2,459.9	-220.9
1978 over 1977	-16	-0.7	3	3.3	-88	3.6	260	260	2,239	-119.5

Table A.4 Data used in sectoral output and employment change in Scotland, 1962–78 (cont'd.)

	REG EXP	ΔREG EXP	NAT IND	ΔNAT IND	EXP UTIL	ΔEXP UTIL	AGR SUB	ΔAGR SUB	EXPRD TR	ΔEXP RDTR	EXP RDHO	ΔEXP RDHO
1962 over 1961	51	-1.4	329.2	-30.7	205.3	15.4	172.4	-13.6	80.7	0.2	226.6	-21.9
1963 over 1962	52.4	-20.8	298.5	8.1	220.7	10.6	158.8	-15.7	80.9	17.8	204.7	100.9
1964 over 1963	31.6	-1.8	306.6	3.6	231.3	8.3	143.1	-23	98.7	34.4	305.6	36
1965 over 1964	29.8	50.5	310.2	-1.8	239.6	-7.9	120	-6.5	133.1	13.3	341.6	2.7
1966 over 1965	80.3	1.1	308.4	5.7	231.7	-13.2	113.5	-4.9	146.4	41.4	344.3	48.2
1967 over 1966	81.4	42.4	314.1	37.6	218.5	17.1	1C.6	3.2	187.8	0.4	392.5	21.4
1968 over 1967	123.8	76.2	351.7	-25.2	235.6	10.9	111.8	-4.1	188.2	22	413.9	55.1
1969 over 1968	200	25.4	326.5	-30.6	224.7	-19.1	107.7	-5.5	210.2	14.7	469	-13.3
1970 over 1969	225.4	-21.7	295.9	9.4	205.6	-4	102.2	-4.7	224.7	0.6	455.7	61.6
1971 over 1970	203.7	-32.4	305.3	6.5	201.6	-7.1	97.5	-2.3	225.3	19.9	394.1	-20.8
1972 over 1971	171.3	-21.3	311.8	8.2	194.5	-7.6	95.2	-21.2	245.2	-10.9	373.3	-70.7
1973 over 1972	150	14	320	19	186.9	-16.8	74	3.1	234.3	-0.7	302.6	52.4
1974 over 1973	164	14.8	301	77.2	170.1	44.1	77.1	59.8	233.6	2.6	355	73
1975 over 1974	178.8	27.4	378.2	79	214.2	42.6	136.9	-19.2	236.2	-24.6	428	-34.9
1976 over 1975	206.2	-9.6	457.8	-56.1	256.6	-54.5	117.7	-21.3	211.6	-7.5	393.1	-49.7
1977 over 1976	196.6	-66	401.7	-58.1	202.3	-53.3	96.4	-29.2	204.1	-16.4	341.4	-35.8
1978 over 1977	130.2	-20	343.6	-70	149.0	56.6	67.2	-22.3	187.7	14.6	305.6	-32.1

Bibliography

Alexander, Sir K. J. W., 'Developing the Highlands and Islands', in C. Blake and S. G. E. Lythe (ed.), *A Maverick Institution* (London: Gee, 1981).

Armstrong, H. and Taylor, J., *Regional Economic Policy and Its Analysis* (Oxford: Philip Allan, 1978).

Ashcroft, B. and Taylor, J., 'The movement of manufacturing industry and the effect of regional policy', *Oxford Economic Papers*, vol. 29 (1977), pp. 84–101.

Ashcroft, B., 'The evaluation of regional economic policy: the case of the United Kingdom', *Working Paper No. 12*, Centre for the Study of Public Policy (Glasgow: University of Strathclyde, 1978).

Ashcroft, B., 'The evaluation of regional policy in Europe: a survey and critique', *Working Paper No. 68*, Centre for the Study of Public Policy (Glasgow: University of Strathclyde, 1980).

Bacon, R. and Eltis, W., *Britain's Economic Problem: Too Few Producers* (London: Macmillan, 1976).

Beacham, A., 'The movement of manufacturing industry', *Regional Studies*, vol. 4 (1970), pp. 41–7.

Begg, H., Lythe, C. and Macdonald, D., 'Investment in manufacturing industry in Scotland, 1961–1971: the impact of regional policy', *Occasional Paper No. 3* (Department of Economics, University of Dundee, 1975).

Begg, H., Lythe, C. and Macdonald, D., 'The impact of regional policy on investment in manufacturing industry: Scotland 1960–1971', *Urban Studies*, vol. 13 (1976), pp. 171–9.

Begg, H., Lythe, C. and Sorley, R., 'Expenditure in Scotland, 1971 and 1972', *Occasional Paper No. 2* (Department of Economics, University of Dundee, 1975a).

Begg, H., Lythe, C. and Sorley, R., *Expenditure in Scotland, 1961–1971* (Edinburgh: Scottish Academic Press, 1975b).

Bell, D. N. F., 'EMOS – an econometric model for Scotland', unpublished paper presented to the Scottish Economists' Conference (Edzell, September 1978).

Blake, C., 'The effectiveness of investment grants as a regional subsidy', *Scottish Journal of Political Economy*, vol. 19 (1972), pp. 53–71.

Blake, C., 'Some economics of investment grants and allowances', in A. Whiting (ed.), *The Economics of Industrial Subsidies* (London: HMSO, 1976a).

Blake, C., 'The productivity of labour in Scottish manufacturing', *Occasional Paper No. 5* (Department of Economics, University of Dundee, 1976b).

Blake, C., 'Labour productivity: an exercise in classification', *Occasional Paper No. 19* (Department of Economics, University of Dundee, 1981).

Blue Book, see Central Statistical Office, *National Income and Expenditure*.

Blunden, J. *et al.*, *Regional Analysis and Development* (London: Harper & Row for Open University Press, 1973).

Brown, A., *Framework of Regional Economics in the United Kingdom* (Cambridge: CUP, 1969).

Buck, T., 'The impact of British regional policies on employment growth', *Oxford Economic Papers*, vol. 28 (1976), pp. 118-31.

Buck, T. and Lowe, J., 'Regional policy and the distribution of investment', *Scottish Journal of Political Economy*, vol. 19 (1972), pp. 253-71.

Bulmer-Thomas, V., 'The regional accounting framework', *Research Monograph No. 5* (The Fraser of Allander Institute for Research on the Scottish Economy, 1978).

Burdekin, R., *The Construction of the 1973 Scottish Input-Output Tables* (Peterlee: IBM UK Scientific Centre, 1978).

Business Monitor, Report on the Census of Production, 1970, Summary Tables, C154; Industry Reports, C2-153; Report on the Census of Production 1971, Summary Tables, PA1002; Industry Reports, PA101-PA603. Departments of Trade and Industry, Business Statistics Office, HMSO.

Buxton, N., 'Economic growth in Scotland between the Wars: the role of production structure and rationalisation', *Working Paper 1977-78, No. 3* (Edinburgh: Department of Economics, Heriot-Watt University, 1977).

Cambridge Economic Policy Group, *Cambridge Economic Policy Review* (July 1980).

Cameron, G., 'The national industry strategy and regional policy' in D. Maclennan and J. P. Parr (ed.), *Regional Policy: Past Experience and New Directions* (Oxford: Martin Robertson, 1979).

Campbell, A. 'Changes in Scottish incomes, 1942-49', *The Economic Journal*, vol. 65 (1955), pp. 225-40.

Caves, R. *et al.*, *Britain's Economic Prospects* (London: Allen & Unwin, 1968).

Census of Production, 1970 and 1971, see *Business Monitor*.

Central Scotland, a Programme for Development and Growth, Cmnd 2188 (Edinburgh: HMSO, 1963).

Central Statistical Office, *Annual Abstract of Statistics*, vols. 106, 109, 111, 112 (London: HMSO, 1969, 1972, 1974, 1975).

Central Statistical Office, *Input-Output Tables for the UK, 1963* (London: HMSO, 1978).

Central Statistical Office (CSO), 'Preliminary estimates of regional gross domestic product', *Economic Trends*, no. 241 (November 1973), pp. LXI-LXXIII.

Central Statistical Office (CSO), 'Agricultural and food statistics: a guide to official sources', *Studies in Official Statistics*, no. 23 (HMSO, 1974).

Central Statistical Office, *Regional Statistics*, no. 12 (London: HMSO, 1976).

Central Statistical Office (CSO), 'The measurement of changes in production', *Studies in Official Statistics*, no. 25 (HMSO, 1976a).

Central Statistical Office (CSO), 'United Kingdom regional accounts', *Economic Trends* (November 1976b), pp. 78-90.

Central Statistical Office (CSO), 'Regional accounts: preliminary estimates for 1975', *Economic Trends* (June 1977a), pp. 96-100.

Central Statistical Office (CSO), 'Regional accounts: further estimates for 1975, including regional fixed investment', *Economic Trends* (November 1977b), pp. 79-96.

Central Statistical Office (CSO), *Regional Accounts* (London: HMSO, 1978a).

Central Statistical Office (CSO), 'Regional accounts: further estimates for 1976', *Economic Trends* (November 1978b), pp. 79–99.

Corden, W., 'Monetary integration', *Essays in International Finance*, no. 93 (Princeton, NJ: University of Princeton, 1972).

Cox, M., Devlen, J. and Lythe, C., 'Expenditure in Scotland 1961–75', *Occasional Paper No. 13* (Department of Economics, University of Dundee, 1979).

Deane, P., *Colonial Social Accounting* (Cambridge: CUP, 1953a).

Deane, P., 'Regional variations in United Kingdom incomes from employment, 1948', *Journal of Royal Statistical Society*, vol. 116, part II (1953b), pp. 123–35.

Department of Agriculture and Fisheries for Scotland, *Agricultural Statistics (Scotland)* (Edinburgh: HMSO).

Department of Employment, *Family Expenditure Survey* (London: HMSO).

Department of Agriculture and Fisheries for Scotland, *Scottish Agricultural Economics* (Edinburgh: HMSO, annual).

Department of Employment Gazette, 'New estimates of employment on a continuous basis: employees in employment by industry, 1959–73', vol. LXXXIII, no. 3 (March 1975, pp. 193–202).

Department of Employment Gazette, 'New estimates of employment on a continuous basis: United Kingdom: 1959–74', vol. LXXXIII, no. 10 (October, 1975, pp. 1030–36).

Department of Employment Gazette, 'New estimates of employment on a continuous basis: regional data: employees in employment by industry order groups, 1965–75', vol. LXXXIV, no. 8 (August 1976a, pp. 839–50).

Department of Employment Gazette, 'New estimates of employment on a continuous basis, employers and self-employed, 1961–74', vol. LXXXIV, no. 12 (December 1976b, pp. 1344–9).

Department of Trade and Industry, *Census of Production, 1968*, Report No. 157 (London: HMSO, 1974).

Dewhurst, J. H. L. and Lythe, C., *Temptress: Model of the Scottish Economy* (provisional title), (Aberdeen University Press, 1982).

Draper, P. and McNicoll, I., 'The new Scottish input-output tables: the importance of UK and foreign trade for Scotland', Fraser of Allander Institute *Quarterly Economic Commentary* vol. 4, no. 4 (April 1979).

Drucker, N. and Drucker, H., *The Scottish Government Yearbook 1980* (Edinburgh: Paul Harris, 1979).

Education in Scotland (Edinburgh: HMSO, annual).

Fessey, M. and Browning, H., 'The statistical unit in business inquiries', *Statistical News*, no. 13 (1971), pp. 13.1–13.5.

Firn, J., External Control and Regional Policy, *in* G. Brown (ed.), *The Red Paper on Scotland* (Edinburgh: University Student Publications Board, 1975), pp. 153–69.

Forbes, D. and Lythe, C., *Expenditure in Scotland 1961–1979*, Department of Economics, University of Dundee, forthcoming mimeograph, 1982.

Forsyth, D., *US Investment in Scotland* (New York: Praeger, 1972).

Fraser of Allander Institute, *Quarterly Economic Commentary* (October 1981).

Gaskin, M. and MacKay, D., *The Economic Impact of North Sea Oil on Scotland* (Edinburgh: HMSO, 1978).

Government of Northern Ireland, Digest of Statistics (Belfast, HMSO).

Henderson, D., 'Consumers' expenditure in Scotland 1962–1977', *ESU Discussion Paper No. 9*, Scottish Economic Planning Department (1980).

Highlands and Islands Development Board, *Annual Reports* (Inverness).

H. M. Treasury, *Estimates of Central Government Revenue and Expenditure Attributable to Scotland for the Financial Year 1967–1968* (London: HMSO, 1969).

Hochwald, W., 'Conceptual issues of regional income estimation', in *Regional Income*, Studies in Income and Wealth, National Bureau of Economic Research, vol. 21 (Princeton University Press, 1955).

Holland, S., *Capital versus Regions* (Basingstoke: Macmillan, 1976a).

Holland, S., *The Regional Problem* (Basingstoke: Macmillan, 1976b).

Hood, N., Reeves, A. and Young, S., *European Manufacturing Investment in Scotland*, unpublished report commissioned and prepared for the Scottish Development Agency (1980).

Hood, N., Reeves, A. and Young, S., 'Foreign direct investment in Scotland: the European dimension', *Scottish Journal of Political Economy*, vol. 28 (1981), pp. 165–85.

Hood, N. and Young, S., 'U.S. investment in Scotland – aspects of the branch factory syndrome', *Scottish Journal of Political Economy*, vol. 23 (1976), pp. 279–94.

Hood, N. and Young, S., *European Development Strategies of US-owned Manufacturing Companies in Scotland*, Report for the Scottish Economic Planning Department (Edinburgh: HMSO, 1980).

Howard, R., *The Movement of Manufacturing Industry in the U.K., 1945–1965*, Board of Trade (London: HMSO, 1968).

Inland Revenue, Board of, *Inland Revenue Statistics* (London: HMSO, annual).

Input–Output Tables for Scotland, 1973, see Scottish Input–Output Project (SIOP).

Jefferson, C., 'A regional model of the Northern Ireland economy', *Scottish Journal of Political Economy*, no. 25 (1978), pp. 253–72.

Johnston, T., Buxton, N. and Mair, D., *Structure and Growth of the Scottish Economy* (London: Collins, 1971).

Jones, D. T., 'Output, employment and labour productivity in Europe since 1955', *National Institute Economic Review* (August 1976).

Jones, T., 'Sectoral income and multiplier effects: Scotland, 1963', *Occasional Paper No. 1* (Department of Economics, University of Dundee, 1975).

Kaldor, N., 'The case for regional policies', *Scottish Journal of Political Economy*, vol. 17 (1970), pp. 337–47.

Keeble, D., 'Industrial mobility: in which industries has plant mobility changed most? – a comment', *Regional Studies*, vol. 9 (1975), pp. 297–9.

Kellas, J. G., *The Scottish Political System* (Cambridge, CUP, 1975).

Kent-Smith, D. and Pritchard, A., 'Further estimates of regional gross domestic product', *Economic Trends*, no. 259 (May 1975), pp. 87–91.

Kent-Smith, D. and Hartley, E., 'United Kingdom regional accounts', *Economic Trends*, no. 277 (November 1976), pp. 78–90.

Lewis, T. M. and McNicoll, I. H., *North Sea Oil and Scottish Economic Prospects* (London: Croom Helm, 1978).

Local Financial Returns for Scotland, Scottish Office, Scottish Development Department, HMSO, Annual.

Lythe, C., 'The Scottish economy in 1980', in D. I. MacKay (ed.), *Scotland 1980, the Economics of Self-Government* (Edinburgh: Q. Press, 1977).

Lythe, C., Begg, H. and Majmudar, M., 'Expenditure in Scotland, 1961–73', *Occasional Paper No. 6* (Department of Economics, University of Dundee, 1977).

Lythe, C., Begg, H. and Sorley, R., 'Shift-share analysis and the assessment of Scottish economic performance, 1959–71', *Occasional Paper No. 4* (Department of Economics, University of Dundee, 1975).

Lythe, C., Dewhurst, J. H. L., Parrillo, S., Cox, M. and Devlen, J., 'Temptress: an economic model of Scotland', *Occasional Paper No. 15* (Department of Economics, University of Dundee, 1979).

Lythe, C. and Majmudar, M., *Scottish Gross Domestic Product 1961–1971: an Exercise in Regional Accounting and Analysis* (Department of Economics, University of Dundee, 1978).

Lythe, C. and Majmudar, M., 'An appraisal of the social accounts for Scotland for 1973', *Occasional Paper No. 10* (Department of Economics, University of Dundee, 1979).

Lythe, C. and Majmudar, M., 'Scottish gross domestic product statistics for 1961–71', *Journal of the Royal Statistical Society* (1981), Series A, vol. 144, pp. 352–9.

Lythe, S. G. E. and Butt, J., *An Economic History of Scotland 1100–1939* (Glasgow: Blackie, 1975).

Majmudar, M., 'Regional income disparities, regional income change and federal policy in India, 1950–51 to 1967–68: an empirical evaluation', *Occasional Paper No. 7* (Department of Economics, University of Dundee, 1977).

Majmudar, M. and Lythe, C., 'Government and Scottish economic performance', *Social Science Working Paper No. 38* (Paisley College of Technology, 1981).

Marquand, J., 'Measuring the effects and costs of regional incentives', *Government Economic Series, Working Paper No. 32* (1980).

Maurice, R., *National Accounts Statistics, Sources and Methods* (London: HMSO, 1968).

Millan, B., 'The Scottish Office and the U.K. Economy', in C. Blake and S. G. E. Lythe (ed.), *A Maverick Institution* (London: Gee, 1981).

Milne, Sir David, *The Scottish Office* (London: Allen & Unwin, 1975).

Ministry of Agriculture, Fisheries and Food, 'The new index of agricultural net output', *Economic Trends*, no. 77 (March 1960, pp. viii–xii).

Ministry of Health Annual Reports, HMSO.

Moore, B. and Rhodes, J., 'Evaluating the effects of British regional policy', *The Economic Journal*, vol. 83 (1973), pp. 87–110.

Moore, B. and Rhodes, J., 'Regional policy and the Scottish economy', *Scottish Journal of Political Economy*, vol. 21, no. 3 (1974), pp. 215-35.

Moore, B. and Rhodes, J., 'Regional economic policy and the movement of manufacturing firms to development areas', *Economica*, vol. 43 (1976a), pp. 17-31.

Moore, B. and Rhodes, J., 'A quantitative analysis of the regional employment premium and other regional policy instruments', in A. Whiting (ed.), *The Economics of Industrial Subsidies* (London: Department of Industry, HMSO, 1976b).

McCrone, G., *Scotland's Economic Progress, 1951-1960* (London: Allen and Unwin, 1965).

McCrone, G., 'The application of regional accounting in the United Kingdom', *Regional Studies*, vol. 1 (1967), reprinted in Blunden, J. *et al.* (1973).

McCrone, G., *Scotland's Future: The Economics of Nationalism* (Oxford: Blackwell, 1969).

McCrone, G., 'The location of economic activity in the United Kingdom', *Urban Studies*, vol. 9 (1972), pp. 369-71.

McDermott, P., 'Multinational manufacturing firms and regional development: external control in Scottish electronics industry', *Scottish Journal of Political Economy*, vol. 26 (1979), pp. 287-306.

McDowall, S. and Begg, H., *Industrial Performance and Prospects in Areas affected by Oil Development* (Edinburgh: HMSO, 1981).

MacKay, D., 'Industrial structure and regional growth: a methodological problem', *Scottish Journal of Political Economy*, vol. 15, no. 2 (1968), pp. 129-43.

MacKay, D. (ed.), *Scotland 1980, the Economics of Self-Government* (Edinburgh: Q. Press, 1977).

MacKay, D. and Mackay, G., *The Political Economy of North Sea Oil* (Oxford: Martin Robertson, 1975).

MacKay, R., 'Employment creation in development areas', *Scottish Journal of Political Economy*, vol. 19, no. 3 (1972), pp. 287-96.

MacKay, R., Evaluating the effects of British regional policy – a comment', *The Economic Journal*, vol. 84 (1974), pp. 367-72.

MacKay, R., 'Regional policy in the U.K.: the effect on employment', in R. Grant and G. Shaw (ed.), *Current Issues in Economic Policy* (Oxford: Phillip Allan, 1975).

MacKay, R., 'Important trends in regional policy and regional employment: a modified interpretation', *Newcastle Discussion Papers No. 22* (Department of Economics, University of Newcastle-upon-Tyne, 1977).

Maclennan, D. and Parr, J., *Regional Policy: Past Experience and New Directions* (Oxford: Martin Robertson, 1979).

National Health Service Scotland Acts: Annual Reports (Edinburgh: HMSO).

National Income and Expenditure (Blue Book), Central Statistical Office (London: HMSO, 1972, 1973, 1975, 1976, 1977, 1978, and 1980).

Nevin, E. (ed.), *The Social Accounts of the Welsh Economy, 1948-56* (Cardiff: University of Wales Press, 1957).

Nevin, E. (ed.), *The Economics of Devolution* (Cardiff: University of Wales Press, 1978).

Nevin, T., in A. M. El-Agraa (ed.), *The Economics of the European Community* (Oxford: Philip Allan, 1980).

Nordhaus, W. and Tobin, J., *Is Growth Obsolete?* Fifteenth Anniversary Colloquium V. National Bureau of Economic Research (Cambridge: CUP, 1972).

North, D., 'Location theory and regional economic growth', *Journal of Political Economy*, vol. 63 (1955).

Odell, P. and Rosing, K., 'A simulation model of the development of North Sea Oil province, 1969–2030', *Energy Policy* (1974).

Organisation for Economic Co-operation and Development (OECD), *Issues of Regional Policies*, report prepared by A. Emanuel (Paris: OECD, 1973).

Pearce, D., 'World energy demand and crude oil prices to the year 2000', *Discussion Paper 80-12* (Department of Political Economy, University of Aberdeen, 1980).

Pottinger, G., *The Secretaries of State for Scotland 1926–76* (Edinburgh: Scottish Academic Press, 1979).

Registrar General for Scotland, *Censuses of Population, 1961 and 1971* (Edinburgh: HMSO, 1978).

Report of the (Kilbrandon) Royal Commission on the Constitution, Cmnd. 5460 (London: HMSO, 1973).

Richardson, H., *Regional Economics* (London: Weidenfeld and Nicolson, 1969).

Rostow, W. W., *The Stages of Economic Growth* (Cambridge: CUP, 1963).

Rymes, T., *On Concepts of Capital and Technical Change* (Cambridge: CUP, 1971).

Salter, W., *Productivity and Technical Change*, 2nd edn. (Cambridge: CUP, 1966).

Schofield, J., 'Macro evaluations of the impact of regional policy in Britain: a review of recent research', *Urban Studies*, vol. 16 (1979), pp. 251–69.

Scottish Council Research Institute (SCRI), 'A survey of European investment in Scotland', *SCRI Studies No. 2* (1973a).

Scottish Council Research Institute (SCRI), 'The location of European companies in Scotland', *SCRI Studies No. 3* (1973b).

Scottish Council Research Institute (SCRI), 'U.S. investment in Scotland', *SCRI Studies No. 4* (1974).

Scottish Development Agency, *Labour Performance of US-owned Plants in Scotland: A Research Report* (Glasgow: SDA, 1979).

Scottish Economic Bulletin, No. 13, 'Relative performance of incoming and non-incoming industry in Scotland' (Scottish Office, HMSO, 1979).

Scottish Economic Bulletin, No. 15, 'Recent trends in earnings in Scotland' (Scottish Office, HMSO, 1978).

Scottish Economic Bulletin, No. 18, 'EEC regional policy and the Scottish Economy' (Scottish Office, HMSO, Summer 1979).

Scottish Economic Bulletin, No. 22, 'Transport costs in Scottish Manufacturing industry (Scottish Office, HMSO, Spring 1981).

The Scottish Economy 1965–1970: a plan for expansion, Cmnd 2864 (Edinburgh: HMSO, 1966).

Scottish Education Department, *Scottish Educational Statistics* (Edinburgh: HMSO, annual).

Scottish Input-Output Project (SIOP), *Input-Output Tables for Scotland 1973*, The Fraser of Allander Institute, University of Strathclyde, The

Scottish Council Research Institute Limited, IBM United Kingdom Scientific Centre (Edinburgh: Scottish Academic Press, 1978).

Scottish Office, *Scottish Abstract of Statistics* (Edinburgh: HMSO, annual).

Scottish Statistical Office, *Digest of Scottish Statistics* (Edinburgh: HMSO).

Short, J. and Nicholas, D. J., *Money Flows in the U.K. Regions* (London: Gower, 1981).

Smith, B., 'Industrial mobility: in which industries has plant location changed most?' *Regional Studies*, vol. 9 (1975), pp. 27-8.

Sorrell, A., 'Some pitfalls in the use of net output statistics', *Statistical News*, no. 12 (1971), pp. 12.5-12.8.

Stafford, J., The development of industrial statistics, *Statistical News*, no. 1 (1968), pp. 1.7-1.10.

Stillwell, F., Regional growth and structural adaptation, *Urban Studies*, vol. 6 (1969), pp. 162-78.

'Stuck in the slow lane', *The Economist*, 24-30 October 1981.

Tait, A. A., 'Financial institutions and monetary policy', in D. MacKay (ed.) (1977).

Thirlwall, A., 'A measure of proper distribution of industry', *Oxford Economic Papers*, vol. 19 (1967), pp. 46-55.

Thomson, J., 'The framework of industry in Scotland: an analysis of the Scottish input-output table', *SCRI Studies No. 8* (1977).

Toothill Report, *Inquiry into the Scottish Economy 1960-1961* (Edinburgh: Scottish Council (Development and Industry), 1961).

Townroe, P., 'The supply of mobile industry: a cross-sectional analysis', *Regional and Urban Economics*, vol. 2, no. 4 (1973), pp. 371-86.

Townroe, P., 'Settling in costs and mobile plants', *Urban Studies*, vol. 13 (1976), pp. 67-70.

Tyler, P., Moore, B. and Rhodes, J., 'New developments in the evaluation of regional policy', unpublished paper delivered to SSRC Urban and Regional Studies Group (1980).

Wanhill, S. R. C., 'Econometric model of the Welsh economy', unpublished Ph.D. thesis (Bangor: University College of North Wales, 1978).

Welch, R., 'Immigrant manufacturing industry established in Scotland between 1945 and 1968: some structural and locational characteristics', *Scottish Geographic Magazine*, vol. 86 (1970), pp. 134-47.

Welsh Statistical Office, *Digest of Welsh Statistics* (Cardiff: HMSO).

Whitaker, T., 'Monetary integration: reflections on Irish experience', *Moorgate and Wall Street* (Autumn, 1973).

Whiting, A. (ed.), *The Economics of Industrial Subsidies*, Department of Industry (London: HMSO, 1976).

Wilson Committee, *Committee to Review the Functioning of Financial Institutions: evidence on the financing of industry and trade*, vols. 4 and 6 (London: HMSO, 1978).

Wilson, T., 'Regional policy and the national interest', in D. Maclennan and J. Parr (ed.) (1979).

Woodward, V., 'Regional social accounts for the United Kingdom', in National Institute of Economic and Social Research, *Regional Papers I* (Cambridge: CUP, 1970).

Yuill, D. and Allen, K., 'Regional development agencies in Europe: an overview', Scottish Economic Planning Department, *ESU Discussion Papers No. 4* (1981).

Index